OUT-PATIENT TREATMENT OF ALCOHOLISM

T0366810

BROOKSIDE MONOGRAPHS

Publications of the
Alcoholism and Drug Addiction Research Foundation,
24 Harbord Street, Toronto 5, Canada

Under the general editorship of
P. J. GIFFEN, Department of Sociology, University of Toronto
R. E. POPHAM, Alcoholism and Drug Addiction Research Foundation

OUT-PATIENT TREATMENT

OF

ALCOHOLISM

A Study of Outcome and Its Determinants

DONALD L. GERARD, M.D.

Research Center for Mental Health,
New York University

GERHART SAENGER, PH.D.

Mental Health Research Unit,
Department of Mental Hygiene, State of New York;
and Department of Psychiatry,
New York State Medical School (Up-State Division)

Brookside Monograph No. 4

PUBLISHED FOR THE

ALCOHOLISM AND DRUG ADDICTION RESEARCH FOUNDATION OF ONTARIO

BY UNIVERSITY OF TORONTO PRESS

Foreword

"What are the results of our investment in treatment services for alcoholics?" This question was presented to a meeting of the Committee on Classification and Nomenclature of the North American Association of Alcoholism Programs (then called the National States Conference on Alcoholism) on October 29, 1955. Many of the members of the NAAAP were concerned about the answer to this question and hopeful that an answer could be found through research. Accordingly, at the 1955 annual meeting, the membership authorized the establishment of a working committee to consider the problem. This committee was given power to seek financial support for a suitable research project, and to enlist scientists to undertake the investigation. Eventually, funds were made available by the United States government through its National Institute of Mental Health, and two scientists, in the persons of Doctors Donald L. Gerard and Gerhart Saenger, were employed to undertake the study.

Active research (including a two-year pilot study) was carried out over a period of 5 years—from February 1957 to June 1962. Eight out-patient clinics and related in-patient facilities, operated by state alcoholism programs in the eastern United States, provided the study sample. The main objectives were: (1) to secure a picture of contemporary clinic treatment of alcoholism in the United States, and (2) to develop suitable standards for the evaluation of treatment offered in alcoholism clinics. The following questions were asked and answered: (a) What kinds of patients with drinking problems come to state-supported alcoholism clinics? (b) What kind of treatment is offered? (c) What changes take place in the patients? (d) To what extent is change related to the characteristics of patients and/or the treatment provided?

v

Those who have attempted evaluation studies of clinical programs are well aware of the formidable methodological problems involved. The description of a treatment experience, adequate for scientific purposes, is a highly complex matter. In addition to the details contained in the recording of the interview with the patient, an understanding of such subjective factors as the quality of the patient's relationship with the therapist and the attitudes of the therapist towards the patient is required. All factors in this highly complex interrelationship are important in assessing the reasons for the therapeutic outcome.

The location of patients following discharge from the clinics, and the reliability (or lack of same) of the information provided by the patients, are among the many difficulties with which the scientist must cope if his results are to have significance. It is a great tribute to the scientific ability and persistence of Doctors Gerard and Saenger that these problems, and many others, were solved more than adequately in the study reported here.

Some of the findings reported in this study will startle some of the more tradition-bound therapists. Those who believe strongly in "drug therapy" should carefully note that the data in this study raise doubts as to the value of such widely used drugs as barbiturates, vitamins, and tranquillizers in the out-patient treatment of alcoholism. On the other hand, antabuse (disulfiram) does appear to have a positive influence on treatment results. However, the authors are careful to point out that the more favourable outcome for those who took antabuse may reflect characteristics (for example, motivation) of those given the drug rather than a specific effect. Those who promote "psychiatric therapy" for all alcoholics should note that patients treated by internists (or an internist in conjunction with a social worker) "were significantly more likely to improve than patients treated by other professionals."

Perhaps one of the most important points illustrated by this study is the need to base treatment on a clear diagnostic evaluation of the alcoholic syndrome manifested by the patient, his personality structure, social and cultural milieu, and attitude towards himself and his world. Some of the results, therefore, may not reflect as much on a particular treatment modality as on a failure to match the treatment to the pathology of the patient. That this fundamental concept should require emphasis in this day and age illustrates the unfortunate gap between scientific knowledge and its practical application to the therapeutic process.

In addition to the method and instruments used by Doctors Gerard and Saenger, which represent important contributions in themselves, the results of their investigation are decidedly of significance to all alcoholism programs in the United States and Canada, and in at least some European countries. The Alcoholism and Drug Addiction Research Foundation is most pleased to include this study in its scientific monograph series.

H. DAVID ARCHIBALD,
Executive Director,
Alcoholism and Drug Addiction
Research Foundation of Ontario

Preface

DURING the five years when the study on which this book is based
was carried out (from February 1957 through June 1962), and
during the following three years which were needed to analyze
the data and prepare the manuscript for publication, we have
enjoyed the encouragement, advice, and assistance of many
people in our own and allied fields. We should like not merely
to acknowledge their roles in the research, but also to express
our gratitude to this veritable community of colleagues.

The study originated within the North American Association
of Alcoholism Programs; without their sponsorship and continuing
interest the research would have been neither conceived nor
carried out. To Mr. David Archibald of Toronto, Dr. Jay Bright-
man of Albany, and Dr. Ebbe Hoff of Richmond, we owe a special
debt. The initial academic setting of the study was the Yale (now
Rutgers) Center for Studies on Alcohol; we wish to acknowledge
the help given to us by their staff in the conceptualization of the
research and the establishment of the complex administrative
structure which the geographic dispersion of the study made
necessary. The late Raymond J. McCarthy played an especially
important role in these regards.

More than fifty clinicians, social workers, psychologists, psychiatrists, specialists in internal medicine, nurses, and so forth made
the direct observations of patients in the collaborating clinics.
Their identities, as well as the identities of the clinics themselves,
have been concealed in the text to emphasize that our interest
was in the interrelationships discerned, and not in the personalities or points of view embodied in these clinics at those points in
time. They know who they are, and may recognize themselves
in the text—we hope without displeasure.

Because the study cut across the disciplines of psychiatry,
public health, sociology, and psychology, we had occasion during

the study to turn for advice and criticism to a distinguished panel of consultants. We wish to acknowledge the aid given us by Professor Ernest Gruenberg, Columbia University College of Physicians and Surgeons; Dr. Herbert Hyman, Columbia University, Bureau of Applied Social Research; and Dr. Isidor Chein, New York University, Research Center for Human Relations. Their methodologic acumen in the processes of sampling, data analysis, and inference strengthened our instruments and provided wisdom to guide their use.

Two of our research associates, Renee Wile, M.S.S., and Lucy Grow, M.S.W., contributed immeasureably to the clarification and amelioration of the human problems entailed in the execution of this research project. Without their heroic efforts, this difficult enterprise would never have been accomplished. Immersed in the procedural methodology, thoroughly familiar with the instruments to whose development they contributed so much out of their extensive social work experience, they traveled from north to south, from coast to cornfield, to share their understanding with the collaborating clinicians.

Next, we wish to express our appreciation to those often unsung colleagues, our secretaries, Mary Donchian, Barbara Evica, Phyllis Yenis, and Maren Grossman, whose sense of identification with the aims of the project, whose active intelligences, and whose administrative skills contributed so much to the execution of the research.

Finally, we wish to express our appreciation to the staff of the Alcoholism and Drug Addiction Research Foundation of Ontario, especially to Mr. Robert E. Popham, for generous help in the editorial and technical processes of publication.

D.L.G.
G.S.

Contents

List of Tables

OUT-PATIENT TREATMENT OF ALCOHOLISM

I. The Design of the Study

1. INTRODUCTION

THIS BOOK reports the findings of a study of alcoholism treatment in the out-patient clinics and related in-patient facilities of state-supported alcoholism programs. The specific aims of the research were briefly as follows: (1) to develop a uniform system of techniques and instruments for standardized and quantifiable follow-up studies of patients treated for alcoholism in out-patient clinics; (2) to apply the techniques, instruments, and experience gained in the first, methodological portion of the project to the follow-up of random samples of alcoholics of various characteristics and from diverse treatment settings. It was hoped that the many data thus obtained might contribute to the knowledge of the complex disorder "alcoholism."

But what is alcoholism? It is common knowledge that there are persons whose pattern of alcohol use is harmful to them; that is, when they continue long enough to exhibit certain patterns of excessive use, there occur deleterious social, medical, and psychiatric consequences. However, to decide that a person is really an "alcoholic" in the same sense that one decides that a person suffers from rheumatic heart disease is still largely a matter of unsatisfactory semantics and as yet unestablished diagnostic conventions. Keller has written an excellent review of the problems involved in the definition of "alcoholism." Alongside the World Health Organization definition of alcoholism[1]* he has proposed the following: "Alcoholism is a psychogenic dependence on or a physiological addiction to ethanol, manifested by the

---

*"Alcoholics are those excessive drinkers whose dependence upon alcohol has attained such a degree that it shows a *noticeable* mental disturbance or an interference with their bodily and mental health, their inter-personal relations, and their smooth social and economic functioning; or who show the prodromal signs of such developments."

3

inability of the alcoholic consistently to control either the start of drinking or its termination once started. . . ."[2] Thus, alcoholism becomes a type of interaction between a person and available unlimited quantities of alcoholic beverages. However, because the clinician is rarely able to observe the alcoholic when the latter is actually drinking, he (the clinician) depends on history, inference, and judgment to determine whether or not a person's drinking is indicative of mal-functioning with respect to his health or social (interpersonal) or economic well-being.

Not surprisingly, it was observed that clinical staff dealing with patients who sought help because of troubled interaction with the use of alcoholic beverages *rarely, if ever*, attempted to determine to what extent the appellation "alcoholic" or the syndrome "alcoholism" was relevant to the management or treatment of such patients. They might seek to make such diagnoses as schizophrenia, sociopathic personality, or cirrhosis of the liver, and to describe how patients' problems with alcohol were related to these or to any other conditions, but there was very little interest in *clinically codifying the fact or degree of involvement* with alcoholic beverages *per se*.

Although it was found that the clinics collaborating in this study sometimes referred patients for special care elsewhere, there was no evidence that any patient was turned away because his drinking problem was considered not severe enough to warrant treatment. Whether this practice was salutary or regrettable is not to be decided here. However, for the purposes of this research, the concept "alcoholism" or the designation "alcoholic" referred to those persons who *seemingly had a problem related to the use of alcoholic beverages* (subjective) *which led them to the attention of a state-supported alcoholism clinic* (indubitable fact). In effect, the term "alcoholism" was used to refer to any or all of the manifold syndromes of troubled functioning and/or impaired health in which alcohol use was an invariable element, and the term "alcoholic" to refer to a person with any of these syndromes.

Apart from the individual who has a problem with alcoholic beverages, there are important social problems associated with alcohol use. These include absenteeism, traffic accidents, family problems, public intoxication and brawling, bootlegging and associated criminality, and the medical morbidity and mortality in which alcohol use is implicated. To what extent such problems are linked to individuals who are acknowledged to have a drinking problem and to what extent to persons who are not acknowledged to have a drinking problem is an important question in its own right, but not one to which this research could make any contribution. Indeed, the interest of public health and welfare personnel in the control of alcoholism has been stimulated by concern for both the individual with a drinking problem and the social problems surrounding the use of alcohol in society.

2. SOME RECENT INSTITUTIONAL HISTORY

The control of alcoholism has been a matter of serious social concern, probably for as long as alcoholic beverages have been used in complex societies. In the United States the most dramatic attempt at social control of alcoholism of this century was the experiment with prohibition, that is, the Volstead Act and the Eighteenth Amendment (1919). This effort to deny the pleasures of alcoholic beverages to all, for the sake of obviating the harm which excess by the few created,[3] was not based on any scientific inquiry into the needs involved, or into the probable efficacy of an attempt to deny the satisfaction of these needs arbitrarily. Some of the unanticipated consequences of this legislation were the prohibition gangster, the rum-runner, and the institution of the speakeasy, bathtub gin, moonshining, and misuse of methyl alcohol. In any case, it became apparent that a valuable source of tax revenue and employment in the alcoholic beverages industry was being denied the economy.

When the prohibition amendment was repealed in 1932, there were no scientifically gathered figures to indicate the extent of the alcoholism problem in the United States during or before the prohibition period; nor were the influences of repeal on the morbidity associated with alcoholism evaluated subsequently. However, in recent years increasing evidence has accumulated to

5

suggest that the extent of excessive usage of alcoholic beverages by men, women, and adolescents of most social classes is impressively large, despite attempts to "educate" the population to drink with prudence; and there is indication that a considerable number of men, and to a lesser degree women, are suffering from the physical illnesses and social pathology which are believed to be associated with the excessive use of alcoholic beverages.

By the end of the 1930's two significant movements to cope with the alcohol problem in the United States had developed.[4] Though not antithetical in aim, these movements are quite different in approach, motivation, and historical background. The first is Alcoholics Anonymous (AA), the history of which has been described by its membership[5,6] and studied by sociologists and psychiatrists. In the words of the masthead of the AA publication *The Grapevine*, the organization is "a fellowship of men and women who share their experience, strength and hope . . . that they may solve their common problem [that is, their use of alcohol]." A program of group meetings and discussion, and of support by the sober for the intoxicated rests not on a carefully thought-out preliminary rationale, but on the personal experiences gleaned by members in helping each other; public confessions are usually a central feature of these meetings, and restraint of persons from drinking, rescue work, and informal help with monetary, employment, family, and other problems are important supportive activities. Two of the central tenets of AA philosophy are that members believe in a non-denominational God on whom they must lean, and that they continue to be alcoholics, even though sober.

Among the thousands of groups which compose AA, there are widespread differences in program, membership, and leadership. However, because of the informality of the groups, there are no records or statistics that will permit scientific evaluation either of the alcoholic population who are able to participate regularly in AA or of the efficacy of its program. On the basis of his study of a number of successful (that is, prolongedly abstinent) members of a particular AA group, Zwerling[7] has reported that this organization offers comradeship to the isolated, satisfies dependency needs "without shame and with little incitement to rebellion," gives opportunity to express omnipotent and even sadistic needs in a socially valuable context, and offers the possibility for a more adaptive "ritualization of non-drinking," that is, the regular "getting-together with the boys," away from the family and with a central preoccupation about drinking, yet without drinking. AA is entirely non-professional in outlook, has little if any interest in studying the etiology or course of alcoholism, and regards alcoholism as a peculiar "allergy" to alcohol based on some ill-defined bodily or emotional processes which must be dealt with through avoidance of the noxious agent and by acquiescence to and permeation with its philosophy. Although the medical profession is acceptable to AA for assistance in the psychophysiologic and pathophysiologic consequences of alcoholism, as the ministry is for support in spiritual crises, basically AA believes that it is the fellowship of alcoholics which offers the best means to reach and influence another alcoholic.

The second movement grew out of the Yale University Laboratory for Applied Physiology and its "Studies on Alcohol" section, some of the origins of which have been described by Haggard.[3] The work of this group and of the Yale Plan clinic—a multidisciplinary group for the study, management, and treatment of persons with drinking problems—has in turn fostered the development of a number of organizations for the scientific study of alcoholism. One of the particularly influential groups of this nature is the North American Association of Alcoholism Programs (NAAAP). Much of what can be said about it is generally true of such organizations as the National Committee on Alcoholism, National Council on Alcoholism, and various state and provincial councils on addiction and alcoholism; however, for simplicity and discussion the NAAAP is used here as a major social or institutional representative of the scientific outlook towards alcoholism.

This group has looked towards a better control of alcoholism as an individual and social problem, through learning more about the psychologic, physiologic, and social etiologic factors in alcoholism; through applying insights and techniques from medical, psychiatric, and casework treatment of individuals who have problems in social adaptation, impulse control, or frank mental illness; and through support of study which, on a broad scientific

7

base, considers the manifold factors in alcoholism. Under the aegis of the NAAAP, programs of clinical casework and of public and professional education and research in alcoholism have been established in many of the states of the United States and the provinces of Canada. Its membership (technically speaking, the various state programs are the members; the individual representing the state program in a secondary sense may be described as the membership) consists of a scientifically oriented group of heterogeneous professionals who are engaged in a variety of public health, administrative, research, clinical, and educational roles. Although there are persons involved with the NAAAP whose interest in the problems of alcoholism may have been motivated by their own difficulties with alcohol, they are by and large professionally qualified for their work, unlike AA persons whose primary competence is considered to be their own successes or failures in exorcising the demon rum.

Some of the basic assumptions of the NAAAP (and the related organizations cited above) are that: (1) alcoholism is a heterogeneous syndrome, both *socially* in terms of the vast differences in the nature of the persons involved and the degree of impairment of social functioning and status associated with alcoholism, as well as *medically* in terms of the vast differences in extent and reversibility of the pathological physiology associated with alcohol intake at the expense of other dietary substances, notably proteins and vitamins; (2) alcoholism should be approached as a *disease* rather than as a vice; and (3) alcoholism can be treated in special clinic programs involving the use of a team of specialists—medical, psychiatric, and social. It was towards this third assumption that the present research was particularly oriented.

3. EVALUATION RESEARCH IN ALCOHOLISM

In 1955 the NAAAP became responsive to an important current in contemporary public health psychiatry, specifically the growing interest in evaluative research of clinical activity and programs. It is unnecessary to go into the rationale and manifold functions of evaluation research in psychiatry. That it is an important

8

problem has been cogently argued by Burnett and Greenhill,[8] by Felix and Clausen,[9] and by Kotinsky and Witmer,[10] and that these arguments have been regarded seriously is attested to by the voluminous literature on evaluation research which has grown up in the past ten years. In different ways these authors make the point that it is not unreasonable to expect that all therapeutic modalities, and particularly those supported by public money, ought to have a built-in program of evaluation. But as Rosenfeld[11] has put it, there are significant scientific as well as practical reasons why every clinical activity should have such a program; namely, if clinical activity rests on a body of scientific assumptions the latter should be tested in their application to practical affairs, and if evaluation implies questionable effectiveness both practical tactics and underlying scientific assumptions require clarification.

Review and critical evaluation of the working practices and accomplishments should be a part of each clinic's responsibility. In actuality, the need to satisfy the demand for service rarely permits such an evaluation to be made. Furthermore, there are few clinicians with sufficient research bent who can, or will, design and implement a program of evaluation; nor are there general standards for the individual clinic to rely on in an attempt to review and evaluate its own work. Although there are certain logical requirements in any program of evaluation,[12] the particularities of a clinical problem or area call for differences in approach and procedure which are not necessarily applicable from one field to another; for example, the criteria that would be valid in evaluating the outcome of treatment of certain neuroses would not be applicable to the outcome of treatment of delinquents or persons with a manic-depressive psychosis.

That there should be evaluation in the sense discussed above; that it should be done predominantly *by the clinics*; that the procedures and the approach should be related to the particularities of alcoholism in these clinics; and that through active participation in the systematic study of patients at intake and at follow-up the clinic personnel should gain experience in the complexities of research and organize a basis for future evaluation research on their own—all these considerations were taken into

9

account by the NAAAP in lending its sponsorship to the research outlined in this book. Reported here is the attempt to create *meaningful standards* for evaluating the work of clinics engaged in treatment of patients with drinking problems, and to apply these standards to the following questions: (1) what kinds of patients with drinking problems come to these state-supported clinics? (2) what kind of treatment is offered them? (3) what changes take place in the patient? and (4) what are the relationships among these changes and the variables pertinent to (1) and (2)? Because there was a variety of clinical programs within the collective framework of the NAAAP, it was possible to compare a number of clinics simultaneously, and thus to investigate the influences of a variety of treatment programs on a variety of patients, as well as to draw inferences about the interaction between alcoholism and its treatment on a broader level than the examination of a single clinic would permit.

4. OVERVIEW

An overview of the course and development of this research project is presented here so that the details of the methodology and findings of the elaborate survey which follow can be understood in proper context.

The reader is reminded that the authors were not giving clinical and research direction to an alcoholism clinic. Rather, their function was to organize and synthesize the process of data collection, to study what was done for and what could be learned about alcoholic patients, without creating major revisions in the on-going patient-clinic interactions. Thus, for example, the authors did not request that the clinician identify some of their (the authors') interests by exploring the family backgrounds and early relationships of alcoholic patients because such a procedure would have created a major revision of the clinics' approaches to meeting the needs of alcoholic patients. Furthermore, because the clinics were to do this research in addition to their usual responsibilities, the amount of professional time that could be devoted to it had to be severely limited. On the basis of conference and discussion with the collaborating clinics, it seemed feasible to request that a clinic give eight hours per week of *total* professional staff time; for example, the general physician associated with the clinic might give two hours, the psychiatrist another two hours, and the social worker four hours each week. When one considers that these eight hours a week spanned at least two years, one realizes that the total time contribution of the clinics was indeed generous.

The specific aims of this research project, as described above, indicated that the study would proceed in a sequence of (partially) overlapping phases. These can be differentiated into three major segments. First there was the initial, primarily methodological phase—the *pilot study*—which developed and tested various instruments for the description of patients at the time they initiated contact with the clinics, for the summarizing of intake evaluation of the patients and of patient-clinic treatment interactions, and for the re-evaluation of patients at follow-up interviews. As a result of the insights obtained through the pilot study, a manual of operations was prepared; included were sampling procedures, the use of the research instruments, the structure of record-keeping, the transmittal of data from clinics to research staff, the time table of operations, and so forth—in short, the whole complex operating schema. The second segment or the *main study* involved the subsequent application of the instruments and procedures to a sample of patients and clinics. Finally, the data collected in the main study were reviewed, coded, and entered on IBM cards; various statistical operations were performed and interpreted; and qualitative data were reviewed and interpreted. This phase of the research was the *data analysis*.

(a) *Pilot Study*

As a first step in the development of instruments and procedures for use in and by alcoholism clinics, the authors decided to establish relationships with and to study the customary working practices, particularly clinical recording, of four clinics. Those chosen were located in four major eastern cities, and differed among themselves in therapeutic approach, in patient population, and in administrative organization; it was felt that if the instruments were developed in these heterogeneous settings their

11

general applicability to state-supported out-patient alcoholism programs would be maximized. Although most of the staff of each of these clinics were to be involved in the study, a liaison person from each played a major role in the collaboration.

The research staff met often with the staffs of the pilot study clinics, both in formal conferences and in informal conversation. The aims of the project were discussed and clarified, and the interest of the clinic staffs in the process and the problems of evaluation research was stimulated. At the same time, the clinic staffs reported their understanding of their working practices as well as their approach to the treatment of alcoholism based on their conceptual orientation towards this complex syndrome. Initially, it had been hoped to include a searching and extensive inquiry into many of the facets of alcoholism through systematic study of case material. Such a task did not seem unreasonable to the pilot study clinics, because they felt that they studied a sufficient proportion of their patients in depth to permit a contribution to the understanding of the background of alcoholism, as well as of the patients' current functioning and of the interactions occurring in treatment between patients and therapists.

A primary task in the pilot study was to identify the breadth and depth of the data which could be systematically collected in usual clinical procedures, and subsequently obtained from records. Consequently, a data availability study was made, for which purpose a record abstract form, in effect a questionnaire addressed to the clinics' records, was developed. The records chosen in each of the four pilot study clinics covered a representative sample of patients who were first seen in the year prior to the authors' relationship with the clinic. The record abstract form, which was then applied to this sample, gathered information on certain major areas such as health; family relationships, historical and current; social relationships, past and present; employment and vocational history; and history of pathology associated with alcohol use. Statistical collation of these forms indicated that the process of recording in these clinics was rarely supervised, critically reviewed, or systematically structured beyond the requirements of certain identifying data. In consequence of this fact, data describing the patient's adjustment and relationships at work, with his parents or children, with his spouse, and with persons out of the context of work or family were characteristically either absent or meager. When presented with these findings, the collaborating clinics displayed incredulity and defensiveness. Because they took an active role in analyzing their own records, they could not disclaim the facts of their recording, but their reaction was to contend, in effect, that they really knew much more about the patient than they *reported* in the record.

This claim led to the second phase of the pilot study, in which three research instruments, the intake information form, the intake case review, and the intake check list (see Appendix), were presented to the clinics. These forms were devised on the basis of the clinics' expectations about what they usually knew about their patients, and about the interactions between their patients and the treating staff. The clinics were asked to record the knowledge that they obtained about patients through customary interviewing procedures and according to the topical headings or explicit questions asked in these research instruments; in this manner, the clinics were to write up four new patients each month. When, after six months' experience, these data were collected and reviewed, it was realized that the expectations of what the clinics learned systematically and regularly about their patients were still too high. The forms were therefore revised and modified over and over again in accord with the experience of re-applying them to successive samples of patients, until, in their final versions, they simply defined certain minimal expectations or *standards* for the description of all patients.

These forms may be summarized as follows (see also Appendix). The intake information form, which was used to record information systematically obtained at the first interview, presented identifying data, for example, age, sex, race, religion, marital and educational status; data relevant for tracing the patient at followup; a preliminary description of the patient's employment and occupational adjustment; observations of the patient's personal hygiene and general appearance, and of his health and drinking status on the day he first appeared in the clinic. The intake case review was a narrative review of the case, to be written within six weeks after the date of the patient's first visit. Certain minimal

13

standards for the initial clinical understanding of a patient with a drinking problem were formulated, and their presentation defined in a topical review of the patient's history and adjustment (with particular emphasis on the *year* preceding intake) in the areas of health, drinking, family relationships, social relationships, occupational adjustment, treatment experience, clinical observations, extent of activity at the clinic, and the clinic staff's impression of the patient's treatability. The intake check list required that the clinic make certain categorical decisions, choosing the category which best described the staff's understanding of the patient (with emphasis on the *month* preceding intake) apropos eleven topics. The latter paralleled those in the intake case review, thus reinforcing expectations by serving as a reminder to collect certain minimal information, in order that these categorical choices could be intelligently made.

At the very beginning of this research, it had been hoped to obtain systematic data from the collaborating clinics without imposing any change at all into their dealings with their patients. To some degree, varying from clinic to clinic, some changes were imposed, particularly in the study of patients' personal relationships and social adjustment, but the extent of change was minimized through the clinics' reactions and their participation in the work of devising the instruments. Thus the final forms developed for studying patients at intake represented a level of demand for data collection and recording somewhat, but not exorbitantly, in excess of customary clinical practice; that is they demanded a greater degree of systematization, but did not require any activities tangential to customary practice.

The third phase of the pilot study involved the development of an instrument—the treatment record (see Appendix)—which would describe what the clinics did for the patients as well as their observations and impressions of the patients in the course of treatment. This task was complicated by the fact that the treatment of patients in alcoholism clinics may involve relationships between patient and general physician, psychiatrist, social worker, medical student, nurse, minister, or other treating person. The relationships between the patient and an internist who is discussing the former's anxiety and the efficacy of a tranquilizer in

14

controlling it are quite different from those between the patient and a psychiatrist who, in seeking to understand the provocation of anxiety, is looking to an interaction between the patient and a significant figure in his environment. Therefore the goal was to develop an instrument which could be used in any of these varying treatment relationships, that is, which could communicate some of the major structural features of the interactions with minimal emphasis on the subtle aspects of the relationships. To be filled out by the interviewing person each time the patient was seen for an individual interview, the treatment record, in its final version, presented the date, duration, location, and purpose of the interview; summarized what was given to the patient in the form of drugs, recommendations, or special planning; indicated which areas were discussed in the interview; reviewed the recent status of his health and drinking; and abstracted in check list form the clinician's observations of the patient during the interview.

Like the intake forms described above, the treatment record was developed on the basis of conversations and conferences with the clinic staffs, then tried out, clarified within the research staff, interpreted to the participating clinics, used on groups of patients, and then revised. The final version of the form embodied the fact that it was feasible to get a record only of the most structural aspects of the treatment situation. There were two reasons for this development: first, most of the clinicians involved were not sufficiently confident in their work, in their judgment, and/or in their relationship with the researchers to give the latter free access to their thoughts and feelings about their interactions with patients (this factor probably was as it should have been because it was not the role of the researchers to offer case supervision); secondly, the treatment record had to be devised so that it could be filled out in a few minutes after a treatment session with a patient.

Because a small proportion of patients were seen in group therapy, a form was also devised in this phase of the pilot study to summarize the extent and nature of the participation of the patient in group therapy sessions. This out-patient group therapy form inquired about the patient's verbal activity in initiating or responding to communication about his life experiences, relationships, feelings, and drinking problem, or about those of other

15

patients in the group; codified the nature of the patient's emotional reactions in the course of the session; and recorded the patient's drinking behavior in the interval between the previous and current sessions if this datum was obtained in the course of the group meeting.

Although the researchers were aware of the enormous difficulty of describing "what goes on in therapy," and although they consequently limited the range of data to be obtained by the treatment record and by the out-patient group therapy forms (see chapter IV), there were still some major problems in getting the clinicians to use the forms. In part, this difficulty was due to the burden and discipline of recording treatment at all, for although some social agencies and some psychiatric clinics have a tradition of extensive recording, by and large alcoholism out-patient clinics usually regard recording as a tool for the clinician to use by himself to supplement his own memory, rather than as an instrument for use in research by himself or by others. Another reason for the reluctance to use the forms was that some of the clinicians found it hard to accept that the researchers were *not* defining what should be discussed in a treatment interview, but only *inquiring* about what was discussed.

The reader will observe that no emphasis was placed, either in the intake or in the treatment forms, on what might be termed the patients' "intrapsychic" functioning; nor was any formal use planned for psychiatric diagnoses and examinations, or for the products of psychologic testing. There were two reasons for this procedure: first, these kinds of data are notoriously difficult to treat categorically; secondly, only a minority of patients were examined or tested by psychiatrists or psychologists. Furthermore, the clinics did not systematically study and record the subtleties of intrapsychic processes or interpersonal relations in their continued relationship with the patient in treatment because only a very few patients came more than a few times to the clinic (see chapter IV); because the emphasis was placed on supportive and suppressive therapy, that is, largely on the patient's current problems, not on his total life situation; and because the amount of time per patient interview and the number of patient interviews per month were insufficient to admit the exploration of trans-

16

ference phenomena through which the emotional significance of certain types of experience and relationships could be ascertained. For a psychoanalytic or depth-psychologic understanding of alcoholism, this approach has limitations, but whether it impairs the care of patients with a drinking problem is of course a moot point.

The fourth stage of the pilot study was directed at organizing and executing the follow-up phase. Prior to its initiation, however, the authors had the opportunity to conduct a retrospective follow-up study for the Connecticut Commission on Alcoholism in which they gained extensive experience in the tracing of patients and follow-up interviewing, very often outside of the clinic itself. Some of the difficulties experienced in this retrospective study led to the incorporation of certain questions into the intake research instruments used in the pilot study, because it was learned that the data thus obtained would facilitate the later tracing of the patient. In the pilot study there were no major problems in defining which data should be obtained at follow-up, because by design these data were modelled upon those requested at intake. If comparable information apropos the patient's functioning were obtained at two points in time, measures of change could be devised, and a basis laid for ascertaining improvement, not merely in the area of drinking, but for a broad segment of the patient's total life experience and functioning. Thus, the research instruments used at follow-up were a follow-up observation sheet, a follow-up case review, and a follow-up check list (see Appendix), and in large measure both the forms themselves and the procedures for the tracing and follow-up interviewing of patients corresponded with those developed during the intake phase of the study.

Because a single interview might be all that could be depended on for reviewing the status of the patient roughly one year after intake, the extent of the inquiry at follow-up was minimized. On the other hand, the earlier research experience mentioned above had indicated that a patient very often is able to communicate at greater length about himself in the context of a follow-up interview than during his initial visit to the clinic.

Although the general plans and procedures for the main study

17

were worked out in the pilot study, there was one significant methodologic addition initated in the course of the main study. This instrument was called a pre-follow-up review (see Appendix), by means of which the clinics had the opportunity to correct or reformulate their understanding of certain aspects of the patient's status and function from incomplete or erroneous impressions obtained at intake. Furthermore, on this pre-follow-up review they would report those data which would aid in exploring the patient's status at follow-up (for example, that he had been in jail for a certain six months' period), or data which might contribute to the process of tracing the patient and thus perform a necessary prerequisite for the follow-up interview.

Prior to the experience of conducting the follow-up phase of the pilot study, it had been envisaged that several follow-up interviews, at several points in time, would be done on the patients in the sample studied by the collaborating clinics. However, it was learned here that the amount of work necessary to do a follow-up study, even at one point of time after intake, was so great that the clinics could not undertake to participate in serial follow-ups. Consequently, the original design was revised, and a single follow-up interview planned. In this context, there was some concern that false inferences might be drawn about the status of the patient at intake in relationship to that at follow-up and to the treatment he received, especially if there was an insufficient time lapse between intake and follow-up. Obviously, a very brief interval, such as one month, might be very misleading, but, on the other hand, there is never any certainty about the ultimate outcome of a patient's treatment for a chronic disease, short of following him from treatment to the time of his death. Also, on the basis of a collateral statistical investigation which used information from three sources and which was carried out in the pilot study to clarify the influence of a single follow-up at an interval of one year after intake (see chapter v), it was concluded that such a follow-up study need not grossly distort the data; this information failed to show significant relationships between the interval separating intake and follow-up and the status of patients at follow-up.

In the terminal phase of the pilot study, Mr. R. G. McCarthy, one of the prominent figures in alcoholism research, education,

18

and program development met with the directors of many of the state alcoholism programs at the September 19, 1958, meeting of the NAAAP. Here, he discussed the then current status of the project, the significance and value of the research for future program planning and for knowledge about alcoholism, and the need for their participation in the next phases of the study. There was considerable interest at the level of the clinic directors and the state alcoholism program directors, for they believed that a scientific review of the characteristics of the patients with whom they dealt, of the treatment that was offered, and of the outcome of this treatment would indeed be valuable. Interested persons were asked to take, fill out, and return (to the researchers) forms which were intended to describe the administrative set-up of the various clinics, professional backgrounds of the executive, and treatment staffs (see Appendix).

Those forms that were returned were then reviewed by the researchers as a basis for selecting clinics to assist in this study. Naturally, the chief concern was whether there was an on-going treatment program of broad enough caliber that the statistically complex studies planned on could be undertaken. Of the eighteen state programs east of the Mississippi* that responded, sixteen clinics which seemed to have a large enough professional staff and a large enough patient population were selected. On the basis of further correspondence and site visits, four of these clinics were eliminated, two because they had a smaller new-patient case load than they had realized, and two others because they were actually insufficiently financed or staffed to contribute professional staff time to research without slighting their service responsibilities. Furthermore, it was learned that most of the sixteen alcoholism programs received only marginal support relative to the extent of the problem with which they were intended to cope (see chapter II).

(b) Main Study

As with the pilot study, formal and informal conferences were held on the grounds of the twelve chosen clinics and also in New York. A manual of procedures, which was prepared out of the

*Programs west of the Mississippi were excluded because of budgetary considerations.

experience gained in the pilot study (see Appendix), was presented to the clinics for study prior to these meetings. The forms and procedures were discussed and reviewed, and minor accommodations to the particular practices of certain clinics were devised.

Sampling procedures were worked out for each clinic. Generally, samples consisted of the first nine new patients seen each month, the over-all intent being to study approximately 100 such patients from each of these clinics. For those clinics whose total annual intake was in the range of 100 cases, all patients would have to be included. However, because some clinics had an intake very much in excess of 100 cases a year, a critical review of the sampling procedures was made to ascertain whether a biased, rather than a representative sample was being selected. For example, the first nine new patients of the month in a clinic were compared to the total new case population of the previous six months. Because the data indicated that the first nine new patients seen each month did not differ by age, sex, marital status, education, occupation, or duration of alcohol problem from the total intake of the month, it was inferred that the mode of selecting patients used here provided a sample representative of the clinic's new-patient population.

Of the twelve clinics which began work in the main study, three dropped out in the course of the intake phase. One withdrew because its budget was cut unexpectedly by the state; it thus became impossible to retain certain personnel without whom the clinic was no longer in a position to contribute the eight hours staff time per week which this study entailed. Another clinic dropped out, despite the interest of its medical director, because —for a mixture of administrative and personal reasons—its staff members were overburdened with other responsibilities and commitments and/or were defensive about their own work which would, indeed, implicitly come under some scrutiny in the course of the study. The third clinic withdrew because of dissension within its staff about the value and feasibility of such a study. A fourth clinic was able to participate through the intake phase of the main study, but had to drop out in the follow-up phase, despite, various attempts to carry out a considerably modified follow-up program; this drop-out occurred in the context of widespread confusion and administrative problems, not primarily on the level of this clinical operation, but rather on the level of the entire system of social welfare in the state which was being severely weakened by the "economy drive" of a new governor. Thus, data describing the status of the patients at intake and the treatment these patients received were obtained from nine clinics, but data describing the status and functioning of these patients at follow-up from only eight clinics.

The main study was divided into three phases, the intake phase, the treatment phase, and the follow-up phase, the general structure of which can be illustrated by following the course of a clinic's activities with a hypothetical patient.

INTAKE PHASE. Mr. John Jones was the first new patient to come to Clinic X in January 1959. On the basis of data gathered at his first visit an intake information form was filled out. Between one month and six weeks after his first visit to the clinic, based on review of the clinic's records and informal conferences among the staff who had contact with Mr. Jones and/or with his relatives or other collateral sources, the intake case review was written and the intake check list was filled out.

TREATMENT PHASE. Beginning with the patient's first visit to the clinic, for every formal interview or group session a treatment record or out-patient group therapy form was filled out. This collection of treatment data was continued for one year after the date of intake, and did in fact overlap in time with the intake phase.

FOLLOW-UP PHASE. Eleven months after intake, Mr. Jones's clinical records were reviewed and an informal conference held with the clinic staff. As a result, a pre-follow-up review was prepared. One year after intake, the follow-up evaluation began, first by tracing the patient and/or collaterals, then by attempting to arrange a follow-up interview either at the clinic, at the patient's home, at an institution, or wherever would be relevant or feasible. Efforts to follow-up the patient continued for at least three months (after which time it could be decided that the patient was neither traceable nor interviewable). The follow-up data were then brought together on a follow-up observation

21

sheet, follow-up case review, and follow-up check list. Information from telephone calls, correspondence, interviews with relatives or spouses, death certificates, social agency inquiries and reports, and so forth were incorporated into these documents, as was the material obtained in the follow-up interview.

The intake phase lasted for twelve months. Therefore the collection of treatment data could continue for as long as two years, that is, from the date of Mr. Jones's first visit to one year after the date of intake of Mr. Z., who was the last patient in the sample (the ninth patient in the twelfth month of intake). The follow-up phase lasted twelve to fifteen months, that is, from the anniversary of Mr. Jones's intake to three months after the anniversary of Mr. Z.'s intake. Altogether, the main study required about two and a half years from the beginning of the intake phase to the completion of the follow-up phase.

(c) *Data Analysis*

Long before the final coding of the data and their statistical analysis, a great deal of work was directed at the "raw" data as these were received from the clinics. These data were subjected to persistent, if not incessant, critical examination by the research staff. At one level, this scrutiny consisted merely of observing that all data requested in the research instruments were obtained. At another level, it involved reviewing the data in a clinical perspective, for example, to see whether the data reported in the qualitative write-up of the case (intake case review) were consistent with those offered in the intake check list and intake observation sheet. Furthermore, the research social workers looked to these documents for some sense of clinical comprehension.

When the recording of the case material by the clinics did not seem altogether satisfactory, a number of appropriate alternatives were taken. Sometimes, a simple mail or phone inquiry to the clinic was all that was required. When the problems were more complex, the research social worker discussed the case with relevant persons in the course of her monthly visit to the clinic. Because of their detailed interest in the cases in the sample studied, and because of their own clinical backgrounds and experience, the research social workers were able to obtain data from the clinics at a higher level of clinical validity than would have been possible had their relationships with the clinics consisted merely of the supervision of a mechanical process.

After about half of the sample of patients in the study had completed the intake phase, an intake code guide was devised to summarize in categorical form the data that had been received. This code guide was written and re-written and applied to the intake data; reliability checks were then made to ascertain the level of intercoder agreement. Differences in coding were discussed, and the code guide re-written and re-applied until the level of intercoder agreement reached approximately 95 per cent. Those areas which could not be coded at this level of reliability were removed from the guide, and put aside for later consideration in a qualitative or casuistic context. Similarly, code guides were devised for the treatment and follow-up data.

In addition to these code guides from which the proportions of patients in certain categories and the interrelationships between certain categories might be studied, indices were prepared which generalized about the patient's functioning on the basis of the coding of several areas. For example, the index of social stability gave each patient a rating based on the summation of data from three relevant areas of social functioning, his marital status, his residential setting, and his employment status. If the patient was either single, or divorced or separated, he was assigned two points; if he resided alone or in an institution or was a transient, he received two points; if he was unemployed or unable to work, he received two points. The range of points for this index (and similarly for the other indices) was zero to six, zero points indicating that the patient's social stability was not grossly impaired as measured by these three criteria, and six points indicating that his social stability was very poor, that he did not have any apparent stable ties in a marital, familial, or occupational context. If the data were lacking for any one of the three criteria areas,* for example, for residential setting, the patient would be assigned one point, rather than either zero or two. If the data

*Although the level of reporting was far more complete than prior to the research, perfectly complete data collection was never achieved.

were lacking for as many as two of the three criteria areas, the patient was excluded from statistical analyses involving cross-tabulations or comparisons between this index and any other index or categories. Further details on the construction of the indices, the assumptions underlying them, and the statistical procedures which were utilized are described in subsequent chapters where appropriate; the indices themselves are presented in the Appendix.

II. The Research Setting: Alcoholism Clinics

1. INTRODUCTION

IN ORDER that the reader can obtain a picture of the kinds of settings in which treatment was given to the alcoholic who came to a publicly supported special clinic, this chapter presents a review of the eight out-patient clinics which participated throughout the intake and follow-up phases of the study.

These eight clinics were treatment agencies within state alcoholism programs which, to varying extents, also engaged in educational, research, and co-ordination activities. However, on the basis of statistical material prepared by the North American Association of Alcoholism Programs, it was quite clear that these clinics were not representative or typical of alcoholism services in the United States. For example, the 1960 budgets of the alcoholism programs of which they were a part varied from $93,000 to $459,000, a range of budgetary support which, to a statistically significant degree, exceeded that of the state programs not in the study (the Mann-Whitney U-Test indicated that the difference in these ranges was highly significant: $p =$ less than .001). Moreover, their greater budgetary support was not countered by a greater demand for service, for the range of new patients which these eight clinics served in their out-patient facilities in 1960 did not differ from that of the clinics in the alcoholism programs which did not participate in the study. This finding agreed with the researchers' impression that the clinics which participated through the intake and follow-up phases of the study were "stronger" than those which dropped out of the study in the terminal phase of the pilot study, and, also, that they were probably stronger than the clinics in those programs which did not offer their participation.

Because the reader is likely to be interested in evaluation research, some of the problems encountered in the mediation of clinician-researcher interactions are also reviewed here. Parenthetically, the setting in which the patients are treated might itself influence the outcome of treatment—as measured by changes in the adaptation and functioning of the patients. This is a factor independent of the structure of the treatment experience of an individual patient, because two patients might receive highly similar forms of treatment (for example, therapeutic interviews by a psychiatrist), in settings which differ markedly not only physically, but also psychologically in terms of the relationships within the clinic staff, the relative stability of the clinic staff, the level of clinic morale, and so forth.

It is important to emphasize that these clinics and the state programs of which they were a part were continually in the process of growth and change, and that the descriptions presented below indicate only how they appeared to the researchers in the years of study (1959–61). The clinics are presented anonymously, identified here and throughout the book by capital letters, to emphasize that the interest of the study was not in evaluating critically or pointedly the clinics or state programs *per se*, but rather solely in gaining an understanding into the role which they as social institutions might have played in influencing the outcome of treatment. Although anonymity is hopefully preserved, and although certain minor details which might identify the clinics to the reader have been altered or disguised for this purpose, there is still a chance that the person knowledgeable in this field may be able to identify them.

Clinic A

This clinic was part of a medium-sized general hospital in a run-down neighborhood of a small industrial city. The orienting attitude towards the treatment of alcoholism in the clinic was that alcoholism is related to psychological difficulties, and that the problems of the patient should be viewed as a whole, in the hope of improving his general adjustment. The staff consisted of a part-time director who was a psychoanalytically oriented psychiatrist, and three well-trained full-time social workers who were also responsible for a substantial amount of social work with the non-alcoholic patients of the hospital. Over the years the obvious sincerity and skill of the chief social worker had communicated itself to the medical staff of the hospital, and she was constantly approached on behalf of patients and community problems. The psychiatrist functioned as a diagnostician and as leader of one therapy group to which the more disturbed patients were assigned. Most of the patients were seen individually rather than in groups, predominantly by the social workers who consulted with the psychiatrist as needed.

The hospital administration was somewhat reluctant to admit alcoholic patients to its wards, but the clinic could send patients to a psychiatric treatment hospital which was maintained by the state in another community and where patients could be hospitalized for six weeks. The clinic felt that it did not receive the full co-operation of the state-sponsored in-patient service for alcoholics, and that patients were often *not* encouraged to return to the clinic after hospitalization. Ironically, the social workers at this clinic were also asked to do intake studies for all alcoholic patients applying for admission to the psychiatric treatment center.

Any resident of the state was eligible to receive service at Clinic A. It was perhaps for this reason that well-to-do alcoholics in the community did not accept this clinic for themselves, whereas a considerable proportion of economically marginal and impoverished persons did. Apart from the question of economic status, the clinic served a large proportion of residentially unstable persons. Fees for service could be set and requested, but they were rarely required or collected here.

Staff relationships were good, but in the course of the study an experienced worker resigned to take a better-paid job; her replacement was less experienced in psychiatrically oriented casework and required more time from the supervising social worker. Some months later, another worker resigned to become a housewife, and more pressure was put on the chief social worker who believed that the needs of patients should be met quickly regardless of numbers.

The collaboration of this clinic in the main study was hampered and delayed by the staff's manifold responsibilities other than

27

those of treating alcoholics, by the special difficulties of tracing patients of marginal adjustment, and by staff turnover and difficulties in finding as highly trained replacements. Throughout, however, interest and concern with the patients and what happened to them were manifested by diligent, though dilatory, co-operation.

Clinic B

This clinic was part of the local Department of Health. It was housed in a Department of Health building in a lower class urban area which was noted as a stopping-off place for transients. The clinic served a population of almost a million. The orienting approach of this clinic towards the treatment of alcoholism was that alcoholism is a symptom of a psychiatric disorder requiring the services of a multidisciplinary psychiatric clinic. The staff consisted of a half-time director who was a psychiatrist, two full-time psychologists, four full-time social workers, one of whom supervised the others, a part-time internist, and a full-time public health nurse. All except the nurse and the internist were trained in interviewing. There was a loose liaison with a public hospital to which patients requiring in-patient care could be transferred, by ambulance if necessary.

Because treatment was multidisciplinary, most patients were seen by several members of the staff. The public health nurse saw patients initially, got some background data, dispensed medication prescribed by the physician in his absence, and arranged for physical examinations as needed. The patient was then referred for psychiatric or social work evaluation, or was discussed in conference with the psychiatrist and assigned to a group or to individual therapy; individual psychotherapy was done by all the staff. Some patients were carried by two persons, one for psychological help and the other for physical assistance. Everyone but the public health nurse also did group therapy. Groups were started in this clinic as a means for coping with a large intake, but also for screening out unmotivated persons in order to assign more promising candidates for the limited treatment time available. Originally, the groups were all known as "orientation groups"; a number of them developed willy-nilly into treatment groups, especially for less verbal patients.

Intake in Clinic B had been as high as thirty new cases per month, and intake policy shifted three times during the researchers' acquaintance with the clinic. At first, all comers were seen; then only those patients who came three times were screened and assigned for therapy; and then again all comers were eligible for treatment. The shifting intake policy reflected the clinic's concern over the fact that there were a large number of transients who applied to the clinic for emergency treatment of medical-psychiatric correlates of alcoholism while en route to another area, and who did so clearly without intention or motivation to continue in treatment beyond crises or discomfort.

One of the clinic social workers was assigned half-time to help alcoholics before the municipal court, and many alcoholics were referred by the court on a *non-voluntary basis*. These patients were not considered by the staff to be well motivated for continued treatment. Fees were charged, but collected very infrequently.

The work of the clinic was handicapped by three changes in directorship in the time the clinic was known to the researchers. The position was at most part-time, so that many of the administrative tasks and decisions were delegated to the senior social workers, especially when the director was a neophyte in the field of alcoholism and/or when he was not interested in administrative detail. This weakness in direction accentuated personality conflicts among the staff. Although all the clinic workers were trained professionals, several of them appeared to be fairly indifferent to the needs of the patients. Furthermore, there were many marked differences in professional background and orientation, and many power struggles within the staff which were facilitated by the weak administration. The whole staff expressed frustration with the many patients who were felt to be "hard core" (the clinic's term) alcoholics, which fact might also have contributed to the typically low morale of the clinic.

The researchers' work with the clinic was affected by the nature of the patient population; intake information was often meager when the patient came only once, and the very large percentage of transient patients made follow-up difficult and time-consuming for the staff. However, in this clinic, the researchers had the benefit of a liaison person who was interested in research and prodded the workers when they procrastinated about completing the work. At the same time, when clinic morale was low and personality conflicts flourished, the interest of the liaison person was also inconsistent.

Clinic C

This clinic was located in a large predominantly industrial city. During the intake phase of the study it was housed in the same building as the Department of Welfare near the city skid-row area, but during the follow-up phase it moved to the out-patient and aftercare building of a small state hospital in the outskirts of the city. The clinic was defined as psychiatric with a primary interest in experimentation with drugs as a means of increasing the accessibility of alcoholics to psychotherapy. It was directed throughout the study by a psychiatrist who worked full-time for the first year of the research relationship, and half-time in the second year. He took responsibility for both psychiatric and medical care. There were two full-time and one part-time social worker, a part-time psychologist, and a group therapy consultant who worked with the social workers. All were well trained.

Although there was no direct affiliation with an in-patient service, the clinic could send patients to three state hospitals in the area; two of these kept alcoholic patients for ten days and one for sixty days. Treatment at the clinic was usually individual, patients being seen by the director and the social worker at the same visit. In the course of the researchers' relationship with the clinic, two therapy groups for patients and spouses were begun, and, although they failed to work out, there was always interest and experimentation in this area.

Intake was about thirty patients per month, residence in the state being the only eligibility requirement. Fees were set and accepted, but *rarely* paid. A very large proportion of the clinic's patients were skid-row residents or transients, partly because the clinic had for many years been located in the same offices as the Department of Welfare, and partly, the staff thought, because there had been insufficient interpretation of clinic services to the socially more stable alcoholics in this community.

The administrative direction in Clinic C was strong, and morale and interest in work were high. One social worker resigned during the second year of the study, and the director became part-time instead of full-time because of discouragement about the inadequate budgetary support by the state. Intensely interested in the care and treatment of alcoholic patients, the director administered a particular drug, the use of which increased the case load extensively because more patients returned to the clinic; he then became deeply concerned and annoyed that insufficient services were made available to work with patients whom he believed were made more accessible to psychotherapy through the supportive influence of this drug.

Problems in collaborative work with this clinic were minimal, a reflection of the strong administration and good working relationships within the staff and between them and the research team. Both intake and follow-up were made difficult by the preponderance of skid-row patients who tended to come only once and then were hard to find, and who also were often too sick and/or intoxicated to give very much information about themselves during the one visit they made to the clinic.

Clinic D

This clinic was located in the psychiatric unit of a city general hospital in a large metropolitan area; the hospital was associated with a medical school. The major focus of interest here centered on research; at the time of the study, emphasis was primarily on exploring psychophysiological correlates of alcoholism through studies comparing alcoholic and non-alcoholic populations, and secondarily on studying the usefulness of drug therapy in the treatment of alcoholism. An implicit function of the clinic service was to obtain patients to serve as research subjects.

The staff consisted of a research-oriented medical director who was an internist, four part-time internists, two part-time psychiatrists, a chief social worker who supervised the rotating medical students, a part-time psychologist, one full-time social worker, and a rotating group of psychiatric residents to whom the "best" psychotherapy cases were assigned. Except for those patients referred by social agencies, definite intake appointments were not made in this clinic; rather, there were five "clinics" a week, at any

31

of which new patients could appear and be seen by the social workers. Usually, the patients saw the internist on the same evening, and subsequently many could also see the psychiatrist or the social worker for further evaluation. Whether or not patients were referred for psychiatric diagnosis seemed to depend not only on the mental status of the patients, but also on the need of the training program to give the psychiatric residents experience in evaluating patients with serious drinking problems; about 10 per cent of the patients were seen for psychiatric interviews by these residents. The great bulk of patients were seen by the internists who put a heavy dependence on medication. (As in many crowded clinics, a patient's name was shouted down the corridor when it was his turn to see one of these doctors.) There was one therapy group led by a psychologist, and referrals to the group were made by the psychiatrists. The social workers did no psychotherapy or casework after the original social history; they were heavily involved in other research being carried out by the clinic, being responsible, for example, for recruiting patients for a week's in-patient testing of kinaesthetic reactions on a special service of the hospital.

Intake was open to all persons in the metropolitan area in which the clinic was located, but the patients came mostly from the area closest to the hospital. About 50 per cent of the new patients were alcoholics who had been in-patients in the larger psychiatric hospital of which the clinic was a part. Because alcoholics were admitted to the in-patient service only when they were in *delirium tremens*, suicidal or homicidal, some fairly deteriorated patients were referred from the in-patient service to the clinic. However, clinic patients could be referred for in-patient care only at the discretion of the in-patient physicians with whom the alcoholism clinic did not have close working relationships; for example, the clinic was not informed when its patients were re-admitted to the in-patient service. Fees could be charged, but few patients paid them.

In the life of the study, three staff social workers resigned, and the interest of the chief social worker increasingly shifted from patient care to administrative matters and to supervision of the work of the medical students and student social workers. Uncertainty about the number of patients to be seen at any given clinic, especially an evening one, made for confusion and a sense of pressure on the social workers; also, those social workers interested in treatment were frustrated by the pressures of the large intake (more than thirty new cases per month) and the needs of various on-going research projects. The staff resignations seemed related to these pressures.

The staff of Clinic D was reluctant to continue with the main study after two years' participation in the pilot study because of greater immediate interest in other research being carried on in the clinic, and because of the additional work which the collaborative effort entailed for social workers and medical personnel. If the state administration had not given its active support for continuation of this evaluation study, this clinic would have dropped out. In addition, the researchers had to give considerable extra support, both in money and research supervision, to hold this clinic in the study.

From the very beginning, the clinic regarded the study as an intrusion into its practices, which the researchers noted to be far from the high standards that one might have expected in view of the substantial budgetary support this clinic received. Nevertheless, one social worker was highly co-operative and helpful in coping with the special difficulties of the follow-up phase, in which social work students were involved partly under his supervision. The basic difficulty appeared to lie in the clinic's attitude towards the patient population as a source of material for research rather than as a group of sick persons that the staff hoped to help. In informal conferences between the researchers and clinic staff members, the latter openly voiced and rationalized the above attitudes by pointing out the unsatisfactory state of knowledge about alcoholism and the necessity for basic research without regard to questions of present clinical efficacy.

Clinic E

This clinic was located in a major city of a resort and retirement area. It was set up as a psychiatric clinic with primary interest in psychotherapy. When the researchers began to work with Clinic E, the director was a part-time psychiatrist; another part-time psychiatrist, a part-time psychologist, occasionally a psychiatric resident from a nearby general hospital, a part-time internist, and two full-time trained and experienced social workers completed the staff. Patients were seen first by the receptionist and then, perhaps several times, by the social worker, who in turn referred them to the internist for physical examination or to the psychiatrist for evaluation. Treatment plans were formulated in staff conference. Although the bulk of treatment was individual and handled primarily by the social workers and occasionally by the psychiatrist, one group was carried by the psychologist before he resigned, and another by the director who died in the course of the research relationship; both groups were taken over, one by a social worker, the other by a psychiatrist. Another group, which consisted of wives of alcoholics, was seen off and on by one of the social workers.

In-patient service was available at a state-maintained rehabilitation service for alcoholics where patients were hospitalized for twenty-eight days and treated in large didactic and small therapy groups. This service was at a considerable distance from the clinic, and the amount of effective liaison between the two units was minimal; little or no encouragement was given patients to continue at the clinic after they were discharged from the in-patient service. The only emergency medical treatment available was at the general hospital across the street (from the clinic), from which alcoholics were often sent to a convalescent home (known in the community as a "hell hole") rather than to the state service.

Intake was open only to those patients who had a year's residence in the state, and no court referrals were accepted unless the patient voluntarily agreed to treatment; transients were thus fairly well excluded.

The death of the clinic director and his replacement by the second psychiatrist who was able to give only one-half the time of his predecessor (ten hours a week) meant less time for diagnostic interviews and a cessation of staff meetings. In addition, the clinic social workers had what to them was the time-consuming extra responsibility of covering vacationing staff members at the in-patient rehabilitation center and at one-man clinics elsewhere in the state. Morale consequently was quite poor.

Some of the staff of Clinic E reacted to the research with defensiveness. For example, it was discovered in the "dry run" preceding the intake phase that patients were not being registered after their first visit, but only after they had demonstrated interest in continuing treatment. The purpose of the sampling procedure was then re-clarified, and the staff accepted the arrangement that registration would take place after the first visit. Work was slowed up by the need to adjust to the death of the director and to other demands made on the staff. One of the social workers was continually resistant to contacting patients for follow-up, ostensibly as an invasion of patients' rights, but eventually she did participate in a few. Fortunately, the other social workers saw follow-up as a positive clinical activity and participated in it with considerable zeal.

Clinic F

Located in an industrial and university town, this clinic was one of several set up by the state in its program for the treatment of alcoholics; its functions were well known to persons and agencies in the community. The clinic had always been psychotherapeutically oriented, with a "team" approach; that is, an effort was made to have the patient relate to the clinic as a whole rather than to an individual therapist. The staff consisted of the director who was a half-time internist with many years of interest and experience in the care of alcoholics, two part-time psychiatrists, a part-time psychologist, and two full-time social workers, one of whom supervised the other; all were well trained. Although most of the treatment was carried by the social workers, many patients were seen concurrently by the internist. The psychiatrists served as consultants to the social workers and also carried some patients for individual treatment. Although a psychiatrist and a social worker led a group which had originated from a desire to offer something to the non-verbal patient made anxious by individual therapy, the bulk of treatment continued to be individual psychotherapy attempting to influence the total adjustment of the patient. The psychologist contributed psychometric and projective test data for selected cases. Treatment plans were discussed in a staff meeting once a week.

This clinic had the use of a small voluntary state hospital designated exclusively for the care of alcoholics. Although situated some distance from Clinic F, the hospital made its services available to those referred by the clinic. A half-way house for the chronic alcoholic was also at the disposal of Clinic F.

Intake, which was open to all state residents without regard to their level of sobriety or income, varied monthly from nine to twenty patients who were referred from many social agencies and clinics in the community as well as by other patients. Patients came from all strata of social and economic stability, from transients to established suburbanites.

Although the staff appeared to have genuine interest and skill in helping patients, its functioning was handicapped by administrative and intra-staff conflicts. The over-all director of the state program was not trained in the "helping professions," and there was need for an over-all medical psychiatric director and a director of social service. In the course of the research relationship, there were three new social workers, and, more important, a power struggle between the administration and two of the social workers. One of the social workers became so involved in personal antagonisms that at one point she was unable to see patients; the atmosphere at the clinic became extremely tense, so that both morale and interest in work were low.

The research work was affected by these staff problems. The chief social worker left in the middle of the study, and his replacement resented the additional work of the on-going study. In addition, the study became a football for the warring factions in the clinic to the point that the researchers felt obliged to subsidize fully the follow-up phase of the study to assure its completion.

Clinic G

Constituting the major element in a state alcoholism program, this clinic was housed in a large general hospital which was part of a university medical school in a middle-sized university and industrial capital city. The state program was administered by a social worker who was concerned with personnel problems and the smooth functioning of the program. Its medical direction was provided by a neuropsychiatrist who imbued the whole state program with his orienting attitude towards the treatment of alcoholism. Thus, the primary goal of all the clinics in the state program was to achieve abstinence rather than to deal with or modify the underlying psychologic problems of the patients; indeed, it was felt to be an error to delve into problems and preferable to offer reassurance. Consistent with this policy, Clinic G was the only one of the eight clinics in the study which made extensive use of antabuse.

Clinic G offered both in-patient and out-patient care. Though some patients were seen initially on an out-patient basis, patients at Clinic G were accepted primarily for a program of in-patient care followed by aftercare clinic visits. Patients who were admitted to the in-patient services spent five days in the hospital, and after discharge were seen once per month for follow-up by psychiatrists or internists. An effort was made to ensure that patients were sober enough to know they were being admitted to a hospital, but this practice was not always observed. Similarly, patients who showed no conscious bent towards attaining sobriety could be refused admission or care, although this rule was not usually enforced until the patient had been admitted twice without noticeable improvement in sobriety or in the motivation to attain it. Those who were demonstrably psychotic, who drank while on the ward, or who signed out against medical advice were immediately excluded from readmission. The cost of the in-patient service was about $100 for a week of treatment, which fee was assiduously collected by an accounts supervisor. This feature influenced the nature of the patient population, automatically excluding almost all skid-row persons and favoring the admission of patients who were married, employed, and established in the community.

The out-patient service at Clinic G was staffed by the two internists who took care of the patients during their stay in the hospital, by a trained social worker, and by two part-time psychiatrists who offered diagnostic consultation and carried a few patients.

Clinic G had played an important role in the pilot study (see Chapter 1). At the end of the pilot study, it was learned that the burden of the research (together with the responsibility of screening, admitting, and discharging patients from in-patient care and continuing to offer social-work services to the patients and their families) could no longer be carried out by Clinic G in relation to eight to nine new patients each month. Instead of dropping Clinic G from the study, the researchers explored the possibility of continuing within the state program, because the other four clinics which composed the program carried out the same procedures and philosophy of treatment as did Clinic G. (This consistency within the state program was unusual, for in other programs where several clinics operated under the aegis and support of the state, the philosophy of treatment was observed to differ widely from one clinic in the program to the next.) This consistency was due to the fact that both the administrative and medical direction was centered at and intimately associated with Clinic G which was the model and mentor for the state program as a whole. Just as at Clinic G, the outlying clinics would begin treatment of a patient with in-patient care, either at the in-patient service located at Clinic G or in another medical-school hospital service connected with the state program. Following discharge from in-patient care, the patients would continue under the care of the clinic that had arranged for their in-patient care. The same standards for accepting patients were used by the outlying clinics. They were staffed entirely by part-time personnel, by a medical director who would be an internist and by social workers who were untrained according to the standards of the National Association of Social Workers, but who were college educated, usually imaginative, helpful, and devoted to the work of the clinics. Three of the outlying clinics had part-time psychiatric consultation.

Although the term Clinic G is used to refer to all the patients taken into the study from this state program, the reader is reminded that in fact they came from five interrelated clinics, Clinics G^1, G^2, and so on. Problems in carrying out the research came from two sources; first, there were the logistic problems of training and supervising the staff of five units within the state program in the research procedures. Secondly, there were the problems growing out of the fact that the entire state program consistently carried out its medical rather than psychosocial orientation; the lack of formal training, experience, and clinical judgment in the psychosocial framework of the research made the collection of psychosocial data an arduous task for the untrained social workers, and exceptional research supervision was required from the research staff.

Clinic H

Located in a medium-sized city in a primarily agricultural region, this clinic was oriented towards group and milieu therapy. An effort was made to have patients relate to the clinic as a supportive entity, to see the clinic as a place where they could come to relax as well as to seek treatment. To this end, there was a well-equipped lounge where staff members made themselves available for casual conversation with patients. Also, when the occasion demanded, patients were brought into the treatment program of other patients as sources of transportation, moral support, and so forth.

The staff consisted of a full-time "admissions counsellor," a full-time receptionist, a full-time nurse, a part-time medical director, and between fifteen and twenty part-time staff members including internists, psychiatrists, ministers, a psychologist, and an occupational therapist. None of these staff members except the psychiatrists and psychologist had formal training in interviewing, but all had a genuine interest in learning from one another. Initial procedures were unusual in this clinic. The patient was seen first by the admissions counsellor who explained the voluntary nature of the service, and next by the receptionist. He then returned to the admissions counsellor who set up daily appointments over a week's period for a social history, a meeting with the medical director, a psychiatric interview, an orientation meeting with movies, a physical examination, pastoral counselling, a meeting with the occupational counsellor, and, for many of the patients, a self-administered Minnesota multiphasic personality inventory. Following these appointments, the patient chose a group to attend. These groups were led by ministers, psychiatrists, and internists and met once a week. There was also an occupational therapy group which met twice a week and a group for spouses. Physical therapy at the clinic consisted mainly of a vitamin and tranquilizer regime usually dispensed by the nurse. Patients in need of in-patient care had to be sent to a state-maintained rehabilitation center in another part of the state, while those in need of prolonged medical care or religious counsel were referred to their own physicians or religious leaders. Intake in this clinic was limited to persons who had one year's residence in the state and who came to the clinic sober (in theory but not always in practice). There was a $25 intake fee which could not be waived, but which was usually paid in small installments; this policy excluded some marginal patients.

It was difficult to evaluate the influence that the lack of formal clinical training had on the functioning of the clinic. Certainly, the atmosphere was more casual and less "professional" than at some of the other clinics, and may have had both positive and negative connotations for patient care. The wide range of disciplines represented in this setting was an interesting aspect of the service.

At the outset of the study the researchers' summaries presented a challenge and a threat to the personnel of this clinic who had never attempted to formulate an overview of the patient. After time-consuming attempts it was learned that intake data could be obtained better if the researchers abstracted from the clinic staff's own forms and notes than if the staff was required to use the research instruments. By the time of the follow-up, the personnel was reassured and felt comfortable enough to write adequate case reviews for us.

Because the reader may find it difficult to recall the salient and differentiating features of these clinics, the following summary tabulation is offered. It has been compiled by the authors; other summaries might well describe these multi-faceted treatment contexts with quite different emphases.

Clinic A: social casework, a high level of empathy, sympathy, and "giving" attitude to the patients.

Clinic B: group and individual therapy of good professional caliber in a context of poor morale and high pressure of work.

Clinic C: drugs to enhance the patient's accessibility to psychotherapy; high morale in the face of an impoverished and unstable patient population; strong medical direction.

Clinic D: predominant emphasis on research rather than service; treatment *quid pro quo*, that is, patient given "something" so that he would co-operate with the research needs of the clinic.

Clinic E: highly selective in determining who would be treated with psychotherapy which was provided by caseworkers; weak medical control or supervision.

Clinic F: individual casework and a high level of interest in patients in the context of a weak central administration.

Clinic G: de-emphasis on examination of and concern with psychologic problems; suppression and conscious control encouraged.

Clinic H: a high level of enthusiasm and concern for helping patients with a combination of club house, settlement house, and group therapy by largely non-psychiatric, predominantly part-time staff.

2. SOME GENERALIZATIONS ABOUT ALCOHOLISM CLINICS

On the basis of impressions and observations acquired through experience in the collaborative research, certain generalizations can be made about these publicly supported treatment services—predominantly out-patient services—for alcoholics. Few of the observations that follow are likely to be found in public reports to or by boards because they refer to issues which are talked about by professionals in this field, usually among themselves, seldom to a wider audience.

In the opinion of the researchers, all these clinics suffered from the burdens of their task, that is, of helping patients with severe drinking problems. Not only did the clinics know that many social agencies and psychiatric clinics were loath to treat patients with

41

drinking problems, but they also knew why, for they were all too familiar with the special difficulties of working with such patients: alcoholics' poor motivation for change; their propensity for getting into serious external difficulties which often called for enormous investment of staff time, frequently in apparently hopeless causes; the frequency of treatment drop-out without discussion, much less against advice; the missed appointments; the provocative late-comings; and so forth. In fact, the alcoholism clinics operated in a state of such intense awareness of these difficulties that they anticipated failure rather than success. (Although other clinical fields also experience treatment difficulties their "failures" are usually not quite as conspicuous as are those in the field of alcoholism; that is, chronic mild depression, inability of the person to achieve to the level of his abilities, and the maintenance of private anxieties, symptoms, and inhibitions, are never as dramatic as wife-beating, public intoxication, drunken driving, and crises in health.) Prior to this evaluation study, the staffs of the alcoholism clinics stated that they had not been satisfied with the outcome of their efforts; consequently, they later developed an intensified defensiveness about their work, and also attempted to make themselves feel more successful by altering their intake policies, in the hope that they would maximize the proportion of patients who might improve in their drinking and social relationships.

Another problem was that the staffs of the alcoholism clinics very often regarded themselves as the "poor relative" in the hierarchy of professional prestige and support. Certainly, it is a fact that many competent people leave the field of caring for alcoholics to enter greener pastures, leaving behind a mixture of professionals, of whom some are indeed quite competent, and others, less competent. Among psychiatrists, work with alcoholics is often regarded as a good background, as something to experience, but not to stay with. The effects of this attitude on the morale of the "more competent" who remain is deleterious. Furthermore, their professional position is undermined by the relatively large proportion of non-professionals working in this field, as well as by the conflict with the ex-alcoholics, who, on the basis of their personal experience with alcoholism, claim to be better equipped to help alcoholics than the professionals are. Despite the known difficulties and frustrations entailed in dealing with alcoholics, these clinics, by and large, were not given the budgetary or professional support which might offer compensation for the special difficulties that the work entailed. The staff were not better paid; their case loads were not smaller; special inducements to hold or attract the most experienced and skilled were non-existent. In effect, the communities which sponsored these clinics expected them to do a good job in taking care of alcoholic patients, but did not give them ample support for this task; even if the inadequacies were recognized, service expectations were not lowered.

One of the major consequences of this climate of failure and insufficient support was a high turnover in staff—a turnover which is believed (although the comparative data are not available) to be much higher than that in mental hygiene or child guidance clinics, given the same number of years of operation.

3. SOME GENERALIZATIONS ABOUT COLLABORATIVE EVALUATION RESEARCH

During the course of the relationship between the eight clinics and the researchers, the latter, as noted above, experienced certain difficulties in mediating clinician-researcher interactions. Because these problems are perhaps of broad applicability to evaluation research, some of them are presented below; also discussed are attempts made to solve them.

(a) Sponsorship and Participation

The first general problem area had to do with the discrepancy between sponsorship and participation, that is, with the fact that the sponsorship of the evaluation activity came from administrative levels, but the participation and effort on behalf of the research was the responsibility of non-administrative personnel. Naturally, the clinic personnel had mixed feelings about the additional uncompensated work which the study required, and perhaps even more about the additional responsibility which was imposed upon them. Administrative persons can be quite cavalier in deciding that clinic workers easily have time available for a research project. That some of the administrators in the clinics studied may actually have made a correct assumption only enhanced the defensiveness on the part of the clinic personnel.

The researchers tried to cope with this problem by establishing a relationship with the clinic staffs in which the latter felt free to communicate their complaints and resentment. Many hours were spent in trying to educate them about research and involve them in the study through informal discussions about the problems of alcoholism and the treatment of this syndrome. Despite these efforts, the researchers were not wholly successful in involving the clinic staffs, especially the part-time medical personnel whose interest in working at the clinics often was based on the wish for additional income with a minimum investment of additional time. In some clinics, it was particularly difficult to get these physicians to fill out the treatment forms, not so much because of the few minutes this task required, but more because it represented an intrusion into their independent attitude.

The follow-up phase realistically added considerable burden to the work of the clinic staffs, because new patients continued to come into the clinic at about the same rate as they had during the intake phase of the study, and no clinic reduced its intake in order to carry out the follow-up study. The intake phase of the study undoubtedly had been an extension, to varying degrees, of customary clinical activity, whereas the follow-up phase introduced a set of procedures and activities entirely foreign to their regular practices. Thus, by the time the intake phase of the study had been completed, the initial warm readiness to grant time for research had dissolved with the pressure of the clinics' continuing service requirements.

There were problems at two levels, the first of which concerned the rights of patients. A number of social workers involved in the follow-up phase believed that tracing and inquiring about the functioning of a person who no longer sought their help was an unwarranted invasion of the patient's privacy, and might militate against his ever returning to the clinic. In discussing this matter with the workers, the researchers supported the concern for patients' rights and tried to bring to the workers' attention the fact that the entire purpose of the study was to acquire more and better knowledge about alcoholism, so that better services might be rendered to patients. Examples were cited of patients who were in dire need of help and who experienced a follow-up interview not as an expression of hostile curiosity, but rather as an expression of professional concern which led them to return for treatment. It is interesting to note that this problem did not come into discussion in any of the preliminary contacts during the pilot study, or during the intake phase of the study; rather it struck the minds of many of the collaborating social workers only after they had actually participated in follow-up evaluations.

At another level, the follow-up study meant additional work for the individuals involved without additional support from the clinics. It called for night work, weekend work, home visits, diligent inquiry by mail and by telephone to patients as well as to collaterals and other agencies. Fortunately, the clinics had by this point invested sufficiently in the research so that the researchers could in part make up for the additional burden by special payments out of research funds. On the basis of what had been learned in the pilot study about the time and effort required, a schedule of payments was drawn up so that the social worker would be paid for home visits even if they were unfruitful.

(b) Change and Growth

The second problem had to do with the fact that the collaboration was a challenging experience, calling for both change and growth. The research design required that the data be collected by the staffs of the participating clinics in the hope that they would become familiar with research procedures and would continue an interest in research, specifically in evaluation, after the collaboration was concluded. For many of the clinic workers whose professional training for research interviewing was meager or incomplete, the method of recording intake data for the study required them to function at a somewhat higher level than was customary for them; they were asked to conceptualize, to think diagnostically, to think about the meaning of information they were acquiring, and to attempt to get a fuller grasp through

45

collecting a standardized minima of information. For the more experienced workers, on the other hand, these same aspects of data collection were considered antithetical to theoretical concepts which they had evolved in the course of their training or their experience with alcoholics; in particular, they had to submerge partially their own theories and related treatment approaches in the cause of research—a procedure which implicitly challenged the correctness of their points of view. Here again, the researchers attempted to cope with these issues through open discussion of ideas and feelings.

One example of the challenge presented to the experienced staff related to the widespread concept, particularly in social work, of "accepting the patient where he is" when he first comes for help; the workers were afraid that any structured approach towards studying the patient at intake might disturb his precarious defensive equilibrium. Notably they would assiduously avoid inquiry into the patient's social activities and relationships, feeling that this area would be especially sensitive because the patient might not wish to have the putative emptiness of his life exposed and discussed. Fortunately, the researchers had data to demonstrate that the drop-out rate of patients who were studied with the minimal standards established for the study was no greater than that of patients who were approached in this more protective fashion. Parenthetically, the question of what constitutes a proper intake study in a clinic is a serious problem within many psychiatric clinics.

(c) Research versus Treatment

The third problem had to do with the emotional and practical issue of "research versus treatment." By and large, the clinic staffs were orientated towards "helping" and not towards "research." They were afraid that patients would be considered as guinea pigs, that patients would be asked questions which were merely to satisfy the arcane interest of the researchers and which would be irrelevant to the helping process. They were afraid that the research staff might not understand practice and might not be sympathetic to the realities of working in a clinical setting. Fortunately for the purposes of the research, the research staff in fact were not unsympathetic, by and large having as much of an interest in the helping activities as did the clinic staffs themselves, and expressing their interest in conferences and in informal discussions with the clinic staffs about the problems of dealing with certain of their patients. Conversely, for at least one "research-oriented" clinic, the researchers' interest in helping the patients conflicted with the staff's more limited or at least different research goals to which the breadth of psychosocial understanding was irrelevant.

Finally, it was important for the researchers to clarify some of the clinicians' misunderstandings of research. For example, there was one point of distinction which to a research-trained person seems superficial, yet for many clinicians is a difficult point: the research instruments were addressed to the clinic's understanding of the patient, not to the patient; that is, these forms were not marketing survey questionnaires to be held in hand while "interviewing," but rather modes of systematic study reporting data acquired in clinical interaction.

(d) Personalities

Fourthly, there was the ubiquitous problem of "personalities." There were times when tempers ran short, when nagging met with passive obstructionism, when back-biting and mild slander were indulged in. But because the researchers believed that accepting and dealing with the matter of personalities was inherent in evaluation research (as it is in any interdisciplinary research), they aimed to establish a relationship in which free discussion permitted the ventilation of hostility and a task-oriented resolution of the difficulties encountered in the operation of the study. It may have been fortunate that they were never in a position to fire the clinic staffs with whom they worked. In consequence of the nature of the interrelationship between clinic personnel and researchers, the latter were able to obtain a high level of co-operation, and therefore a high percentage of follow-up interviews on a population of patients expected to be elusive, resistant, and defensive.

4. SOME GENERAL RECOMMENDATIONS

Some general recommendations can be made from our experience, recommendations which the researchers believe may be applicable to evaluation research in other clinical areas: (1) it is extremely important that the working staff participate in the decision to take part in the study; (2) it is preferable to over-estimate than to under-estimate the required work; (3) the implications of the special work for regular service responsibilities should be clarified and accommodation to this planned for in advance; (4) research instruments should be constructed in a fashion geared to the realities of practice—they should be as brief as is consistent with the needs of the research; (5) it is crucial that a democratic researcher-clinician group be established, so that inevitable resentments, confusions, and defensiveness be prevented from undoing the work or interfering with its course; (6) the development of a liaison person who can act as intermediary between researchers and clinicians is an extremely helpful adjunct, because the clinics accept prodding or criticism from their own staffs with better grace than from the research staff.

A final recommendation is the warning that although money is a helpful adjunct to maintaining the interest and participation of the clinic staffs in the more arduous phases of evaluation research, by itself it is remarkably ineffectual. No amount of it can buy their interest, and participation without interest, as a general rule, produces valueless material. As was mentioned in the introductory chapter, one of the clinics was not able to continue in the follow-up phase because of the disintegration of the structure of social welfare of which it was a part, and no amount of money was effectively able to enhance the workers' interest, when the meaninglessness of their work, in view of the circumstances in which they were operating, became evident to them.

III. Characteristics of Clinic Patients at Intake

1. INTRODUCTION

BECAUSE SOME picture of the characteristics of the patients who came to the out-patient clinics is a necessary background to the understanding of patient participation and treatment, this chapter reviews and summarizes a large quantity of statistical material indicative of the status and functioning of patients at the time of intake. Although the authors have tried to organize and present these data in as meaningful and interesting a fashion as possible, the reader is warned that this is the kind of chapter which the non-statistically minded might find arid or dull.

Three topics are covered. First, there is the alcoholism of the patients; that is, as a group, to what degree did their dependence on alcohol (to paraphrase the statement of the World Health Organization Expert Committee[1]) reach such a point as to show noticeable mental disturbance, or interference with their bodily or mental health? Secondly, there are the identifying social characteristics of the patients. It is hoped that such a description of patients who came to the state-supported alcoholism clinics is of interest to persons concerned with the public health aspects of psychiatry, as a basis for comparison with other ill or deviant populations, for example, out-patient or in-patient psychiatric patients, prisoners, and so forth. As far as possible, the identifying social characteristics are compared with those of the general population. Although the skid-row stereotype of the alcoholic is no longer as viable as it was when Straus and Bacon[13] reported their study of the alcoholism clinic populations of nine states, these current data offer a replication of the hypothesis that "the alcoholic" is not grossly different from other members of the

society in which he lives. The third topic concerns the characteristics of the patients' social functioning (when they first came
to these clinics for help); that is, how disrupted were their personal relationships? how well could they work, or were they
working at the time of intake to the clinics?

2. THE ALCOHOLISM OF THE PATIENTS

As was pointed out above, the clinics did not systematically or
explicitly evaluate the relevance—or the extent of the relevance
—of the concept "alcoholism" for their patients. However, they
did, to some extent, assemble certain data which could be related
to what the authors regard as the central concepts in the World
Health Organization Expert Committee discussions on and definition of alcoholism:[1] dependence on alcohol, noticeable mental
disturbance, and interference with mental or bodily health.
Although there is no consensus on criteria for these terms, they
are useful constructs around which the clinical data can be
organized and presented.

(a) Dependence on Alcohol

The psychophysiologic nature of dependence on alcohol is a
complex and unresolved issue. With the opiate drugs, dependence
is unquestionably a biologic process which entails the maintenance of a certain level of a substance to sustain apparently
normal bodily function; even decerebrate dogs and the new born
infants of addicted mothers suffer from the withdrawal of
opiates.[14] The most explicit evidence for dependence on alcohol
comes from the extreme experimental situation devised by Isbell,[15]
in which acute withdrawal of alcohol from chronically intoxicated
(more than forty days of consecutive intake of alcohol at co-ordi-
nation-impairing levels) subjects precipitated convulsions and/or
psychotic reactions. Whether alcoholics outside the laboratory
sustain such prolonged intoxication or not cannot be said, although
it is known that this situation certainly occurs much less frequently
than do "rum fits" or *delirium tremens*. But whether there is a
"real" pharmacological dependence on alcohol or not, the indi-

vidual may *believe* (or the clinician may infer) that he has such a pathological need for alcoholic beverages, a belief which may of course significantly affect his drinking behavior (or his clinical management).

(i) BELIEF OF PATIENTS. Only 56 per cent of the patients unequivocally believed that they were alcoholics, that is, that they had a pathological need for alcohol which was beyond their control; another 15 per cent related ambiguously to this question; and 24 per cent unequivocally denied that they were alcoholics. Although only slightly more than half of the patients were sure that they were alcoholics, clinical observers felt that the total picture—the history, reports from collaterals, and the clinic staff's own observations—indicated that 92 per cent of the patients had serious drinking problems and might be regarded as alcoholics, at least in the perspective of the month preceding intake. Of these, 85 per cent had gross difficulties in their lives associated with their use of alcohol, either within their families (67 per cent) and/or in their extrafamilial relationships (62 per cent), that is, work, school, social relationships. A small proportion of the patients were abstinent at least for the month preceding intake, a fact requiring special discussion (see below).

(ii) OBSERVED BEHAVIOR OF PATIENTS. Another source of conviction about dependence on alcohol was the observed behavior of patients during their relationships with the clinics. It is assumed here that the person who is not dependent on alcohol would not drink in the context of his interaction with the clinic to which he reports because he would be attempting to achieve or display abstinence or control over the use of alcoholic beverages. However, 42 per cent of the patients were obviously under the influence of alcohol at their first visits to the clinics, either exhaling an odor of alcoholic beverages or telling of the use of alcohol that day (11 per cent), being grossly intoxicated (12 per cent were mal-co-ordinated in locomotion and speech), or suffering from a "hangover" (19 per cent). Furthermore, about the same proportion of patients (42 per cent) continued to use alcohol during the course of their contacts with the clinics.

(iii) HISTORY OF DRINKING. Although the details were not regularly reported by the clinics, the patients admitted to the use of

51

alcohol and to episodes of intoxication or excessive use going back many years. For the 686 patients (77 per cent) for whom such data were available, more than half (54 per cent) had been using alcohol to excess for ten or more years. About a quarter (22 per cent) had been using alcohol to excess for five to nine years, and about the same proportion (23 per cent) for less than five years; of the latter group only 2.7 per cent admitted excessive use for less than one year.

For slightly less than half the patients (407 cases) data were available as to whether or not they had had relatively long periods of abstinence. Of 229 cases, 55 per cent had never since their drinking began had a period of abstinence as long as six months; 33 per cent had had one period for as long as six months; 5 per cent had had several such periods; and 6 per cent had had some such period of abstinence but it was not known whether this was singular or recurrent. It was conjectured that the "no reports" which were returned on this question for the majority of the patients probably signified that there never had been such a period of abstinence in the drinking lives of these patients.

Obviously these data were a poor source of verification concerning dependence on alcohol, because the general adult population is not typically abstinent, especially not in the states studied where social drinking among adults is the rule rather than the exception. However, when it was assumed that abstinence is a desirable episode in the life of an alcoholic, and that the clinicians' appraisal (92 per cent had drinking problems) was correct, it was concluded that as a group these patients rarely had been capable of prolonged abstinence in the more than five years of excessive use of alcohol which was typical of this population.

(iv) CONSCIOUS MOTIVES FOR DRINKING. It was thought that the motives and the setting of drinking might cast some further light on the question of dependence. Although it was assumed that the main non-pathologic reasons for drinking alcoholic beverages are dietary, social, and religious, the patients almost never interpreted their drinking in such terms. Fifty-six per cent drank for relief of psychological symptoms, especially anxiety and depression; 14 per cent sought alleviation of physical symptoms or discomfort, such as menstrual cramps, peripheral vascular disease, arthritis; 28 per cent felt that they drank because they could not stop, which of course was the most appealing type of evidence for the fact of, or the belief by patients in, their dependent need for alcohol. On the other hand, 11 per cent boldly asserted that they had no need to stop drinking because their drinking was completely under their control; parenthetically, they were sometimes acutely intoxicated while making this assertion.

Whatever the motives of a person's drinking may be, as consciously experienced and expressed, there are certain situations where drinking is unquestionably supported by the social setting, for example, cocktail parties, and weddings, and where it might be regarded as freer from dependence on alcohol than is drinking taking place outside of such settings. However, the data indicated that 37 per cent of the patients drank alone; another 34 per cent drank with casual acquaintances; and only 11 per cent drank in the setting of their family or with close or intimate friends. Thus, only a small minority did their drinking in settings which themselves might be supportive of drinking, and the remainder drank in contexts where the individual's drinking might be inferred to be motivated by dependence on alcohol.

(b) Noticeable Mental Disturbance

By and large the drinking of the patients seen in these NAAAP clinics had not reached a point where there were such noticeable mental disturbances as disorientation in time and place, memory loss, or aphasic states; such gross disorders of perception as delusion and hallucinations; or such mentally determined disturbed bodily states as the various hysterical or conversion symptoms. Patients with such mental disturbances, even though the symptoms were ostensibly or probably related to alcoholism, were more apt to be found in such facilities as mental hospitals, and neurologic and psychiatric clinics. Similarly, those patients who suffered from such syndromes as Korsakoff's or Wernicke's, or from alcoholic hallucinosis rarely came or were brought to the NAAAP clinics.

However, there were noticeable mental disturbances, which

were not infrequently reported as elements in the current life history of patients. The data indicated that these patients sometimes had symptoms of mental disturbances of a transitory nature, the most common form of which was the "blackout," an episode of amnesia for events occurring in the context of acute intoxication. As with all amnesias, as Schilder has pointed out,[16] there may be forces inhibiting the return of registered experience in which both physiologic and psychodynamic factors may be involved. Thirty per cent of the patients reported this disturbance of memory in the year preceding intake.

The most common syndrome associated with alcoholism was *delirium tremens*, 15 per cent of the patients being known to have had this acute medical-psychiatric disturbance in the year preceding intake. However, there were widespread differences among the clinics with regard to the prevalence of these mental disturbances: at Clinic D, where the main source of intake was the in-patient service of the associated psychiatric teaching unit, 50 per cent of the patients had had blackouts and 44 per cent *delirium tremens*, whereas at Clinic E almost 50 per cent of the patients had had blackouts, but only 10 per cent *delirium tremens*.

To summarize, the majority of the patients who came to the state-supported alcoholism clinics had not suffered and were not suffering from noticeable mental disturbances except of a transitory nature. That they might suffer from such disturbances in the future of course was not unlikely.

(c) Interference with Mental or Bodily Health

Did the use of alcohol interfere with the patients' mental health? There were two considerations here: was their mental health impaired? if so, was it owing to the use of alcohol? With regard to the first question, it is the common experience in an out-patient or an in-patient service that whenever a psychiatrist evaluates a patient with a drinking problem he will make a psychiatric diagnosis. If he does not make such a diagnosis as personality trait disturbance, psychosis of undetermined origin, or organic brain condition, he will undoubtedly affirm that the patient suffers from a personality pattern disturbance called addiction. From this perspective, all patients with a drinking

54

problem suffer from impaired mental health. Moreover, because nearly all psychiatrists tend to regard the excessive use of alcohol as symptomatic of emotional disturbance, by definition all persons with a drinking problem can be considered impaired in their mental health.

The second question—whether this emotional disturbance was related to the use of alcohol—could not be answered from any of the data collected by the clinics with whom the researchers worked. However, because in most cases the answer would depend on the observer's frame of reference, it was probable that, in the context of today's psychodynamic influence in psychiatry, the patients' impaired mental health preceded and was dynamically related to their excessive use of alcohol and not vice versa; however, a certain number of patients might be considered to have been more impaired in their mental health through the excessive use of alcohol.

When an attempt was made to approach this question without reference to these ambiguities, there were some limited data on the extent of involvement with psychiatric facilities, or on illnesses or diagnoses, preceding the patients' first contacts with the clinic. For example, 8 per cent of the patients were treated for depression in the year preceding their first contact; 5 per cent had suffered from a sexual problem; 7 per cent had been treated for some unspecified mental illness; and 4 per cent had had some kind of medical treatment for nervousness, anxiety, or depression, that is, treatment outside of an institutional psychiatric setting. In short, the majority of the patients (more than 75 per cent) were not seen in settings where psychiatric diagnoses might have been made prior to the first visit to the NAAAP clinics. Had they been, and had their drinking history been known, it was most probable that all of them would have been assigned some psychiatric diagnosis.

Had the patient's dependence on alcohol impaired his bodily health? To some degree, each episode of acute intoxication impairs bodily health, though such impairment may very well be only transitory or functional. For example, many of the patients suffered some disturbances of sleep (45 per cent) such as insomnia or restlessness, or of appetite (46 per cent) in the year preceding intake. Although the data were not generally clear on this point, the bulk of the evidence indicated that these functional disturbances occurred while patients were in phases of acute intoxication or hangover, rather than while relatively abstinent.

The question posed above had to be refined so that it asked instead whether there were relatively persistent interferences with bodily health. Although some alcoholics first came to the clinics in grossly poor health, the majority of those studied first came in good health. It was conjectured that those obviously suffering from late complications of cirrhosis of the liver were to be found more commonly in medical or surgical wards or clinics. Also, although tuberculosis is regarded as a not infrequent occurrence among persons with serious drinking problems and vice versa, it was considered that those suffering actively with tuberculosis were more likely to be found in the special facilities for patients suffering from this disease.

Two-thirds of the patients described their health as good when they first came to the clinic. Of the remainder who reported that their health was generally not good, one-half (16 per cent) described it as fair, indicating that they could function despite certain health problems, and the other half (16 per cent) reported themselves as in poor health, stating that their lives were grossly affected by one or another type of illness. Supporting the patients' appraisals of their health were data obtained from the informal recording of the medically untrained clinic staffs: only 7 per cent of the patients were observed to be grossly ill at intake, that is, excluding the acute or recent effects of bouts of intoxication; another 17 per cent appeared not well, but it was unclear in the minds of the clinic observers whether this state was a result of acute or recent effects of alcohol, or whether it was representative of a persistent bodily disturbance associated with alcoholism.

The influence of alcohol use as a factor impairing the bodily health of the patients studied by these clinics was not determinable from the data. Because any illness may be aggravated by alcohol use or by its behavioral or dietary consequences, it is impossible to know the relation between illness and alcohol use without a careful and detailed review of the patient's medical history. Thus pneumonia may be the outcome of a chilling which a person received when comatose or asleep in the open; head injuries may be sustained when someone under the influence of alcohol is driving a car; or an ulcer may perforate or bleed profusely because of the irritant effect of alcohol. Such detailed study of the patient's health was rarely a part of either the initial or the later work-up of the patients. In fact, medical evaluation varied markedly from clinic to clinic: in some of the clinics, Clinic G for example, a thorough medical work-up, including a number of laboratory tests, was part of the routine study of a patient; in others, an internist was called upon when the non-medical personnel were alerted to conditions requiring the attention of a specialist.

Despite these differences in medical evaluation, there was remarkable consistency from clinic to clinic in the medical conditions reported and observed in their patients. Nineteen per cent of the patients were suspected to be suffering from some kind of gastrointestinal illness. The figures, which ranged in a normal curve from 10 to 34 per cent, did not reflect availability of internists or opportunity for special medical study. In slightly more than half of these cases, gastrointestinal illness was diagnosed; in the remainder it was suspected, looked for, but not confirmed. The most common gastrointestinal illness was peptic or gastric ulcer, which occurred in 3.5 per cent of the patients. Because peptic or gastric ulcer is a fairly common condition, occurring in as many as 10 per cent of the general male population—at least according to health surveys and reviews of post mortem examinations—the data did not indicate gross over-representation of the disorder in clinic patients.[17] Cirrhosis of the liver —the classical instance of alcoholism's interference with bodily health—occurred in only 3.2 per cent of the patients in the year preceding intake, and gastritis and miscellaneous gastrointestinal illnesses in another 3.7 per cent.

The extent of alcoholism of the patients who came to the outpatient voluntary services of the NAAAP clinics may be briefly summarized. First, those data which had some, though admittedly loose, association with dependence, suggested that a weak majority of the patients accepted themselves as "alcoholics," but that the clinicians considered almost all patients to be suffering from drinking problems. In the course of their contacts with the clinics, almost half the patients were observed to be using alcohol despite the "anti-alcoholic" character of their relationships with the clinics. Most patients had been using alcohol to excess for more than five years, and very few for less than a year. Since they had first begun drinking, most patients had not had periods of prolonged abstinence. Their conscious motives for using alcohol were almost never social, religious, or dietary; they drank alone or with casual companions, and only rarely with close friends or relatives, which fact suggested that dependency on the use of alcoholic beverages, rather than social supports for drinking, was probably the major determining factor.

Secondly, most of the patients did not have any "noticeable mental disturbances," except those of a transitory nature such as blackouts and *delirium tremens*. Thirdly, the patients' mental health could be regarded as impaired by definition, but not usually by the evidence of psychiatric observations or of treatment or diagnoses prior to their first contacts with the NAAAP clinics. Their bodily health in the majority of cases was good, except in the context of acute intoxication, when disturbances of sleep and appetite were not infrequent.

Those patients who did suffer from noticeable mental disturbances or whose mental and bodily health was impaired through the use of alcohol probably did not find their way to these clinics. A survey of the prevalence of ill health associated with alcoholism would have to incorporate samples of patients in the state mental and tuberculosis hospitals and in the general hospitals, as well as those patients handled by private physicians.

3. IDENTIFYING SOCIAL CHARACTERISTICS

The social characteristics of patients are of growing significance and interest to the clinician as well as to the social scientist, for, as Hollingshead and Redlich have pointed out, the kinds of treatment offered are often determined by the social class positions of patients.[18] Also, Straus and Bacon have suggested that patients' motivations to participate in treatment may reflect their social stability;[13] those in a marginal or dependent position have little to lose by continuation of their alcoholism—apart from their lives —whereas those who have social positions that are worthy of sustaining or defending are likely to be better motivated to stop drinking or to accept help.

(a) Social Stability

Three aspects of social status being considered as criteria of stability, it was possible to divide the patient population of the clinics into four groups, ranging from one in a maximally stable position which therefore was worth sustaining, to one in a minimally stable position where little was left to uphold. These criteria were based on whether the patient at intake was (1) married, (2) living with his family, and (3) regularly employed.

The first group consisted of those patients who fulfilled all three criteria. Thirty-one per cent were in this maximal position. Parenthetically, the data contrasted with the findings previously reported by Straus and Bacon.[13] In the present sample, 35 per cent were married and living with their wives, compared to 53 per cent in the earlier study, although in both samples 66 per cent could be described as residentially stable, that is, living in some kind of permanent family setting. Forty per cent of the present sample were regularly employed at intake, compared to 7 per cent of the group described by Straus and Bacon.

Twenty-eight per cent of the patients fulfilled two of the criteria, and 23 per cent, one; 18 per cent, those likely to be found in a skid-row or comparable social setting, fulfilled none. There were considerable differences between clinics: for example, at Clinic C, 22 per cent of the patients were married, 47 per cent not living alone, and 32 per cent regularly employed, whereas, at Clinic G, 69 per cent of the patients were married, 90 per cent not living alone, and 51 per cent regularly employed at intake. Later in the book the authors report on the relationship between social stability (as measured in terms of these criteria), and the motivation for treatment and maintenance of abstinence.

(b) Occupational Status

When the clinic population was looked at from a demographic standpoint, the occupational status of the patients was found to be remarkably similar to that of the general population, with one exception; that is, very few farmers (less than one per cent) used the clinics. Whether this latter fact reflected that farmers rarely became alcoholics or that the clinics were inaccessible to farm areas was not known. Certainly, the clinics were not located in rural areas.

(c) Educational Level

The educational background of the clinic population differed from that of the general population. According to the 1950 census 14 per cent of males had attended college, whereas the proportion of the clinic population was 16 per cent. Thirty-five per cent of the male population had attended high school, compared to 53 per cent of the clinic population; and 51 per cent of the general population had education at the grammar school level only, compared to 31 per cent of the clinic population.

(d) Race

Although the racial distribution of the patients resembled that of the population as a whole (15 per cent of the patients were colored), this similarity was probably an artifact of restrictive intake policies. Thus the proportion of Negroes seen in the southern clinics was substantially smaller than would be warranted by their representation in the population. With certain very rare exceptions in its history, Clinic G did not accept Negroes for treatment. Clinic H accepted them for individual treatment, a type of treatment which they rarely gave, but not for group treatment, which was the clinic's preferred treatment approach; nor was participation in the therapeutic milieu encouraged for Negroes. The percentage of Negroes in Clinic B was 42 per cent, about the same as their representation in the population of the area. In contrast, Clinic F saw almost twice as many Negroes (27 per cent) as were found in the population of its city.

Although there is a common prejudice that alcoholism, as distinguished from a propensity for intoxication, is rare among Negroes, official vital statistics show that the occurrence of cirrhosis of the liver and of psychoses associated with alcoholism is about twice as common among non-Whites as among Whites.[19] It can thus be hypothesized that the under-utilization of the state-

60

supported clinics (with some exceptions) by Negroes was part of a "self fulfilling prophecy," to use Merton's well-turned phrase,[20]* rather than a reflection of the low prevalence of drinking problems among Negroes. Only in Clinic F, where a large urban Negro population was accustomed to receiving services on an equal basis with Whites, was the proportion of Negroes consistent with the data in vital statistics, which are in large measure the basis for the estimation of alcoholism prevalence in population groups.[21]

(e) Nativity

Ninety-four per cent of all clinic patients were born in the United States, and of these 77 per cent were third-generation Americans (an additional 4 per cent were Canadians). Considering the heavy influx of foreign immigrants into all of the clinic communities outside the south, the proportion of first- or second-generation alcoholics was therefore smaller than would be expected. It is therefore possible that acculturation is a factor that enhances alcoholism, a point of view which Klineberg proposed in his book on race differences.[22] At least it is an unequivocal factor enhancing patients' coming to state-supported clinics.

(f) Religious Denomination

Almost two-thirds of the clinic population were Protestant and the remainder Roman Catholic. Very few patients were Jewish (one per cent), and those that were were found in cities with very large Jewish populations. This finding was in accord with that of Bales,[23] who in studying drinking among different cultural groups, observed that alcoholism was practically absent among Jews; and with that of Snyder[24] who noted that alcoholism was extremely rare among Jews, but that, with the shift in drinking patterns among third-generation Jews, it might be expected to have been or to have become a problem for this group.

(g) Sex and Age

The sex and age distribution of the patients differed from that of the general population. For example, although there were

*Prejudicial attitudes impede the utilization of a facility; hence the statistics describing utilization "fulfill" the prejudices or prediction that Negroes do not need services for alcoholism.

slightly more women than men in the population as a whole, only one out of every six patients was female—a proportion comparable to that reported in other studies.[25] With regard to age, two-thirds of the patients were in the age group from thirty to fifty; only 9 per cent were younger than thirty years; and only 4 per cent were sixty years of age or older. This age distribution differed from the general population in which 16 per cent of the total adult population over twenty years of age was (according to the census figures for 1960) over sixty. Several factors might have accounted for this difference. First, the age specific death rate may be greater among alcoholics than among the general population, a finding which has been reported elsewhere.[26] Secondly, the older alcoholic did not come to these clinics; older persons who were still alcoholic and suffered longer with this syndrome might have had severe impairments of mental or bodily health which would have taken them to in-patient psychiatric or neurologic facilities, or to medical or surgical clinics where late complications with cirrhosis would be treated.

(h) Marital Status

The compilation of statistics about the marital status of patients with drinking problems is important from two points of view. First, from the perspective of social psychiatry, it is important to know to what extent these patients are in a position to affect harmfully the lives and welfare of those others in the community with whom they have direct, intimate, and prolonged relationships, specifically their wives and children. Secondly, from a prognostic perspective, the married alcoholic may have a greater chance of improvement than the alcoholic who has no wife or children, because the wife and children exert pressure on him to give up drinking, and because he stands to gain the support of their increased appreciation and respect. Both the pressure to abstain and the rewards for abstinence are lacking for the single alcoholic. Although some wives of alcoholics may have a stake in the perpetuation of their husbands' drinking problems, recent data[27] suggest that this phenomenon is not frequently relevant to the drinking problems of married alcoholics.

The data indicated that almost all the patients (85 per cent) had been married at some time in their lives; 21 per cent had been married two, three, or more times. However, at the time they came to the clinics, only about half (47 per cent) of the patient population were married. Of these, 11 per cent were currently in second or third marriages; 34 per cent were currently either separated or divorced; and another 4 per cent were widowed. The frequency of divorce and separation among the clinic patients was about twice as high as that among the general population. Of those patients who had been married at some time, more than half had been divorced or legally separated; according to census figures, roughly one-quarter of marriages in the general population ended in divorce or separation.

The prospective social impact that alcoholism had on the families of the patients was further highlighted by the fact that 67 per cent of the patients had children, and 47 per cent of their children were minors (below twenty-one years of age), mostly between eight and twenty years of age; thus the children had already been exposed to their parents' drinking problems for many years.

4. SOCIAL FUNCTIONING

Just as there is an extensive literature depicting alcoholics as persons with severely impaired adjustment patterns,[28] so the data on the state-supported clinics indicated that, despite marked individual differences in social adjustment within the group, many of the patients had serious difficulties both in their personal relations and in their roles as workers.

(a) *Personal Relationships*

The patients' personal relationships were overtly disturbed or meager. For example, the above data on divorce and separation suggested that many patients had not been able to cope with the vicissitudes of marital life. Also, the data on the year preceding intake showed that about 13 per cent of those patients who were legally married at intake were out of touch with their wives. Of those who were still with their spouses or who maintained some relationship with them, 79 per cent had "poor marital relationships"—defined for purposes of this study as involving marked complaints about, or unhappiness or dissatisfaction with, the marital partner, whether these are expressed by the patient or the spouse. For only 8 per cent of those patients who were currently married were such complaints completely absent from the records. In one-third of all marriages, the marriage was currently on the verge of dissolution or had already been functionally dissolved, although the patient was still legally married and the formal separation had not taken place. In another third, the marriage was marked by severe and usually frequent arguments, verbal abuse, or beatings. In one-fifth, the spouse explicitly described the mate with the drinking problem as undesirable or sick, or as a cause of major trouble. Interestingly, complaints about financial irresponsibility, or about infidelity or other sexual difficulties were expressed in relatively few cases (one in seven and one in fifteen, respectively).

It was found that the patients' relationships with relatives were generally described as better than those with spouses. Almost all (all but 8 per cent) of the marriages of the patients were overtly troubled when the patients came to the clinics, whereas the great majority of relationships between the patients and their families of origin were reportedly not severely troubled (81 per cent). This difference might have reflected the fact that the patients had very much less contact with their relatives than with their spouses. However, the fact that there were no complaints expressed by the parents or siblings about a patient, or vice versa, did not clarify the *quality* or "normality" of the relationship, which might indeed have been characterized by extreme emotional dependency, passivity, or mutually acceptable sado-masochistic interactions.

Evidence of the meagerness of the patients' interpersonal relationships was obtained from the clinic descriptions of the patients' friendship patterns. In this sample of patients, only 30 per cent maintained that they had close friends; 41 per cent reported only casual acquaintances; and 11 per cent stated that they had no friends. Data were not obtained in 18 per cent of the cases; because this "no data" group was composed almost entirely of transients and of patients who were living alone, and considering what was known in general about the lives and relationships of this unattached group, it could be assumed that these patients would belong to the groups who had only casual acquaintances or no friends.

Data clarifying the social relationships of the patients at the time of intake were obtained by inquiring about the social participation and activities of the patients. About two-thirds of the patients for whom data were available led an extremely isolated existence; of these 31 per cent described their activities as "solitary" in character—reading, going to movies, watching television, or most often doing nothing, and an additional 34 per cent characterized their social lives as limited to drinking with casual acquaintances or strangers. Of the remaining one-third, 16 per cent described their activities as limited to family life (that is, they stayed at home after work and on weekends with parents, spouses, or children); 5 per cent devoted the major part of their social lives to AA activities; and only 14 per cent described what might be regarded as full or normal social lives which included participation in activities shared with other family members, mutual visiting with friends, and/or involvement in organized social activities.

Although alcoholism is regarded as a frequent concomitant of asocial and deviant behavior, the latter was noted only in a minority of patients who came to the state-supported clinics. Twenty-one per cent engaged in overt physical aggression or threatened violence when drunk; 11 per cent drove their cars while under the influence of alcohol; and 3 per cent had been involved in automobile accidents associated with drinking. Arrests or summons to appear before a court for offences related to drinking were noted for 37 per cent of the patients; most of these had been arrested or summoned more than five times, and another large proportion between three and five times. However, the data pertinent to assessing the prevalence of asocial and deviant behavior were insufficient: in half the cases, this aspect of the patients' lives either had not been investigated or had not been recorded. Consequently, the above figures were minimal estimates of the actual frequency of such difficulties in social adjustment.

(b) Relationship to Work

A person's ability to work and to maintain himself in his work is another important index of his social functioning. When women patients who were housewives, and those patients who were elderly and retired were excluded from the data collected for analysis, only 41 per cent of the patients were regularly employed at intake; 52 per cent were unemployed and on the labor market; and another 7 per cent were in an ambiguous position with regard to work, describing themselves as free-lance workers, as seasonal workers, as holding temporary jobs, and so forth. Because it was probable that most of these latter patients (the 7 per cent) were really not regularly employed at such occupations but rather were saving face by presenting themselves in these terms, and in order that possible misinterpretations based on this ambiguity would be avoided, the group was excluded from the following more detailed observations about the work adjustment of the patients.

The employed patients, by and large, had a fairly stable current work history: 71 per cent of them had been holding the same job for at least the year preceding intake; another 29 per cent had been at the same job for less than a year; and only 7 per cent of the patients had been recently employed at the job they had at intake, that is, had been working at it for one month or less. Of the employed patients, 24 per cent presented themselves as having no problems at work; 40 per cent reported having serious problems such as absenteeism, difficulties in their relationships with their bosses and fellow-workers, and difficulties in performing the tasks involved; and the balance reported having occasional difficulties of this nature.

The unemployed patients, as far as could be determined, were not unemployed primarily because of either age or illness. Unemployment was heaviest among the unskilled workers, (61 per cent), although it was also relatively high among the patients who were trained in the professions (54 per cent), and fluctuated between 43 and 53 per cent for the remaining major occupational groupings. However, there was one interesting exception: that group of patients who might best be described as "small business" men had the lowest unemployment rate, that is only 20 per cent unemployed at intake. Presumably, having no boss or few co-workers to cope with, and not being required to keep to authoritatively defined hours or schedules, they were protected from the consequences of such difficulties as absenteeism, a common factor leading to loss of employment among alcoholics.

The duration of unemployment was as follows: 24 per cent were recently unemployed, that is, had lost a job a month or less preceding intake; 37 per cent had been out of work from one to six months; and of the balance (41 per cent)—those who had been out of work over six months—three out of four (30 per cent of the 41 per cent), had been unemployed for more than a year.

Of all the working age male patients, 64 per cent (586 cases) had had some kind of regular employment in the year preceding intake. Fifty-five per cent or slightly more than half (322 of 586) had lost a regular job: in 40 per cent of these cases drinking was unquestionably the cause; in another 40 per cent drinking was implicated as a factor but whether this was the actual reason for job losses was not entirely certain; and in only 20 per cent of the cases were factors other than drinking undoubtedly the causes of job losses.

The occupational histories of patients during their adult years showed that only 14 per cent reported that at work they had never had trouble related to drinking. The remaining cases had had a variety of occupational difficulties: 43 per cent had had difficulty because of absenteeism; 32 per cent had been fired because of their drinking habits; and another 32 per cent had left their jobs because they disliked the work, because they had fought with bosses or fellow-workers and had been dismissed as a consequence, or because they had had difficulties in the actual tasks involved so that they suffered in their work performance. Although there was no control group which could be used for comparative purposes, it was interesting to note that 30 per cent of the patients showed downward occupational mobility probably associated with their alcoholism; 65 per cent showed no change in the status of their work; and 5 per cent reported some upward mobility. Downward occupational mobility was sometimes expressed in extreme forms; for example, one patient, a lawyer by education, was working as a dishwasher at the time of intake to the clinic. A less extreme example was that of a patient who had been a skilled machinist and foreman and who at the time of intake was working on a production job using a drill press; thus, he no longer had managerial responsibilities and worked at a far simpler task.

Of those who had had jobs in the year preceding intake, 30 per cent actively disliked the work; 10 per cent had a neutral, accepting attitude towards the work, feeling that this was the way in which they had to make a living and that it did not matter whether they liked it; and 60 per cent described certain personal satisfactions derived from their work. Again, it was very difficult to evaluate these percentages without a control group.

In summary, the functioning of the patients with regard to work was characterized by extensive individual differences. However, the typical, or at least the modal, pattern for the patients was that they were probably unemployed at intake; they probably had lost their jobs in the year preceding intake; and they had had troubles maintaining themselves in jobs because of their drinking. In the atypical group of patients who were regularly employed at the time of intake and who had been on the same jobs for quite some time, there were also tendencies towards troubles at work because of drinking. Thus, for both groups, absenteeism and difficulties in personal relationships with bosses and fellow-workers were the common types of problems in the work area.

IV. The Nature of Clinic Treatment

1. SOME METHODOLOGICAL CONSIDERATIONS

A TRULY adequate description of a treatment *experience* is a highly complex matter, entailing not only the problem of abstracting the details of interview recording, but also an understanding of such subjective factors as the quality of the patient's relationship with the therapist as well as the therapist's attitudes, both conscious and unconscious, towards any patient, and especially towards the particular patient with a drinking problem. Furthermore, although any given interaction between patient and therapist may be brief, and although little may be overtly said or done, even such an encounter may be fraught with benign or malign implications or consequences.

In this large-scale study, the researchers did not have access to the minds of the patients, or to the minds of the many and diversely trained therapists who collaborated in the study. What were systematically available were the *public* or *outer, readily categorized features* of the treatment experience, that is, the details of the treatment *situation* to which (from the researchers' perspective) the patients were exposed, and in which (from the patients' perspective) they participated. Hereafter, the term treatment situation has been used to indicate these outer aspects of the treatment experience.

Later in this book attempts are made to formulate the more subjective or attitudinal aspects of the treatment experience for selected samples of patients (see chapter vii). At that time discussion centres on the alcoholic as a patient, describing in more clinical and qualitative terms such variables as his motivation for treatment, the nature of his participation in treatment, and the factors which brought him to treatment. For the present, however, discussion is restricted to a detailed review of two aspects of the treatment situation:

First, what was the treatment situation available to patients in the state-supported alcoholism services? How often and how long did the patients come to the clinics? Was treatment given to their relatives? Who saw the patients? How many patients were given group therapy? What drugs were used? To what extent did differences in these treatment factors induce the patients to maintain contact with the clinics?

Secondly, who received what type of treatment? What was the influence of the patients' social characteristics on the treatment offered to them? To what extent did social characteristics act as a determinant of the type of treatment received?

2. THE TREATMENT SITUATION

(a) Extent of Contact

If one accepts the premise that alcoholism is difficult to influence, one must likewise consider that to hold the patient in a relationship to the supportive or controlling potentials of treatment is of singular importance. Therefore a good deal of attention is paid here to the simplest public or "outer" aspects of the treatment experience, that is, to the extent and duration of contact of the patients with these clinics, and later in this chapter to the variables which influenced the type of treatment received.

The extent of contact that patients suffering from drinking problems had with the specialized treatment services made available for them was typically meager: about half the patients (52 per cent) came no more than four times to the clinic, and only one out of every five patients participated in treatment relatively persistently, coming at least ten times in the course of the year between intake and follow-up (see Table 1). The median duration of contact with the clinic was about one month. Forty-eight per cent of the patients maintained contact with the clinic for no longer than a month after their initial visit, and 30 per cent for no longer than eight days after the intake visit (see Table 2). Only about one in every four patients had relatively prolonged contact with the clinic, that is, for six months or longer subsequent to intake.

TABLE 1
Extent of Patients' Contacts with Clinics

No. of visits	Patients No.	Patients %		
1	138	17		
2	107	13		
3–4	165	21		
5–6	98	12		
7–8	76	11		
9–10	50	6		
11–12	32	4		
13–16	47	6		
17–20	20	3		
21+	56	7		
Minimal contact (<5)			410	52
Moderate contact (5–10)			224	28
Persistent contact (>10)			155	20
Totals	789	789	100	100

TABLE 2
Duration of Contact between First and Last Visits in the Course of the Study Year

Duration of contact	Patients No.	Patients %		
<8 days	237	30		
8–14 days	49	6		
15 days–one mo.	97	12		
<2 mos.	77	10		
<3 mos.	54	7		
<4 mos.	37	5		
<5 mos.	32	4		
<6 mos.	24	3		
6–9 mos.	75	9		
9–12 mos.*	113	14		
Brief duration (< one mo.)			383	48
Moderate duration (one-6 mos.)			224	28
Prolonged duration (> 6 mos.)			188	24
Totals	795	795	100	100

*Some of these patients were still in treatment at the clinics at the time of the follow-up interviews.

From these statistics alone, it was evident that most alcoholic patients were not held by the clinics. A review of individual cases provided further evidence that the extent or duration of

71

contact was far less than the patient's troubled clinical state would warrant. For example:

Mr. A.T., who was a patient at Clinic H, came to the clinic three times in the interval between intake and follow-up. He came each time in crises related to physical ill health associated with his alcoholism, but he did not return for the appointments which were offered to him. At follow-up, he was located and interviewed in jail. The patient had little recollection of his visits to the clinic and questionable insight into any need for further treatment or service, despite his present alcohol-related difficulties.

Mr. E.A., a patient at Clinic F, came to the clinic six times in the course of the year after intake. He then broke his contact with the clinic. Subsequently he continued to drink, was in jail and in a mental hospital, impregnated a young lady out of wedlock, acquired gonorrhea and possibly syphilis, and finally found his way to a residence for (hopefully) rehabilitable, unattached, and unemployed men. Ten months after intake, he returned to the clinic through the support of the director of this residence.

For purposes of categorical description and statistical analysis, the patients were arbitrarily divided into groups according to both the extent and the duration of their contacts with the clinics. With respect to *extent* of contact, three groups were defined: the first or minimal contact group consisted of those patients who visited the clinics no more than four times; the second or moderate contact group came more than four times but not more than ten times; and the third or persistent contact group came more than ten times. From the perspective of *duration* of contact, three groups were also distinguished: the brief duration group of patients was seen by the clinics for less than a month after their first visits; the moderate duration group had contacts of one to six months; and the prolonged duration group was in contact for longer than six months.

There was relatively little difference among the clinics with respect to the extent and duration of their contacts with patients (see Tables 3 and 4). Clinic H, however, tended to keep patients longer than other clinics (36 per cent versus 12–23 per cent), perhaps because this clinic offered a club house, settlement house atmosphere, as well as clinic services of a more conventional nature.

TABLE 3

COMPARISON OF THE EXTENT OF CONTACT OF PATIENTS IN THE EIGHT
CLINICS IN THE STUDY YEAR

Clinic	No. of Patients	Extent of contact as % of clinic's patients		
		Minimal	Moderate	Persistent
A	84	54	28	18
B	108	55	24	21
C	99	67	19	14
D	105	50	27	23
E	100	42	40	18
F	106	63	21	16
G	104	55	33	12
H	91	27	37	36

TABLE 4

COMPARISON OF THE DURATION OF CONTACT OF PATIENTS IN THE EIGHT
CLINICS IN THE STUDY YEAR

Clinic	No. of Patients	Duration of contact as % of clinic's patients		
		Brief	Moderate	Prolonged
A	84	55	27	18
B	108	54	24	22
C	99	57	28	15
D	105	35	25	40
E	100	60	29	11
F	106	51	25	24
G	104	40	28	32
H	91	40	36	24

TABLE 5

RELATIONSHIP BETWEEN EXTENT OF CONTACT AND DURATION OF CONTACT WITH
THE CLINICS IN THE STUDY YEAR

Extent of Contact	Total no. of patients	Duration of contact by no. of patients (% of total no. in parentheses)		
		Brief	Moderate	Prolonged
Minimal	410	327 (80)	55 (13)	28 (7)
Moderate	224	47 (21)	117 (52)	60 (27)
Persistent	152	0	52 (34)	100 (66)

As expected, duration and extent of contact tended to be highly correlated in the groups of brief and minimal, moderate and moderate, and prolonged and persistent (see Table 5). However,

73

there were some interesting exceptions. For example, twenty-eight patients maintained contact for longer than six months, even though their total number of visits was four or less. This group came almost entirely from those two clinics, D and G, which by design did not see patients at frequent intervals; indeed, at these clinics, it was very common for appointments to be made at intervals of one or two months for relatively brief visits. On the other hand, there was another group of exceptions—fifty-two patients who came very often to the clinics (more than ten times, in some cases even more than twenty times) but broke contact after as few as two months following their initial visits.

(b) Treatment of Collaterals

Because patients with a drinking problem are often immersed in complex and presumably pathogenic family relationships, it is frequently regarded as clinically desirable to give counsel, guidance, or treatment to members of their families. Although at intake two-thirds of the patients studied resided with their spouses or with their families of origin, in only one-fifth of all cases (or 30 per cent of those residing with families) were relatives seen at the clinics. In almost all of those cases (95 per cent) the collaterals were the spouses. If spouses were seen, there was some likelihood that one or several other collateral figures might also have been seen, but it was quite exceptional for any of the relatives of unmarried patients to be seen.

The extent of contact that the collaterals had with the clinics tended to be brief. In those cases where collaterals were seen, there was usually only one visit (64 per cent); 24 per cent had two or three visits, and the remaining 12 per cent more than four visits. In other words, in only 3 per cent of the entire treated population (or 25 cases out 797) were collaterals seen in what might be regarded as a context of continuing treatment.

(c) Who Saw the Patients?

At initial visits, the patients received services from several professions. About half the patients, 56 per cent, had some kind of psychiatric evaluation; 61 per cent received a medical examination; and 80 per cent saw a social worker at least once. However, from clinic to clinic, there was a wide range of professional services available at the first or initial evaluation (see Table 6). At one extreme, Clinic E offered a psychiatric evaluation to 80 per cent of its patients, while Clinic G did so for only 18 per cent.

Following initial evaluations of patients, treatment teams utilizing the skills and experience of several disciplines were rarely offered. For only one of every six patients who came at least four times to a clinic was there definite utilization of a team (that is, some collaborative, on-going, cross-disciplinary activity in which a patient was seen by both a social worker and an internist or by a psychiatrist). The "team approach" was in fact used at only two clinics, C and F, where respectively 52 and 28 per cent of the patients who came at least four times were seen by a team; in the remaining six clinics the proportions ranged from only 2 to 10 per cent. In short, typical treatment situations after the initial visits involved patients with one treating discipline.

The main individual treating discipline varied extensively from clinic to clinic. To report the extent to which members of individual disciplines participated in the treatment of alcoholic patients in these state-supported clinics would be quite misleading, because the data were highly distorted by the predominance of a particular treating discipline at one or another clinic.

(d) Group Therapy

Group therapy is regarded as an important treatment modality for alcoholic patients, not only for the practical reason that larger numbers of patients can be treated, but also because of certain theoretical advantages: namely, the intensity of the relationship to the therapist is lessened; the patient is offered support from other group members who suffer with similar difficulties; and the patient may play a far greater variety of roles in the group (listener, supporter, leader, critic, rebel, protagonist, chorus) than he can in the confines of the one-to-one relationship of individual psychotherapy. Because the demand and the stress on the individual patient are lessened in the group, the defensive

75

TABLE 6
UTILIZATION OF CLINIC SERVICES:
EXTENT OF CONTACT THAT PATIENTS HAD WITH VARIOUS STAFF MEMBERS OF THE EIGHT CLINICS

No. of contacts with staff members	No. of patients seen by clinic (% of that clinic's patients in parentheses)								
	A	B	C	D	E	F	G	H	All clinics
TOTALS	84 (100)	108 (100)	99 (100)	105 (100)	100 (100)	106 (100)	104 (100)	91 (100)	797 (100)
Internist									
1	1 (1)	44 (41)	—	15 (14)	55 (55)	38 (36)	16 (15)	12 (13)	181 (23)
2-3	2 (2)	13 (12)	—	32 (30)	20 (20)	26 (24)	29 (28)	45 (49)	167 (21)
4 or more	—	—	—	51 (49)	9 (9)	21 (20)	35 (34)	23 (25)	139 (17)
None	81 (97)	51 (47)	99 (100)	7 (7)	16 (16)	21 (20)	24 (23)	11 (13)	310 (39)
Psychiatrist									
1	20 (24)	53 (49)	30 (31)	33 (31)	50 (50)	31 (29)	9 (9)	59 (65)	285 (36)
2-3	13 (15)	14 (13)	26 (26)	2 (2)	20 (20)	10 (9)	3 (3)	3 (3)	91 (11)
4 or more	8 (9)	3 (3)	28 (28)	8 (8)	10 (10)	6 (6)	6 (6)	—	69 (9)
None	43 (52)	38 (35)	15 (15)	62 (59)	20 (20)	59 (56)	86 (82)	29 (32)	352 (44)
Social worker									
1	24 (29)	28 (26)	40 (41)	67 (64)	33 (33)	39 (37)	13 (12)	19 (21)	263 (33)
2-3	24 (29)	17 (16)	23 (23)	8 (8)	43 (43)	36 (34)	12 (12)	60 (66)	223 (28)
4 or more	33 (39)	17 (16)	36 (36)	3 (3)	22 (22)	30 (28)	4 (4)	9 (10)	154 (19)
None	3 (3)	46 (42)	—	27 (25)	2 (2)	1 (1)	75 (72)	3 (3)	157 (20)
Other disciplines	—	14 (13)	—	—	—	—	10 (10)	3 (3)	27 (3)

distancing of the patient from the treatment situation is expected to be considerably diminished.

Group therapy was available at seven of the eight clinics. However, in spite of the advantages cited above, it was found that only 19 per cent of the patients attended therapy groups. Later in this chapter it is shown how such group therapy as did exist helped patients to maintain their contacts with the clinics.

(e) Drug Therapy

Because alcohol has complex psychophysiological correlates, a variety of medications have for many years played a prominent role in the management of this condition. Most important are the various endocrine substances, dietary supplements, sedatives, tranquilizers, and such relatively specific drugs as antabuse. At the clinics studied, these drugs were used to varying degrees in accord with various theories about the etiology or sequelae of alcoholism. The exception was antabuse (tetraethylthiuran disulfide), a drug which interferes with the breakdown of alcohol, so that partial metabolites of recently ingested alcohol accumulate rapidly in the blood, in turn producing extensive vegetative nervous system disturbance, that ranges from perspiration and flushing in a mild reaction to vomiting, precipitous fall in blood pressure, and coma after even small quantities of ingested alcohol. In certain in-patient settings more dramatic drug treatments, for example, conditioned aversion therapy, the use of lysergic acid, insulin, and apomorphine are used for the treatment of alcoholism, but they were not used in any of the out-patient settings studied.

Only a minority (33 per cent) of the patients were given *no* drugs at all. The majority were given one or several drugs, of which the most common group in the years of this study were the tranquilizers, chiefly phenothiazines. Forty-four per cent of the patients received these drugs. Vitamins were also commonly used by the clinics: 41 per cent of the patients received one or several vitamin preparations. Twelve per cent of the patients were given some barbiturate preparation. Antabuse was given to 7 per cent of the patients, all of them from one clinic. Tolserol or mephenesin was given to 3 per cent of the patients.

77

3. FACTORS INFLUENCING EXTENT OF CLINIC CONTACT

In the management of any chronic illness or social disability, maintenance of the patient's contact with treatment is essential for several reasons. First, if one cannot follow a patient's clinical course, one cannot assess whether he has been helped. Secondly, both psychotherapeutic and medical management have to be fitted to the changing circumstances of the patient's life and the course of his illness. Thirdly, continuity of treatment rather than single treatments is almost always indicated. In this latter regard, it is generally believed that a specially supportive attitude should be used in the treatment of the alcoholic, especially in his early contact with the clinic, so that his self-esteem will not be lowered or his defensiveness reinforced. Without such precautions, the basis for establishing a prolonged relationship between patient and therapist is undermined. With the prevention of early drop-out from treatment particularly in mind, the authors looked at each of the categorically described aspects of the treatment situation reported above as a possible factor enhancing the extent or the duration of the patient's contact with the clinic.

(a) Involvement of Collaterals

The data indicated that when collateral figures were involved, even as seldom as one visit to the clinic, the patients were statistically more likely to maintain contact with the clinics for a greater number of visits and for a longer period of time than when collaterals were not involved in the treatment situation (see Table 7). Unfortunately, the data available from the clinics were not rich enough to clarify the meaning of this finding; for example, it would be important to know whether the spouse who came to the clinic was more interested in having her husband sustain or attain sobriety than was the spouse who did not come to the clinic.

(b) Who Saw the Patients?

Did the particular professional discipline involved in the care of the patient appear to influence the extent of contact that the patient had with the clinic? It is assumed that the treatment of

TABLE 7
RELATIONSHIP BETWEEN INVOLVEMENT OF COLLATERALS AND EXTENT AND DURATION OF CONTACT*

Involvement of collaterals	Extent of contact by no. of patients (% of total no. in parentheses)				Duration of contact by no. of patients (% of total no. in parentheses)			
	Total no. of patients	Minimal	Moderate	Persistent	Total no. of patients	Brief	Moderate	Prolonged
None	648 (100)	347 (53)	192 (30)	109 (17)	646 (100)	327 (51)	169 (26)	150 (23)
Some	149 (100)	72 (49)	32 (21)	45 (30)	149 (100)	56 (38)	55 (37)	38 (25)

*Using the chi^2 test for significance of the difference between distributions, the patients for whom the collaterals were seen had greater contact with the clinics: chi^2 for extent of contact = 14.7, p = <.005; chi^2 for duration of contact = 9.5, p = <.01.

a chronic disorder such as alcoholism requires a long-term relationship between the treatment facility and the patient. Thus, if the clinic is not able immediately to *influence* the patient's status (in respect to his drinking, his health, and his social functioning), at least it should be able to *observe* his shifting needs and problems and to attend to clinical exacerbations or to medical-social emergencies.

Earlier in this chapter, it was noted that the entire armament of professional training and experience was generally available for the initial evaluation of patients. It might therefore be asked whether the omission of one or more of these specialized services influenced the duration of the patients' contacts with the clinics. The data indicated that those patients who did *not* receive a psychiatric evaluation or medical examination were more likely to drop out of the clinics shortly after the initial contacts than were those patients who did receive them (see Table 8A). How-

TABLE 8

EVALUATION AND TREATMENT BY MAJOR CLINICAL DISCIPLINES AS FACTORS RELATED TO EXTENT AND DURATION OF CONTACT

A. EVALUATION

Seen at least once by	Total no. of patients	Duration of contact by no. of patients (% of total no. in parentheses)		
		Brief	Moderate	Prolonged
Psychiatrist				
No	357 (100)	217 (61)	69 (19)	71 (20)
Yes	440 (100)	166 (38)	159 (35)	117 (27)
Social worker				
No	153 (100)	75 (49)	33 (22)	45 (29)
Yes	644 (100)	308 (47)	193 (30)	143 (23)
Internist				
No	308 (100)	200 (65)	66 (21)	42 (14)
Yes	489 (100)	183 (37)	160 (33)	146 (30)

B. TREATMENT

Seen at least four times by	Total no. of patients	Duration of contact by no. of patients (% of total no. in parentheses)	
		Brief or moderate	Prolonged
Psychiatrist	68 (100)	35 (52)	33 (48)
Social worker	135 (100)	72 (53)	63 (47)
Internist	140 (100)	59 (43)	81 (57)

80

ever, the omission of evaluation by a social worker did not influence early drop-out from the clinics.*

Patients who saw the psychiatrist only once were divided into two groups: those who did not return to the psychiatrist after the single visit even though they were referred back to him for further treatment, and those who saw the psychiatrist only once for certain diagnostic purposes and for whom future contact with him was not prescribed. Unfortunately these groups could not be discriminated between, because following a patient's visit to a psychiatrist it was rarely noted explicitly (on the patient's chart) whether or not treatment by the psychiatrist was planned after the first, usually diagnostic interview. However, it was certain that those patients who returned to the psychiatrist for four or more visits undoubtedly were being treated by him.

Although a patient may in fact have received some treatment in fewer than four visits, in order to facilitate statistical comparison this criterion was arbitrarily used to differentiate "treatment" from "evaluation." It was likewise used to define treatment by a social worker and by an internist. The resulting data indicated that the particular profession of the therapist did not influence duration of treatment† (see Table 8B).

(c) Group Therapy

The data indicated quite strikingly that group therapy did facilitate maintenance of the patients' contacts with the clinics (see Table 9). For example, 50 per cent of the patients who were offered group therapy came to the clinics more than ten times, whereas only 12 per cent of the patients who did not receive group therapy came that often. Also, 79 per cent of those who were seen in group therapy maintained contact with the clinics

*The fact that there was no difference in the likelihood of a patient maintaining contact with the clinic whether or not he was seen for *evaluation* by a social worker ought not to be misinterpreted. It seemed unlikely to the authors that this reflected some deficiency in the caseworker's role or in his skill, but rather that there were salient differences between the sample of patients referred to social workers and that of patients referred to psychiatrists or internists. The latter possibility is explored later in this chapter.

†The probability that a patient treated by an internist would maintain contact with the clinic for longer than six months was, however, slightly higher than for a patient treated by a psychiatrist or by a social worker.

81

for longer than one month, while only 45 per cent of those who were not in group therapy maintained contact for this period of time. Similarly, of those who were in group therapy, 33 per cent maintained contact for longer than six months, while of those who were not seen in groups only 21 per cent maintained contact for this period of time. These differences raised the question of case selectivity; that is, did the patients selected for group therapy differ in significant respects from those who were not so selected?

(d) Drug Therapy

To determine whether the prescription of drugs facilitated the maintenance of contacts with the clinics, the authors made comparisons between patients who received no drugs and those who received one or another of five types of drugs, namely, vitamins, antabuse, barbiturates, tranquilizers, or special drugs. Although other drugs were given, the number of patients who received hormonal therapy or muscle relaxants was too small for statistical analysis. Also, because most of the patients who were given drugs continued to receive them throughout their contacts with the clinics, the analysis was limited to whether or not the patients were given drugs in their initial visits to the clinics.

The data indicated that the differences between those patients who received drugs and those who did not were statistically significant both for the extent and for the duration of contact (see Table 10A). Notably, those patients who received no drugs were found preponderantly in the minimal contact and brief duration groups. Concerning the relationship between the maintenance of contact and the individual drugs, the differences from one drug to another were minimal (see Table 10B). Although more patients among those receiving antabuse than among those receiving tranquilizers maintained only minimal contact with the clinics, there were no consistent differences between the drugs. Thus, the group receiving antabuse had the largest proportion of patients who maintained contact for six or more months, but the smallest proportion of patients who came for extended treatment, whereas the group receiving tranquilizers had the smallest proportion of patients who maintained contact for six or more months, but

TABLE 9

Group Therapy as a Factor Related to Extent and Duration of Contact

Group therapy received	Total no. of patients	Extent of contact by no. of patients (% of total no. in parentheses)			Duration of contact by no. of patients (% of total no. in parentheses)		
		Minimal	Moderate	Persistent	Brief	Moderate	Prolonged
None	641 (100)	477 (74)	86 (13)	78 (12)	325 (55)	156 (24)	138 (21)
Some	151 (100)	35 (23)	40 (27)	76 (50)	31 (21)	70 (46)	50 (33)

TABLE 10

A. Drug Therapy as a Factor Related to Extent and Duration of Contact

Drugs received	Total no. of patients	Extent of contact as % of total no. of patients			Duration of contact as % of total no. of patients		
		Minimal	Moderate	Persistent	Brief	Moderate	Prolonged
None	259	65.6*	22.8	11.6	63.0	21.6	15.5
Some	536	46.0*	30.7	23.1	41.0	31.4	37.6

*d = 19 per cent; p = <.001.

B. Type of Drug in Relation to Extent and Duration of Contact

Drugs received	Total no. of patients	Extent of contact as % of total no. of patients			Duration of contact as % of total no. of patients		
		Minimal	Moderate	Persistent	Brief	Moderate	Prolonged
Vitamins	328	51.6	24.4	26.9	39.6	31.3	29.1
Antabuse	57	53†	33	14	30	35	35
Barbiturates	93	47	24	29	43	29	28
Tranquilizers	348	39.4†	34.4	26.1	39.2	33.3	27.5
Special‡	93	45	28	27	29	29	42

†d = 13.6 per cent; $S.E.D.$ = 7.4; p = >.10 n.s.
‡A group of experimental drugs, most but not all of which were new tranquilizer preparations.

about the average proportion of patients who came for extended treatment. It could therefore be reasonably implied that the prescription of some drug helped alcoholic patients to maintain contacts with the clinics, but that it probably did not matter very much which drug was given.

Many of the patients received more than one kind of drug. Examination of the use of drugs by clinics separately indicated that some of the clinics prescribed the same drugs for all patients; for example, at Clinic H almost all the patients received both tranquilizers and vitamins. Some of the clinics usually prescribed only one type of drug to each patient, but a few patients received prescriptions for more than one drug. Thus, for most of the clinics it was not possible to interrelate the influence of multiple prescriptions with the extent of contact with the clinics because there was insufficient variance within the sample. However, at two of the clinics, enough cases did fall into each cell of the table to compare those patients who received no drugs, one drug, or several drugs in relation to the extent or duration of their contacts with the clinics.

At Clinic B, the majority of patients were given three drugs singly or in combination: multi-vitamin pills, tranquilizers (chiefly phenothiazines), and barbiturates. A careful analysis of the findings indicated that none of these drugs separately or in combination significantly influenced the extent or duration of contact with this clinic, but that the dichotomy of no drug/some drug continued to discriminate between those patients who maintained brief or minimal contact and those who maintained the contact longer (see Table 11). At Clinic G the principal drugs used were antabuse, tranquilizers, and vitamins. Because the emphasis in this clinic was on helping the patient to maintain contact for a long period of time and not on having him make relatively frequent contact, the authors considered the influence of pharmacotherapy as it affected only the *duration* of contact with the clinic. It was found that there were only trivial differences in the duration of contact among groups of patients receiving these various drugs singly or in combination (see Table 12).

84

TABLE 11
SINGLE AND MULTIPLE DRUG PRESCRIPTIONS AS FACTORS RELATED TO EXTENT AND DURATION OF CONTACT IN CLINIC B

Drugs received	Total no. of patients	Extent of contact by no. of patients			Duration of contact by no. of patients		
		Minimal	Moderate	Persistent	Brief	Moderate	Prolonged
None	21	14	5	2	15	4	2
Vitamins	7	3	2	2	3	2	2
Vitamins and barbiturates	36	26	4	6	24	4	8
Vitamins and tranquilizers	7	2	3	2	2	3	2
Tranquilizers	4	0	2	2	0	3	1
Vitamins, tranquilizers, and barbiturates	20	10	6	4	7	8	5

TABLE 12

SINGLE AND MULTIPLE DRUG PRESCRIPTIONS AS FACTORS RELATED TO DURATION
OF CONTACT IN CLINIC G

Drugs received	Total no. of patients	Duration of contact by no. of patients		
		Brief	Moderate	Prolonged
None	17	7	6	4
Antabuse	24	8	9	7
Tranquilizers	23	8	6	9
Antabuse and tranquilizers	8	1	3	4
Antabuse and vitamins	6	3*	2	1
Tranquilizers and vitamins	10	2	5	3
Antabuse, tranquilizers, and vitamins	6	1	4	1

*Only this small group of patients maintained less contact with the clinic than did the group receiving no drugs.

The reader is reminded that the prescription of drugs in combination may have been or ought to have been based on the clinician's appraisal that the several drugs were indicated for the management of his patients. Consequently, there were undoubtedly biasing factors (for example, extent of psychophysiologic disturbance) determining the placement of the patient in one or another of these groups. That the percentage of patients maintaining contact with Clinic B for six or more months was the same for those receiving vitamins and barbiturates as for those receiving vitamins *and tranquilizers* and barbiturates may have been owing to the fact that the latter group also required certain phenothiazines, without which the patient might possibly have broken contact sooner. Indeed, it would take a study of complex design to elucidate clearly the value of one or several of these drugs as specifically facilitating the alcoholic patient's relationship to the out-patient clinic he attended. As for the differential effectiveness of these drugs in the course of his drinking problem, this question is postponed to chapter vi of this book.

86

4. SOCIAL CHARACTERISTICS OF PATIENTS AS FACTORS INFLUENCING THE EXTENT OF CLINIC CONTACTS AND THE TREATMENT SITUATIONS

Hollingshead's and Redlich's study of the relation between class structure and types of psychiatric treatment provided[18] has been corroborated both directly and indirectly by a number of studies that demonstrate significant relationships between various social-psychologic characteristics of patients and the types of treatment in which they were involved.[29,30] The present study showed a relationship between the overt structural aspects of the treatment situation in the state-supported alcoholism programs and the patients' social stability, but no consistent relationship between the treatment situation and the patients' demographic characteristics (age, race, nativity) or his social class as measured by his educational or occupational status.

The reader is reminded that social stability was measured by means of a composite index, incorporating aspects of the patient's marital status, residential setting, and employment status at intake (see chapter III, 3). On the basis of this index, four social stability groups were differentiated in order of diminishing social stability:

(1) No impairment: married, employed, and living in a familial setting at intake.

(2) Minimal impairment: two of the above three attributes.

(3) Moderate impairment: only one of the three attributes.

(4) Maximal impairment: neither married, nor employed, nor living in a familial setting at intake.

(a) Extent of Contact

The number of visits that patients made to the clinics was found to be highly related to their social stability at intake. Thus, the group at the unimpaired extreme of the index of social stability had the largest proportion (58 per cent) of those patients who attended the clinics more than four times, and the group at the maximally impaired extreme had the smallest percentage (35 per cent) of such patients.

The number of visits that patients made to the clinics was not, however, related to their educational status. About as many patients who had grade school or less education came for more than four visits (49 per cent) as did patients who had some college education. But, paradoxically, a smaller proportion of college-educated patients (14 per cent) than of patients with less education (22 per cent for each of the three other educational groups) maintained contact with the clinics for six months or longer.

Length of contact was not related to occupational status in a consistent manner. Unskilled workers had the smallest proportion (40 per cent) of patients attending more than four times; skilled workers (46 per cent) and service occupations (47 per cent) came next; and the highest proportion (about 55 per cent) occurred in each of the remaining occupational groups. Because these latter categories included clerical workers (that is, white-collar workers in businesses and sales persons), housewives, and a lumped group of business executives, professional persons, and entrepreneurs, it was highly unlikely that differences in length of contact referred to social class differences as expressed in occupational roles.

To summarize, there was no evidence that social class, of which occupational status and educational attainment are commonly utilized as indices, was an underlying determinant of the number of visits that the alcoholic patients made to the state-supported clinics.

(b) Professional Services Utilized

The data indicated that the particular professional disciplines involved in the treatment of patients were quite definitely related to the social characteristics of patients. Just as social stability was strongly related to the extent of contact with the clinics, so it also had the strongest and most unequivocal relationship with the professional services utilized for the patients. In contrast, however, there was no clear-cut relation between educational level or occupational status and extent of treatment received, although the trend was in the expected direction.

When the various professional disciplines were correlated with the patients' social stability at intake, it was found that those patients who were not impaired in their social stability were evaluated and treated by an internist significantly more often than were those patients with maximal impairment of social stability (see Table 13). The pattern for evaluation and treatment by a social worker was strikingly opposite: those patients who were most impaired in their social stability at intake were more likely to be evaluated and treated by social workers than were those who were least impaired. Although internists provided treatment

TABLE 13

SOCIAL STABILITY AS A FACTOR RELATED TO DIFFERENTIAL UTILIZATION OF MAJOR CLINICAL DISCIPLINES

Clinical discipline and social stability	Total no. of patients	No. of patients (% of total no. in parentheses)	
		Evaluated (seen less than four times)	Treated (seen at least four times)
Internist			
High	248	203 (82)	58 (24)
High-medium	226	166 (74)	40 (18)
Medium-low	180	119 (66)	27 (15)
Low	139	77 (55)*	13 (9)*
Psychiatrist			
High	248	133 (54)	23 (9)
High-medium	226	123 (55)	17 (7)
Medium-low	180	107 (59)	16 (8)
Low	139	81 (58)	11 (8)
Social worker			
High	248	188 (76)	40 (16)
High-medium	226	176 (78)	35 (16)
Medium-low	180	148 (82)	38 (21)
Low	139	124 (89)*	33 (24)*

*It is interesting to note that only 55 per cent of the patients of low social stability were *evaluated* by internists, as compared to 89 per cent by social workers. Similarly, only 9 per cent of these same patients were *treated* by internists, compared to 24 per cent by social workers.

for 24 per cent of the unimpaired group of patients, they treated only 9 per cent of the most impaired group, whereas social workers saw in treatment only 16 per cent of the unimpaired group, but were responsible for the treatment of 24 per cent of the most impaired group. There was no relationship between the social stability of the patients and differential availability of psychiatric service.

(c) Group Therapy

The data indicated that social variables had a significant influence on participation in group therapy. When analysis was limited to the treated patients, that is, to those who attended four or more times regardless of modality of treatment, it was noted that 36 per cent of the patients who had completed high school and/or had some college education were in group therapy, whereas only 24 per cent of those who had not completed high school were found in group therapy. Similarly, it was found that 29 per cent of the patients unimpaired in social stability at intake were in group therapy, but that only 12 per cent of the patients with maximal impairment in social stability entered group therapy. The data for occupational status were consistent with those reported above for extent of contact: business and professional persons, entrepreneurs, and housewives had the highest proportion of patients in group therapy; service workers and skilled and unskilled laborers had the lowest percentage.

(d) Drug Therapy

Did the social characteristics of patients influence whether or not they received drugs? Indicating a trend which was not statistically significant but interesting in conjunction with findings reported earlier in this chapter, the data suggested that the more impaired patients were in social stability the less likely they were to receive drugs (see Table 14).

Another interesting finding, about which it was difficult to generalize because it largely reflected the use of drugs in one clinic (G), was that antabuse was given preponderantly to patients of higher social stability (see Table 15). Because antabuse is not a drug which affects the person's emotional status or his biochemistry, but rather is intended to act as a self-imposed punitive barrier in support of the commandment "Thou shalt not imbibe any alcohol," it is understandable that it should have been recommended only to patients who were regarded as likely to want this kind of watchdog.

TABLE 14

Social characteristics	Total no. of patients	Drugs prescribed, by no. of patients (% of total no. in parentheses)	
		Some drug	No drug
Education*			
Low	229 (100)	167 (73)	62 (27)
Low-medium	224 (100)	164 (73)	60 (27)
Medium-high	155 (100)	115 (74)	40 (26)
High	115 (100)	77 (67)	38 (33)
Social stability			
High	248 (100)	180 (73)	68 (27)
High-medium	226 (100)	168 (75)	58 (26)
Medium-low	180 (100)	124 (69)	56 (31)
Low	139 (100)	94 (68)	45 (32)
Occupational status			
Businesssmen, pro- fessionals, and entertainers	109 (100)	73 (67)	36 (33)
Clerical workers	134 (100)	98 (73)	36 (27)
Laborers, servants	489 (100)	342 (70)	147 (30)
Housewives	59 (100)	51 (86)	8 (14)

*Low education means no education beyond grammer school; low-medium indicates some high school; medium-high indicates completion of high school; and high indicates some college or completion of college.

TABLE 15

SOCIAL STABILITY AS A FACTOR RELATED TO THE PRESCRIPTION OF
ANTABUSE

	At all clinics		At Clinic G	
Social stability	Total no. of patients	No. receiving antabuse (% of total no. in parentheses)	Total no. of patients	No. receiving antabuse (% of total no. in parentheses)
High	248	33 (13)	51	28 (55)
High-medium	226	18 (8)	33	18 (55)
Medium-low	180	8 (6)	18	4 ⎫ (26)
Low	139	6 (4)	1	1 ⎭

It was found that housewives were given drugs far more often than were any of the other occupational groups (see Table 14). This probably was a corollary, if not a consequence, of the fact that the housewives in these clinics were evaluated and treated by internists more often than were any of the other occupational groups.

There was also a trend suggesting that patients of higher educational attainment were prescribed drugs less often than were patients in the other educational groups (see Table 14). One could infer that the clinics doubted the intrinsic value of drugs in the treatment of alcoholism and assumed that the college-educated of their clientele would not be interested in what might be a placebo effect. On the other hand, the clinics might have believed that educated alcoholics were much more amenable to verbal interaction. Therefore, the data reported above—that the college-educated patients attended the clinics less frequently than did those with lower educational attainment—might have been a corollary or a consequence of the fact that these patients were given drugs less often than the other patients.

5. SUMMARY

Although half of the patients did not remain in treatment at the clinics for more than a minimal number of visits (one to four) nor for longer than what has been termed brief contact (less than one month), there was a considerable minority of patients (about one in five) who maintained persistent and prolonged contact with the clinics (more than ten visits, longer than six months). Because early drop-out from treatment is regarded as an undesirable event in the out-patient management of any chronic disease, the focus in this chapter has been on evaluating the factors which enhanced the patient's continuing contact with the clinic. The statistical analyses reported in this chapter indicated that these factors were:

(a) Those patients for whom collateral figures (especially spouses) were involved in evaluation and treatment maintained contact longer than did those for whom such collaterals were not involved.

(b) Those patients who participated in group therapy attended the clinics longer than did those who were seen only in individual treatment.

(c) Those patients who were initially evaluated by a physician (either an internist or a psychiatrist) maintained contact longer than did those who were not so evaluated.

(d) Those patients who received drugs from the clinics maintained contact longer than did those who did not receive such prescriptions. It was of interest to note that the type of drug (tranquilizers, barbiturates, antabuse, vitamins) did not demonstrably influence the patients' contact with the clinics—only the fact that some drug or drugs had been prescribed was correlated with the differences in length of contact.

(e) Although *social class*, as measured by education or occupational status, was not associated with the extent or duration of contact with the clinics, the patients' *social stability* was highly correlated with the maintenance of contact with the clinics.

(f) There was a complex interrelationship between the patients' social stability and the treatment they received. The less impaired was the social stability, the greater the likelihood that the patients had collaterals who could come to the clinic, that the patients would participate in group therapy, that they would be seen initially by a physician, and even that they would get prescriptions for drugs. Unfortunately, the sample was not large enough to evaluate or comprehend by statistical analyses why patients with higher social stability were provided with these contact-enhancing factors.

V. Change and the Problem of Improvement

1. METHODOLOGICAL ISSUES

HOW MUCH did the patients change in significant areas of their lives in the interval between intake and follow-up? To what extent did they improve in their functioning and social adjustment? Prior to presenting the data pertaining to these questions, the authors have reviewed, for the critical reader, three methodologic problems which were inherent in the research design and which might have had an influence on the extent of change reported in this study. These problems were: the limitation of the assessment of change to a single follow-up study taking place one year after the patient's intake visit to the clinic; the influence on the data of the fact that the follow-up evaluation was made by the same personnel who were involved in treating the patient—and indeed the whole issue of validity; and the influence on the data of the fact that patients were lost between intake and follow-up.

(a) The One-Year Interval between Intake and Follow-Up

One of the central decisions in planning a follow-up study is the definition of the point in time at which the follow-up interview or interviews should be made. As was pointed out in the first chapter, at the inception of this project the authors had anticipated doing a number of follow-up interviews on each of the patients in the research sample, for example, at six-month intervals from six months after intake to two years after intake, with the hope of establishing such secure contacts with the patients that follow-ups at still longer intervals up to five years after intake (though not necessarily under the same aegis) might be undertaken. However, after more was learned about the time and effort required to conduct a follow-up and to record, transcribe, and

94

analyze the data, these expectations were greatly curtailed. The logistics of the research required the planning of a *single* follow-up study which, one year after intake, would utilize a personal interview supplemented by as many collateral data as could possibly be assembled in the tracing process. Even this method strained the collaborative capacities of the clinics.

An important factor in the selection of the one-year follow-up interval was the avoidance of any hiatus between the intake study activities and the initiation of the follow-up case studies because the clinics could not be expected to maintain an unutilized block of professional time or open up such a block of time at some future point when follow-up activities might begin. Because the research was carried out predominantly by the clinic staffs, such considerations as the maintenance of tempo and of the staff's involvement with the project were highly relevant. Given infinite time, personnel, and money, it was agreed that multiple follow-up interviews and observations were undoubtedly preferable to a single follow-up program. Thus, although the authors were prepared to be "tolerant of imperfection" in mental health research, it was still incumbent on them to evaluate the possible consequences of this logistic decision to do a single follow-up study one year after intake.

Was one year a long enough unit of time in which to observe change in the drinking patterns, health, social relationships, and so forth of alcoholic patients? Would different relationships be observed between the characteristics of the patients, the nature of the treatment received, and the clinical improvement or change or movement, if the period between intake and follow-up were longer than one year, or if there were multiple observations on the same patients at varying intervals?

In general, to assess the influence of a particular treatment on a particular malady, or to study its natural or typical course, one must rely on appropriate statistics—especially when the specific etiology of an illness is not known, and when the goal of treatment is modestly put at arresting a chronic process or at the re-estab-lishment of function, rather than at cure. Indeed, the assessment of treatment of alcoholism may be analogous to the assessment of treatment of certain cancers. Cancer of the breast may apparently

95

be arrested by appropriate intervention, for example, by a radical mastectomy, but hidden seeds may remain to grow and then to destroy. With this type of cancer, five years without recurrence is regarded as fairly certain evidence of cure, while shorter periods of observation without recurrence are held, on the basis of experience, to be an insufficient indication that the disease has been cured or permanently arrested.

The question asked was how long must one observe a patient to assess the influence of a particular treatment upon his drinking problem? Short of observing him to the day of his death, one cannot say with certainty that the patient will never return to the uncontrolled or excessive use of alcoholic beverages (or to other drugs) or, if he is still drinking, that he will achieve sobriety in the future. However, some compromise was needed between the alternatives of making no formal follow-up study at all and of attempting to follow patients with drinking problems from their initial visits to the clinics until their eventual deaths. What difference would it make to the data, and thus to the inferences which might be drawn, if a population of patients with drinking problems were observed only one year after the beginning of clinic treatment rather than for longer intervals?

Three prior studies contributed to the clarification of this question. Davies, Shepherd, and Myers[31] reported on "the first 50 alcohol addict patients" discharged from the Maudsley Hospital in London; these patients were followed for two years by clinic interviews, telephone, correspondence, or personal visits, and data describing their status at monthly intervals were presented in a complex histogram. Among these authors' summary statements, one in particular seemed important: "Nearly 90% of the patients who resumed drinking began to do so within 6 months, and nearly all of these within 3 months after leaving the hospital. Predictions made 6 months after discharge based on the patient's [drinking] behavior during that time would result in a prognostic misclassification (i.e., of their drinking status after 2 years) of less than 20% of all cases in the series." Although these authors did not attempt a prognostic evaluation at one year, they gave enough of their data to permit a reader to do something of this sort: thus, it was estimated that 77 per cent of the patients studied by Davies, Shepherd, and Myers had the same status, in terms of the categories these authors used, for the second year as they had for the first; for 11 patients or 23 per cent there were some differences between the first and second years.

It is notoriously difficult to assess the severity of a drinking problem, and particularly to assess change in it, except when there is a change to complete abstinence at one extreme, or to the grossest disturbances of social relationships and bodily health at the other. When the data presented by Davies and his associates were utilized impressionistically, two of these eleven patients could be classified as having functioned slightly better in their second than in their first year, three as much better, four as slightly worse, and two as much worse. In short, it was concluded that for those patients who did change from the first to the second year of follow-up observation there was about as much movement in one direction as in the other, and that no consistent error was introduced when observation of this cohort of patients was confined to a year of follow-up as compared to a two-year follow-up.

It was also possible to go beyond impressionistic evaluation of these authors' data, by making some quantitative comparison of the patients' drinking behavior in the first and second years of the follow-up study. Arbitrarily a score of zero was assigned for any month in which the patient reported abstinence, one point for any month in which he reported light drinking, two points for heavy drinking but with "social competence" (their term), three points for heavy drinking with "social incapacity" (their term), and four points for institutionalization. It was clear that there was an excellent relationship between the first- and the second-year scoring of this population (see Table 16): thirty-two patients were in the same group of scores in the first year as in the second; twelve were in the adjacent category; and only three had moved more than one group away from their first-year scoring range. One patient could not be fitted into this scheme, because he committed suicide early in the second year after drinking (in the words used by Davies, Shepherd, and Myers) "heavily, though without social incapacity" for eleven of the twelve months of the first year.

TABLE 16

COMPARISON OF FIRST- AND SECOND-YEAR FOLLOW-UP SCORES OF
FORTY-EIGHT ALCOHOLICS, FROM DATA OF DAVIES, SHEPHERD,
AND MYERS

First-year follow-up scores	Second-year follow-up scores by no. of patients*				
	0–9	10–19	20–29	30–39	40–49
0–9	*15*	1	—	—	—
10–19	2	*7*	—	—	—
20–29	1	8	*3*	—	—
30–39	2	—	—	*6*	—
40–49	—	—	—	1	*1*

*The italicized figures indicate the number of patients with the same score range in the first and second years of follow-up.

Gibbins and Armstrong[32] followed the clinical course of sixty-nine patients who received in-patient treatment at the Alcoholism Research Foundation, Toronto, Canada, and who continued to attend as out-patients for at least three visits. The duration of follow-up ranged from nine to fifty-five months. For each of these patients, these authors reported on the length of follow-up, on the number of months of post-admission abstinence, and on the measure of percentage "gain in abstinence" related to the number of months of abstinence in the years preceding admission. It was possible to evaluate Gibbins' and Armstrong's data by dividing their patients into four approximately equal groups based on the duration of follow-up: group I followed 36–55 months; group II followed 26–35 months; group III followed 17–25 months; group IV followed 9–16 months. Each patient was then classified into one of four categories: A was abstinent throughout the entire follow-up period; B was abstinent at least 80 per cent of the months of follow-up; C was abstinent more than 20 per cent but less than 80 per cent; and D was abstinent less than 20 per cent of the months. The abstinence data of the four groups (see Table 17) indicated that there was no significant relationship between duration of follow-up and abstinence status.

Gibbins and Armstrong also analyzed their data in terms of the gain in the number of months of abstinence. If one expressed "gain in abstinence" on a percentage basis, rather than on an absolute basis, the group which was observed for the shortest time after admission would have the largest percentage gain, all

TABLE 17

RELATIONSHIP OF MONTHS OF ABSTINENCE TO LENGTH OF FOLLOW-UP IN SIXTY-NINE PATIENTS REPORTED BY GIBBINS AND ARMSTRONG

Duration of abstinence	No. of patients by months of follow-up			
	Group I (36–55 mos.)	Group II (26–35 mos.)	Group III (17–25 mos.)	Group IV (9–16 mos.)
A. Entire period	3	0	4	4
B. 80% of period	3	6	1	4
C. 20–79% of period	7	7	8	3
D. Less than 20% of period	4	5	4	6
TOTALS	17	18	17	17

TABLE 18

RELATIONSHIP OF PERCENTAGE GAIN IN ABSTINENCE TO LENGTH OF FOLLOW-UP IN SIXTY-NINE PATIENTS REPORTED BY GIBBINS AND ARMSTRONG

Percentage gain	No. of patients by months of follow-up							
	Group I (36–55 mos.)		Group II (26–35 mos.)		Group III (17–25 mos.)		Group IV (9–16 mos.)	
75–99	4		3		4		3	
50–74	2		4		3		3	
25–49	3		2		3		5	
0–24	6		5		5		6	
Loss	2		4		2		0	
50–99		6		7		7		6
Less than 50		11		11		10		11
TOTALS	17	17	18	18	17	17	17	17

other things being equal: that is, if a patient followed ten months after admission was abstinent one month and if he was abstinent in none of the ten months before admission, his gain in abstinence would be 10 per cent; similarly if a patient followed for twenty months after admission was abstinent one month, and in the twenty months before admission he was abstinent for no months, his gain in abstinence would be 5 per cent. Comparisons on the basis of percentage gain provided the sharpest test of the hypothesis that there was no greater "percentage gain in abstinence" for those patients briefly followed than for those who were followed longer. Nevertheless, the data in Table 18 indicated that there were no differences in gain in abstinence associated with the duration of follow-up.

99

The third source of data was a study which Gerard and Saenger made in 1958 for the Connecticut Commission on Alcoholism[26,33] and which was part of an evaluation of the work of this commission in its first ten years of operation. A follow-up of patients treated at the out-patient clinics and the in-patient facility of the commission was designed: every third patient seen for the first time in 1950, 1953, and 1956 was registered into a census of some 1,200 cases. Through probability sampling, three representative samples of patients seen in these years were selected. Comparison of the patients in these three time samples indicated that they did not differ in age at intake, sex, marital status, occupational status, or number of visits, all of which were regarded as gross potential sources of differences in outcome. Table 19 presents some of the major findings of the 1958 follow-up. The data indicated no statistically significant differences in the proportions of patients attaining abstinence in the three time groups. The apparent trend, which suggested that the longer the interval between treatment and follow-up the more abstinent the patients, did not withstand the critical test of the null hypothesis; nor was this trend substantiated when the abstinent and controlled drinkers (the "improved" patients in terms of that study) were combined. There was one *prima facie* sensible and statistically significant finding: more of the patients in the samples which were studied five or eight years

TABLE 19

RELATIONSHIP OF INTERVAL BETWEEN INTAKE AND FOLLOW-UP TO THE GENERAL STATUS AT FOLLOW-UP IN 1958 OF PATIENTS TREATED IN THE OUT-PATIENT CLINICS OF THE CONNECTICUT COMMISSION ON ALCOHOLISM IN 1950, 1953, AND 1956

Follow-up status in 1958	No. of patients	No. of patients by intake year		
		1950	1953	1956
I. Abstinent*	55	24	19	12
II. Controlled drinking	41	14	10	17
(All improved patients: I and II combined)†	(96)	(38)	(29)	(29)
III. Problem drinker	123	35	38	50
IV. Institutionalized	31	6	12	13
V. Deceased‡	49	21	23	5
TOTALS	299	100	102	97

*chi^2 = 4.44; no significant difference for patients in the three time samples.
†chi^2 = 5.66; no significant difference for patients in the three time samples.
‡chi^2 = 13.3, p = <.01; note significant difference here.

after intake were dead than in the sample studied two years after intake—a consequence of increasing age and of continuing alcoholism with its serious medical-surgical complications.*

To review, the data from three follow-up studies which were conducted in different locations, London (England), Ontario, and Connecticut, and which utilized differing criteria, patient populations, and follow-up methodology indicated that the time interval does not influence the statistical patterning of the patients' status at follow-up. In effect, these data supported the present authors' operational decision to follow up alcoholic patients one year after intake. Had the data shown a significant relationship between follow-up interval and follow-up status, such a finding would have placed this decision on a highly unsure footing.

(b) The Problem of Validity

The follow-up interviews and/or the assemblage of other data pertinent to evaluating the status of patients one year following intake were the responsibility of the same clinic staff who did the intake studies and the treatment. Although there is no doubt that all staff would have liked to show an optimal outcome of their clinical practice, this natural urge was balanced by a healthy recognition of the difficulties entailed in treating alcoholics. The clinics were supported in their objectivity by their own tacit expectation that their patients could not be much worse off at follow-up than the patients at other clinics. Their initial defensiveness about exposing the results of their work was quite rapidly undone when they recognized that any comparisons which might be made would be drawn in the framework of a scientific evaluation study. Findings would be presented not merely in terms of percentages of improved patients but rather in relation to the extent to which the patients participated in treatment and to which the over-all level of deterioration in the patients' life situations at intake might impede the clinics' work.

*Age-specific death rates were computed for these three time samples and then were compared with age-specific death rates for men in the state of Connecticut in 1950 from data supplied by the Metropolitan Life Insurance Company. The expected age-specific death rate, based on these figures, was then compared with the actual death rates in those patients followed two, five, and eight years after intake. It was found that the death rates for the alcoholic patients were on the average four times as great as those for the male population as a whole.[26]

With the participating clinics' growing identification with the scientific aims of this research, the main issue *apropos* validity of follow-up data shifted from the eradication of personal or professional bias or vested interest in the results to a shared concern with the problem of accurate assessment of those patients who claimed to be doing well or doing better than they were at intake. This concern was reinforced by the commonplace clinical observation that inaccurate self-reporting by alcoholic patients is usually in the direction of denial of pathology or problems. Thus, if patients claimed to be doing poorly or functioning no differently at follow-up than when they came to the clinics the experience of these clinics indicated that such a statement could be taken at face value.

The assessment of the patient's status at follow-up was based on the interview which probed into the concrete and detailed realities of the patient's life. The final rating of each case for each of the many categories on which the patient was evaluated—that final rating which was coded and punched on the IBM cards for statistical analysis—expressed a clinical judgment formed out of the patient's statements, the patient's appearance, his total life situation proximal to the follow-up interview as known to the interviewer from collateral sources of data, the interviewer's opinion as to the probable veracity of the patient's statements, and the research team's appraisal of all these data. For those interviewed cases for which collateral data were obtained (from family, other agencies, relatives, and so forth by interview, telephone, or correspondence) there were discrepant reports for *only* 2 per cent of those who claimed to be abstinent at the time of follow-up. (There were collateral data for 125 of the 185 patients who claimed to be abstinent at follow-up, and for these there were discrepancies in just three cases.) For the fifty-seven patients who described themselves as controlled drinkers (see below for discussion of this concept) at follow-up, there were collateral data for thirty-four, and discrepant data were presented for only two of these.

Parenthetically, it was the authors' experience that alcoholic patients are much more likely to minimize the medical or interpersonal significance of their drinking rather than to report entirely inaccurately. For example, a patient might describe a seven-day binge (actuality) as a weekend binge (minimization), but he is not as likely to tell a clinically oriented listener that "I haven't had a drink in a year," although he might indeed relate such a story in court or to a hostile relative. Also, alcoholic patients are usually not specially defensive, anxious, or guilty about reporting their drinking behavior, except in contexts which threaten punishment for behavior related to drinking, or in contexts which lead them towards looking introspectively at their motives or at the interpersonal precipitating circumstances of a particular bout of alcoholic excess. Thus, the authors' judgment would have been suspect had they relied on the claims that the drinking patterns had improved or were under greater control, without having probed for the detailed information about those patients' uses of alcoholic beverages.

To summarize, the authors did not have as complete an assessment of the patients' total life situations from sources external to patients or to therapists as they would like to have had in order to make a thorough assessment of validity, but they did have some collateral data suggesting that the amount of error was probably relatively small; and they did have a considerable awareness of the complexities involved in making categorical clinical judgments about patients suffering with alcoholism. The reader will have to decide from the data presented here and later in this book whether particular data or interrelationships described and discussed seem cogent or plausible.

(c) *Loss of Patients between Intake and Follow-Up*

A serious problem to be considered in any follow-up study is the extent of bias derived from the inability to locate and obtain data from all the cases studied and/or treated. To take an extreme example, all the patients who have improved may be willing to participate in an interview that reviews and evaluates their status after they have terminated their contact with the clinics; on the other hand, patients who have not improved may or may not be willing. Consequently, every follow-up study attempts to locate and interview each patient included in the intake sample.

In this study satisfactory follow-up data were obtained for

about 75 per cent of the patients studied at intake. Of the remaining 25 per cent of the patients, about one-fifth were traced but refused to be interviewed; also, other sources of data about these patients were usually not available. (In a few cases partial data about particular aspects of their functioning or only estimates were obtained from their relatives or from professional sources.) About two-thirds of these remaining patients could not be traced.

Had the authors been assured that these patients did not differ in significant respects from the patients for whom satisfactory follow-up data were available, they could have ignored the matter in reporting and evaluating the follow-up data. However, analysis of the intake and treatment data indicated that there were two extremely important differences between patients who were followed up and those who were not, especially for those whom we could not trace. (Full details of the statistical comparisons need not be reported here; briefly, patients who were or were not followed up did not differ in age, sex, race, occupational status, or educational level.) Tables 20 and 21 show that these differences

TABLE 20

RELATIONSHIP BETWEEN PATIENTS' AVAILABILITY FOR FOLLOW-UP AND THEIR SOCIAL STABILITY AT INTAKE

Social stability at intake	Total no. of patients	No. of patients available for follow-up (% of total no. in parentheses)			
		Follow-up refused	Untraced	Deceased	Follow-up completed
High	248 (100)	16 (7)	14 (6)	2 (1)	216 (86)
High-medium	226 (100)	15 (7)	28 (12)	7 (3)	176 (78)
Medium-low	180 (100)	8 (5)	37 (21)	5 (3)	130 (71)
Low	139 (100)	5 (4)	52 (37)	5 (4)	77 (55)

TABLE 21

RELATIONSHIP BETWEEN PATIENTS' AVAILABILITY FOR FOLLOW-UP AND THEIR EXTENT OF CONTACT WITH THE CLINICS

Extent of contact	Total no. of patients	No. of patients available for follow-up (% of total no. in parentheses)			
		Follow-up refused	Untraced	Deceased	Follow-up completed
Minimal	410 (100)	29 (7)	94 (23)	14 (3)	273 (67)
Moderate	224 (100)	8 (4)	28 (13)	3 (1)	185 (82)
Persistent	155 (100)	4 (3)	8 (5)	2 (1)	141 (91)

104

were in social stability at intake and in *extent of contact* with the clinics. Specifically, those patients who were maximally impaired in social stability at intake and those patients who had had minimal contact with the clinics were most likely to be lost to the follow-up study, rarely through refusal to co-operate, usually through the clinics' inability to locate them one year after intake. Because both of these variables are important predictors of change (see below), wherever appropriate this chapter reviews the implications of the above findings about the patients who were not followed up.

2. CHANGE IN VARIOUS AREAS OF THE PATIENTS' BEHAVIOR

Following these methodologic digressions, we may return to the substantive portion of this chapter—to what extent did the patient population change from intake to follow-up? The areas of the patients' lives examined at intake and at follow-up were: (1) drinking, (2) health, (3) social stability, (4) social and familial relationships, and (5) work adjustment.

(a) Drinking

To what extent did the drinking pattern of the patient population change from intake to follow-up? This question entailed the construction of a set of categories describing any person's pattern of use of alcoholic beverages. A rich and descriptive vocabulary has been developed by alcoholics and by professionals treating them to differentiate patterns of excessive drinking, the types of problem drinkers, and so forth.[34] In addition, there are many schemata for conceptualizing and differentiating types of drinkers. For example, an alcohol "addict" may be distinguished from the habitual plateau drinking of the skid-row drinker, for whom the habit is often a means of sustaining his interest in life and his status among his peers. Jackson[35] explored the social-psychological correlates of "solitary" and "sociable," "belligerent" and "non-belligerent," "periodic" and "steady" alcoholics; she noted that there were many patients who shifted from a "periodic" to a "steady" pattern of drinking, while her other quoted terms referred to relatively persistent characteristics. Knight[36] differentiated between reactive, symptomatic, and addictive types of alcoholics. Some psychiatrists find little value in such distinctions, considering the use of alcohol to be a facet of an emotionally disturbed person's life—a mode of coping with anxiety or interpersonal problems; thus, although they would always diagnose the emotional disorder, they might or might not add the diagnosis of alcoholism as a secondary phenomenon.

The present authors made a number of attempts to categorize the drinking patterns of the patients from data presented in the intake case reviews. Although consistent judgments could be made about which categories fitted particular patients, it was found that the categories could not be scaled in such a fashion that movement from one to another could signify unequivocal improvement or deterioration. Furthermore, it was observed that the mode of investigation and description of drinking patterns varied so much from clinic to clinic that no consistent framework could be developed for the comparison of patients from one clinic to another. As a result, the authors fell back on an arbitrary schema which, though it lacked clinical richness and subtlety, at least had the merit of relative simplicity and reliability. Assuming that alcoholism was a serious, chronic disorder which could lead to death or to institutionalization, and if the relevant data were collected, three groups of patients could be defined with considerable precision at any time in a sample of patients with drinking problems. These groups were: I. alive, residing in the community; II. alive, in an institution; and III. dead.

Because all patients were in the first group at intake, movements to groups II and III were evidence of morbid changes in patients' lives, changes which of course might or might not have been entirely related to their uses of alcoholic beverages. Among the patients who were still alive and in the community at follow-up, three types were defined apropos their drinking: type 1 were abstainers for certain defined periods; and both types 2 and 3 still used alcohol, but type 2 were the "controlled," "social," or "normal" drinkers, whereas type 3 were the "problem" drinkers who still had troubles related specifically to the use of alcohol (for example, bouts of intoxication, binges, blackouts, hangovers, arrests for public intoxication, accidents while using alcohol, and so forth, or the debilitation consequent to such events or experiences in the person's physiologic, occupational, or interpersonal functioning). These distinctions between the drinking patterns within group I, and especially between the controlled drinkers and the problem drinkers, were obviously not as simple and precise as the distinctions based on morbidity and social location.

In terms of this schema, how did the drinking patterns of the clinic population in the month preceding follow-up differ from those in the month preceding intake? The data in Table 22 indicated that there were 21.6 per cent more patients who were known to be abstinent and/or controlled drinkers in the month before follow-up than in the month before intake;* these patients could be regarded as improved. On the other hand, 13.2 per cent (106 patients) were out of the community or deceased at the time of follow-up; these patients could be considered more impaired than they were at intake. Thirty-five per cent (280 patients) who were still problem drinkers were regarded as unchanged; one may postulate that were it not for the intervention of the clinics at least some of these patients might have deteriorated.

Concerning the patients for whom follow-up data were not available, it might be assumed that the distribution of their drinking patterns did not differ from those of patients who were traced and interviewed. Pro-rated, these cases would increase the proportion of abstinent or controlled cases at follow-up to 38.2 per cent and the proportion of deteriorated cases to 16.9 per cent (see Table 22). However, there was reason to believe, on the basis of data presented in the next chapter, that these untraced patients were less likely to become abstinent or controlled drinkers than were the patients whose follow-up status was ascertained, and that they were more likely to continue with problem drinking. Had they died or been institutionalized they probably could have been traced. The real increase in the proportion of improved cases between intake and follow-up must, therefore, lie somewhere

*Sixty-seven cases or 8.4 per cent had been abstinent or controlled drinkers prior to the date of intake. At follow-up 239 cases or 30 per cent were known to be abstinent or controlled drinkers for a month prior to the date of follow-up, an increase of 172 cases or 21.6 per cent.

TABLE 22
DRINKING STATUS OF PATIENTS IN MONTH PRECEDING INTAKE AND MONTH PRECEDING FOLLOW-UP

No. of patients in month preceding
(% of respective totals in parentheses)

Drinking status	Intake	Follow-up — All cases	Follow-up — Unknown cases pro-rated	Change in status
Alive				
In the community				
Abstinent	66 (8.3)	180 (22.6)	180 (28.8)	Improved
Controlled drinkers	1 (.1)	59 (7.4)	59 (9.4)	Improved
Problem drinkers	731 (91.6)	280 (35.1)	280 (44.9)	Unchanged
Out of the community				
Through this period		32 (4.0)	32 (5.1)	Deteriorated
Part of this period		55 (6.9)	55 (8.8)	Deteriorated
Deceased		19 (2.3)	19 (3.0)	Deteriorated
Status unknown (no follow-up)		173 (21.7)		Unknown
TOTALS	798 (100.0)	798 (100.0)	625 (100.0)	

between 21.6 per cent (obtained if none of the untraced cases improved) and 30.8 per cent (obtained if improvement rates were the same among traced and untraced cases), but in all likelihood closer to the former than to the latter. These gross over-all statistics did not of course communicate the fact (discussed below) that positive changes in drinking patterns occurred with far greater frequency for certain groups of patients than for others.

In addition to the above comparison of the status of patients in the month preceding intake with that in the month before follow-up, their status was compared for the longer time period of a year before intake and a year before follow-up (see Table 23). Very few of the patients (less than one per cent of the total clinic

TABLE 23

ATTAINMENT OF ABSTINENCE OR CONTROLLED DRINKING AT INTAKE AND
AT FOLLOW-UP

| Drinking status | No. of patients (% of total clinic population* in parentheses) | |
	At intake	At follow-up
Prolonged† abstinence	13 (1.6)	100 (12.5)
Prolonged† controlled drinking	1 (.1)	41 (5.1)
Prolonged† abstinence during the *year preceding* points of observation, but *not at point* of observation	0	20 (2.5)

*Total clinic population was 797.
†Six months or longer.

population) were abstinent for six months or longer in the year before intake, even though a considerable number had been so through the month preceding intake. For example, a patient at Clinic C had a yearly Christmas binge which he carried out long enough to require hospitalization with *delirium tremens*; for the remainder of every year he was abstinent. Such a drinking problem was obviously an extreme rarity, at least for patients who came for treatment to these state-supported alcoholism programs. There were also three patients who had been abstinent for years at the time of their intake, but evidently they were still concerned with the problems of alcoholism.

109

During the year between intake and follow-up there were 100 patients (13 per cent) who were abstinent at follow-up, and who also had been abstinent for at least six months preceding this point of observation. An additional twenty of the patients (3 per cent) said they had had a six-month period of abstinence during the year, although they were obviously problem drinkers at follow-up. Had the clinic staffs observed these patients during such a period of abstinence, and had they reported that the patients had had a "slip," the authors would have been inclined to accept this information without question. However, these patients did not maintain contact with the clinics throughout the year, so both their "abstinence" and their "slip" occurred without benefit of clinical observation. None the less, the authors decided that attainment of abstinence for six consecutive months during the year between intake and follow-up could be used as an index of probable change.

Another forty-one patients (5 per cent) were controlled drinkers at follow-up, and for at least six months. The existence of this substantial proportion of patients who appeared capable of "holding" their liquor or of becoming "social drinkers" suggested that the portion of the Alcoholics Anonymous' creed which says that total abstinence is the only alternative to uncontrolled drinking for the alcoholic is not necessarily part of the reality of alcoholism. There was evidence from prior studies[26,37,38] to indicate that some alcoholics or ex-alcoholics have sustained this "controlled" position for months or years. It might be proper logically and clinically to question or challenge the permanence or stability of this behavior, but to deny its existence for a stated period of time is merely prejudice, not science. Because Alcoholics Anonymous has grown out of considerable practical and personal experience with the troubles of alcoholism, the principle that total abstinence is the proper goal to aim at in the treatment of alcoholics should not be dismissed, as long as it takes into account the fact that some alcoholics are capable of drinking "normally" for some period of time. Later in this book additional data are presented to elucidate this point further.

There were an additional sixty-five patients (9 per cent) who were abstinent at follow-up and who indicated that they had been abstinent for periods of two to less than six months. Although these patients might also have improved, for most of the statistical analyses which follow in chapter VI these patients were placed in an ambiguous "intermediate" group. They were thus separated from those patients who could unequivocally be regarded as improved with respect to drinking, and from those who were regarded as unquestionably still having a drinking problem or who were even more impaired, for example, in an institution.

To summarize briefly, about 18 per cent of the patients were known to be abstinent or controlled drinkers at follow-up, having sustained this pattern for at least six consecutive months prior to the point of observation. In addition, about 12 per cent of the patients might be regarded as somewhat improved with respect to their drinking, because they were observed either to be abstinent in the months preceding follow-up for a period of more than two but less than six months (9 per cent), or to have had prolonged (more than six months) abstinence during the intake/follow-up interval even though they were not abstinent at the time of follow-up (3 per cent).

(b) Health

To what extent had the health of the patient population changed in the interval between intake and follow-up? As was pointed out in chapter III, most of the patients appeared to be in good health when they first came to the clinic. (It was conjectured that those alcoholic patients suffering with evident pathophysiologic changes associated with alcoholism go to medical clinics or to hospitals for care of such conditions, rather than to the special alcoholism clinics.) However, it must be recognized that evaluation of physical health is a highly complex matter, because the organism is composed of many intricately interrelated organs and tissues, each of which is subject to malfunction, infections, infestations, new growths, or trauma; each or any of these conditions may in turn have varying and variable prognoses and consequences for the total welfare and longevity of the organism. Hence, any global rating of health is suspect, except in a well-defined operational context. To make a classic example, should the strong man with severe myopia be considered healthy or ill?

Apart from the extraordinary difficulty of evaluating "health"

111

(whether "physical" or "mental"), the alcoholic patients were not routinely exposed to searching physical examinations at intake and almost never in the context of the follow-up study. Consequently, it was possible to generalize about the patient's health only in terms of his awareness of and/or his concern over his health, as communicated in interviews conducted preponderantly by non-medical personnel. In the authors' opinion, this "health index" was for several reasons the weakest index employed in the study: a minimal concern over or awareness of physical ill health can represent denial of symptomatology as much as it can represent health; a high level of concern may indicate either hypochondriasis or good judgment about bodily ill health; furthermore, the patient may appear to be quite healthy, yet without a searching medical history and appropriate laboratory tests there is no way of evaluating the adequacy of the person's cardiovascular, renal, hepatic, or nervous system functioning. However, on the understanding that the operational context of the generalizations about health was the patient's communication about his health, and not a medical evaluation *per se*, the authors constructed the index out of the following three items:

(1) The patient reported at intake or at follow-up that he was suffering with symptoms of bodily distress, which he cited. These symptoms had been going on for some time and were not ascribed to the immediate effects of alcoholic excess, for example, headaches, gastric distress, or hangover.

(2) In the *month prior* to intake or follow-up, his subjective appraisal of his health was that it was not good.

(3) In the *year prior* to intake or follow-up he had had medical treatment for illnesses outside the context of treatment for alcoholism. (Illnesses which were regarded as trivial or as instances of the multitudinous minor disturbances of adult health, ranging from occasional upper respiratory infections to fungus infections of the feet, were excluded.)

Two points were assigned for each of these items. One point was assigned if data were insufficient to arrive at a rating in regard to one of the above items. If data were insufficient for two items, the patient was excluded from the index rating (position x). Thus, each patient could be rated from zero to six on this index

112

of health at intake and at follow-up, a score of zero indicating no impairment in health, a score of six indicating maximal impairment.

Because the interest was predominantly in change, four theoretical ratings were used to compare movement from intake to follow-up; these were termed improved, unimpaired, impaired, and deteriorated.* The first designation was used to refer to those patients who at intake were impaired at least to some extent, and who at follow-up either were less impaired (for example, moved from a score of four to a score of two) or became apparently completely "healthy" in terms of this index. The term unimpaired covered patients who were healthy at intake and continued to be healthy at follow-up. The rating impaired referred to patients who were impaired in their health at intake and who continued with the same degree of impairment at follow-up. The term deteriorated applied to patients who were more impaired at follow-up than they were at intake; for example, at intake they were symptom-free, but at follow-up they complained of recurrent episodes of abdominal pains.

The findings indicated that the health of about half the patients changed between intake and follow-up (see Table 24). Slightly more patients had improved in their health than had deteriorated. For obvious reasons, deceased patients were included with those patients whose health had deteriorated, even though—to belabor the obvious—a follow-up interview was not feasible. The number of patients whose health was still unimpaired was virtually the same as that of patients who were still impaired in their health. The purpose of discriminating between these two unchanged conditions is made clear later in this chapter where change in one aspect of the patient's life is compared with change in his drinking status.

(c) Social Stability

At several points in this book, the index of social stability is referred to as an important corollary or predictor of such variables

---

*This discussion of change in health can serve as the paradigm for the other indices of change (in social stability, interpersonal relationships, and so forth) to be examined in this chapter.

as the extent or the duration of patients' contacts with the clinics, of aspects of the treatment that patients received, of the availability of patients at follow-up, and, as discussed in the next chapter, of changes in the drinking status of patients.

Did the social stability of the patient population change from intake to follow-up? Because the loss of patients to follow-up was highly related to the social stability at intake, there was an *apparent* gain in the proportion of patients who were maritally, residentially, and occupationally stable (see chapter i for the items upon which this index is based)—from 31 per cent at intake to 36 per cent at follow-up (see Table 25). Similarly, there was a decrease in the proportion of patients who were neither maritally, residentially, nor occupationally stable—from 17 per cent at intake to 13 per cent at follow-up.

TABLE 24

CHANGES IN HEALTH STATUS BETWEEN INTAKE AND FOLLOW-UP

Change in status	No. of patients (% of total no. in index* in parentheses)
Improved	170 (30)
Unimpaired	123 (22)
Impaired	125 (22)
Deteriorated†	150 (26)
TOTAL	568 (100)

*Of the total clinic population of 797 (at intake), 229 were excluded from the health index: 43 because data were insufficient; 186 because they were not in the follow-up sample.
†Includes deceased patients.

TABLE 25

CHANGES IN SOCIAL STABILITY OF PATIENTS FROM INTAKE TO FOLLOW-UP

Social stability	No. of patients (% of respective totals in parentheses)		No. of patients lost to follow-up (% of no. in category at intake in parentheses)
	At intake	At follow-up	
High	248 (31)	216 (36)	32 (13)
High-medium	226 (29)	176 (29)	50 (22)
Medium-low	180 (23)	130 (22)	50 (28)
Low	139 (17)	77 (13)	62 (45)
TOTALS	797 (100)	599 (100)	

114

However, the shift in social stability cannot be entirely accounted for by the correlation between loss to follow-up and mirroring degrees of impairment in social stability at intake, as is illustrated in Table 26. Of the 206 patients whose social stability

TABLE 26

CHANGES IN SOCIAL STABILITY OF THOSE PATIENTS FOR WHOM DATA WERE AVAILABLE AT BOTH INTAKE AND FOLLOW-UP

Social stability at intake	No. of patients at intake	Social stability at follow-up, by no. of patients			
		High	High-medium	Medium-low	Low
High	206	150	30*	20*	6*
High-medium	172	69†	69	29*	5*
Medium-low	128	19†	30†	57	22*
Low	55	4†	4†	8†	39
TOTAL	561				

*Deteriorated in social stability between intake and follow-up.
†Improved between intake and follow-up.

Change in social stability	No. of patients (% of total in parentheses)
Improved	134 (24)
Unimpaired	150 (27)
Impaired	165 (29)
Deteriorated	112 (20)
TOTAL	561 (100)

was unimpaired at intake, fifty-six were observed at follow-up to be impaired in social stability anywhere from a minimal to a maximal degree. At the other end of the scale, of the fifty-five patients who were known to have been maximally impaired at intake, eight had improved considerably (so that at follow-up they were either not at all impaired or only slightly impaired), while another eight had improved slightly, but were still at the impaired end of this spectrum of social stability. In the framework of the four change categories described above (in the section on health), 24 per cent of the patients improved in their social stability from intake to follow-up; 27 per cent continued to be unimpaired; 29 per cent continued to be impaired; and 20 per

115

cent deteriorated. The net increment of impaired over deteriorated was small, but observable.

(d) *Interpersonal Relationships*

An index of social stability is a measure of the patient's capacity to assume the roles and obligations of an adult in the community. From one perspective, absence of impairment in social stability indicates that certain social demands are being met by the person, and that certain limitations are imposed on his mobility. At the same time, these demands and limitations offer him both status and support. Thus, improvement in social stability may be regarded as an indication of growth in the patient's social *niveau*. However, it is only a partial appraisal of his social functioning and relationships. The person may appear to be a pillar of the community, yet be a tyrant at home and an isolate from friendly human interchange.

To what extent did the personal relationships of the patients change between intake and follow-up? Of the 491 patients who were married at intake and about whom sufficient data were available to evaluate the nature of the marital relationships, the marriages of only forty-one (8 per cent) were free of gross complaints. For the remaining 450 patients (92 per cent), the relationships with their spouses were characterized either by withdrawal or lack of relatedness, by physical or verbal abuse, or by complex troubled states which indicated that their marriages were close to dissolution. By the time of follow-up there were only 383 married patients for whom data on marital relationships were sufficient. Of these, 104 patients (26 per cent) indicated that there were no gross marital problems, a gain of 18 per cent over the figure at intake. Because there were more than twice as many patients (104 at follow-up to 41 at intake) without gross marital stress, strain, or unhappiness, the change obviously could not be considered an artifact resulting from the differential loss of patients from follow-up. In short, the patient population seemed to be existing in more harmonious association with their marriage partners at follow-up than they were at intake.

Another way that the extent of change in patients' personal relationships could be determined was to consider the patterns of

116

their social activities in the month preceding intake and the month before follow-up (see Table 27). At intake, 12 per cent of the patients were known to be engaged at least superficially in normal patterns of associations with friends and family, and another 13 per cent socialized at least in the restricted area of family interaction. The majority of the patients (55 per cent) either were solitary persons or restricted their social lives to drinking with casual companions. At the time of follow-up, 18 per cent of the

TABLE 27

SOCIALIZATION PATTERNS OF PATIENTS AT INTAKE AND AT FOLLOW-UP

Socialization pattern	No. of patients (% of respective totals in parentheses)			
	At intake		At follow-up	
Conformal socialization	199 (25)		242 (40)	
Family and peers		95 (12)		106 (18)
Family only		104 (13)		136 (22)
Solitary, a loner	206 (26)		118 (20)	
Casual drinking companions only	231 (29)		110 (18)	
Institution	2 (0)		33 (6)	
AA centred	36 (5)		38 (6)	
No report	123 (15)		61 (10)	
TOTALS	797 (100)		602 (100)*	

*In 195 cases, follow-up data could not be obtained.

patients for whom a follow-up study was made appeared to participate at least superficially in normal patterns of associations with friends and family, and another 22 per cent socialized in the restricted area of family interaction. Overall, there was a 15 per cent gain in conventionally approved patterns of socialization for the patient population. However, this change towards such conformal socialization was due in large part (as described below) to the fact that many of the patients who were lost to follow-up had had impaired interpersonal relations at intake.

Because these data did not, of course, indicate anything about the depth and significance of the patients' social relationships, some clarification of these aspects was sought from the patients' own statements about their friendship patterns. At intake, 30 per cent stated that they had *some* close friends, apart from the associations which were part of their working lives; at follow-up the

117

percentage was only 25. The area of friendship, however, was not carefully explored by these clinics. They assumed, and their data supported their assumption, that the alcoholic who came to these special alcoholism services typically was an isolated person or had severely troubled relations with other human beings. To remind the patient of this situation, to inquire into the nature and quality of his relationships might indeed stir up anxiety without helping him to relate better to the clinician. The apparent slight downward shift noted above might reflect the fact that at follow-up the clinics had better knowledge of the actualities of the patients' friendships. The most conservative interpretation of these data would be that there was no change in the quality of the patients' social relationships.

The relationships between patients and their families of origin were also explored. Of the 739 patients who at intake had contact with their close families (parents and siblings), 294 (40 per cent) had good relationships with one or several of their close family members; that is, there were no overt antagonisms, resentments, unacceptable exploitations, and so forth. At follow-up, there were 528 patients who had contact with close family members, and, of these, 242 (46 per cent) had good relationships with one or several of them. There was therefore a small gain in conformal socialization between intake and follow-up.

An index describing the patient's interpersonal relations was constructed out of the categories from which the above data were abstracted. The items of the index were:

(1) The patient had gross problems in relationship with spouse or (for the patient who was not married at intake or follow-up) with his family of origin.

(2) The patient had no friends or had only casual acquaintances.

(3) The patient had no conformal pattern of associations in the month preceding intake or the month before follow-up; for example, he was in jail or some other institution, was a solitary person, or associated only with drinking companions.

A score of zero was indicative of minimally impaired interpersonal relationships; a score of six was indicative of maximal impairment.

Table 28 illustrates the changes in the patients' interpersonal

TABLE 28

CHANGES IN INTERPERSONAL RELATIONSHIPS FROM INTAKE AND TO FOLLOW-UP

Interpersonal relationships at intake (score on index)	No. of patients at intake	Interpersonal relationships at follow-up (score on index) by no. of patients					No. of patients lost to follow-up (% of no. in category at intake in parentheses)
		0	2	4	6	x*	
0	52	25	12†	6†	3†	1	5 (10)
2	152	24‡	53	23†	16†	6	30 (20)
4	267	29‡	52‡	86	29†	12	59 (22)
6	238	6‡	28‡	44‡	84	8	68 (29)
x*	85	2	17	11	13	9	33 (39)

*Some could not be computed because of lack of data.
†Deteriorated in interpersonal relationships between intake and follow-up.
‡Improved between intake and follow-up.

Change in interpersonal relationships	No. of patients (% of total in parentheses)
Improved	183 (35)
Unimpaired	25 (5)
Impaired	223 (43)
Deteriorated	89 (17)
TOTAL	520 (100)

relationships from intake to follow-up. There was a significant correlation between the loss of patients at follow-up and their level of impairment in interpersonal relationships at intake. Ten per cent of the patients who at intake were unimpaired in terms of this index on interpersonal relationships were lost to follow-up, while at the other extreme of this scale 29 per cent of the patients who at intake were maximally impaired in interpersonal relationships were lost to follow-up. Although this differential loss of patients to follow-up could account, in part, for the decreasing impairment of the patients' relationships with spouses and with families of origin, and for the movement towards conformal socialization reported above, there were extensive individual changes in interpersonal relationships which could not be accounted for merely by the loss of patients to follow-up. Of the 520 patients for whom data were available both at intake and at follow-up, 35 per cent improved—a few of them to a marked degree (score was four points less at follow-up than at intake),

119

and a larger number only slightly (score was two points less). On the other hand, 17 per cent had deteriorated, while the remaining 48 per cent were unchanged. With 35 per cent improving and 17 per cent deteriorating, the patient population known at intake and at follow-up could be said to have gained 18 per cent in interpersonal relationships between intake and follow-up.

What was the significance of these findings? The authors' impression, which cannot be substantiated except through inferences, is that many alcoholic patients have points of exacerbation in their troubled human relationships. They very often come to the clinic at one of such points of crisis in their lives, so that the picture that one gets at intake is not of their usual, perhaps troubled state, but rather of an acute disturbance, of a peak of trouble. At follow-up, they may have returned to the commonplace level of desperation or unhappiness, with which they are able to live without throwing out distress signals.

(e) Work Adjustment

One of the cardinal clinical expectations about alcoholic patients is that they are unable to hold a job. It was noted earlier (chapter iii) that only a minority of the patients were stably employed at or during the year before intake. To determine the extent of change between intake and follow-up, the authors looked at the patients' work from the perspectives of work status, and of adjustment at work with special emphasis on the influence that drinking played in the patients' functioning at work.

Work status was described in terms of two variables: the first, whether or not patients were regularly employed at intake and follow-up; and the second, the duration of their employment during the year preceding these points of observation. Excluding housewives and those for whom data were insufficient, there were 440 patients whose work status could be compared at intake and follow-up. These patients were classified as to whether or not they were employed, and whether or not they had worked for more than six months in the year preceding intake and the year preceding follow-up observation. As above, four functional groups were defined with regard to change. Here, the improved group consisted of those patients who were not employed at intake and/or had worked for less than six months in the year preceding intake; at follow-up they had improved in one or both of these respects. The unimpaired patients were employed at intake, and had worked for six months or more in the year preceding intake; at follow-up, they continued this pattern. The impaired patients were unemployed at intake and/or had worked for less than six months in the year preceding intake; they continued to maintain this same pattern at follow-up. The deteriorated patients consisted of those who were employed at intake and/or had worked for six months or more in the year preceding intake; at follow-up, they had become unemployed and/or had not worked for six months in the year preceding follow-up.

There were two extreme groups. The maximally improved group consisted of those patients who neither were employed nor had worked for six months or more during the year preceding intake, and at follow-up were employed and had worked for more than six months preceding follow-up. The maximally deteriorated patients were employed and had worked for more than six months in the year preceding intake, and at follow-up were unemployed and had worked for less than six months in the preceding year. The data in Table 29 indicated that slightly more of the patients had improved than had deteriorated with regard to work status. The majority of patients had remained unchanged from intake to follow-up.

TABLE 29
CHANGES IN WORK STATUS FROM INTAKE TO FOLLOW-UP

Change in status	No. of patients (% of total in parentheses)	
Improved	119 (27)	
Maximally improved		39 (9)
Unimpaired	116 (25)	
Impaired	131 (30)	
Deteriorated	74 (17)	
Maximally deteriorated		25 (6)
TOTAL	440 (100)	

To what extent had the patient's work adjustment been influenced by alcohol use in the year preceding intake and the year preceding follow-up? At intake, the work of only 17 per cent

121

(95 of 550) of the patients was not adversely affected by the use of alcohol; that is, they had not had problems such as absenteeism, been fired for drinking, or had fights or quarrels while on the job because of alcohol use at work or irritability associated with hang-over. At follow-up, the work of 32 per cent (148 of 465) of the patients no longer seemed grossly affected by drinking. Thus, there would appear to have been a 15 per cent improvement in this aspect of the patients' work adjustment. The evaluation of these percentage differences was complicated by the fact that there was such a considerable number of patients who were fol-lowed up, but for whom data describing this facet of their adjust-ment were not obtained. Furthermore, both the number of patients lost to follow-up, and the number of patients for whom data were insufficient to evaluate work adjustment at follow-up were highly associated with the degree of impairment in work adjustment at intake (see Table 30). Thus, for those patients who had no impairment in work adjustment at intake, only 21 per cent were either lost to follow-up or insufficiently described at follow-up, whereas for those patients who had maximal impairment in work adjustment at intake, 54 per cent were either lost to follow-up or inadequately described at follow-up. It must therefore be concluded that there was probably no significant change in the work adjustment of these patients from intake to follow-up.

(f) Change as an Interrelated Phenomenon

How did change in the patient's drinking behavior influence his adjustment in other aspects of his life? Although there is evidence

TABLE 30

RELATIONSHIP BETWEEN WORK ADJUSTMENT AT INTAKE AND ABSENCE OF DATA AT FOLLOW-UP

Work adjustment (score on index)	No. of patients at intake	Absence of data at follow-up by no. of patients (% of no. at intake in parentheses)	
		No follow-up	No data at follow-up
0	62	11 (18)	2 (3)
2	243	49 (20)	22 (9)
4	188	49 (26)	30 (16)
6	148	42 (28)	38 (26)

that abstinence is far from synonymous with mental health,[39] it is widely recognized that the drinking problem often intensifies the patient's gross or overt difficulties in living. In an earlier study[26,39] it was demonstrated that the patient's drinking status at a point of follow-up was highly correlated with his then current functioning in health, family relationships, work, and so forth. However, because that was a retrospective study, and comparable data describing the patients at intake and at follow-up were not available, the authors could not consider the question of change in the patient's status other than with regard to drinking. Thus remained the tantalizing question of whether this correlation was due to improvement in the drinking status of the physically healthier, better related, and more efficiently working patients or whether in fact it indicated concomitant change.

The data of the present study corroborated these earlier findings, Table 31 indicating the striking correlations between the patient's drinking status at follow-up and his health, social stability, interpersonal relationships, work adjustment, and work status at follow-up. With respect to each of these areas, the patients who were abstinent at follow-up were functioning significantly better than were those with drinking problems.

TABLE 31

RELATIONSHIP BETWEEN DRINKING STATUS AT FOLLOW-UP AND IMPROVEMENT IN FIVE AREAS OF LIVING

Drinking status in month preceding follow-up	No. of patients	% of patients for whom improvement noted				
		in health status	in social stability	in interpersonal relationships	in work adjustment	in work status
Abstinent	179	42	54	25	45	38
Problem drinkers	353	26	33	6	17	21

Because comparable intake and follow-up data were available in the present study, it was possible to answer the "change"-focussed question in a less equivocal fashion than was feasible in the earlier study mentioned above. For this purpose, the patients who were studied at intake and at follow-up were subdivided into three groups in terms of change in their drinking status.

123

Group I consisted of those patients who at follow-up were abstinent and had been abstinent for at least six months as well as those patients who at follow-up were controlled or social drinkers and had been so for at least the previous six months (that is, they continued to use alcoholic beverages, but for at least the past six months they had had no episodes of intoxication or legal difficulties associated with excessive use of alcohol). The next group, group III, consisted of those patients who at follow-up unequivocally continued to have a drinking problem; they were not abstinent at follow-up and they had had no prolonged periods of abstinence or even of controlled drinking in the course of the past year. Group II, which has been excluded from the following statistical analyses and discussions, consisted of patients who were in an equivocal position with regard to the question of improvement or non-improvement in drinking. It was a heterogeneous group of patients who shared only the ambiguity of their positions with respect to change in drinking status, but who were not functionally comparable. Thus, it included those patients who were abstinent or controlled drinkers at follow-up but who had not maintained this status very long; those who were not abstinent at follow-up, but who claimed to have had prolonged abstinence (six months or longer) in the year between intake and follow-up; and those few who were abstinent prior to their first visits to the clinics.

The categorization of change in the other areas of patients' lives followed the same schema as that utilized above; that is, there were those who had improved, those who continued to be unimpaired, those who continued to be impaired, and those who had deteriorated. The relationship of improvement and non-improvement in drinking status to this fourfold schema of change is summarized in Table 32. The data indicated that those patients who in the interval between intake and follow-up had turned their serious drinking problems (characteristic of almost all the patients at intake) into sustained abstinence or sustained controlled drinking had improved and/or maintained an unimpaired status in other areas of their lives more often than had those who continued to have serious drinking problems at follow-up. There was one minor exception to this generalization: only 18 per cent of the patients who were improved in drinking had improved in

124

TABLE 32
CHANGES IN DRINKING STATUS IN RELATION TO CHANGES IN OTHER AREAS OF PATIENTS' LIVES

Drinking status group	No. of patients in group	Change in other areas by % of patients in group				Apparent gain of improved over deteriorated by % of patients in group
		Improved	Unimpaired	Impaired	Deteriorated	
HEALTH STATUS						
I	110	33	25	18	24	9
III	240	29	22	22	27	2
SOCIAL STABILITY						
I	113	18	42	32	8	10
III	264	21	22	37	20	1
INTERPERSONAL RELATIONSHIPS						
I	100	55	10	29	6	49
III	226	15	2	67	16	−1
WORK ADJUSTMENT						
I	74*	57	27	12	4	53
III	188*	31	8	36	25	6
WORK STATUS						
I	85*	28	47	18	7	21
III	205*	22	22	33	23	−1

*Figures exclude a substantial number of patients: about half of them were housewives, and the rest were either patients for whom data were not available or patients for whom the category was not applicable, for example, those who were retired or had prolonged institutionalization.

terms of the index of social stability, whereas 21 per cent of the patients who were unimproved in drinking had improved in social stability. This situation was due to the fact, discussed in chapter VI, that unimpaired social stability at intake was a predictor of change in drinking, so that the number of patients who could improve with respect to social stability was proportionately smaller.

When only those who had changed from their status at intake were considered, it was noted that for group I patients the amount of movement, or the gain in the proportion of patients showing improvement over those showing deterioration, in health, social stability, and so forth was greater than the positive movement or gain for the group III patients. Although the gain was comparatively smaller for the areas of health and social stability, even these differences were statistically highly significant ($p = <.01$). Thus changes in drinking were correlated with changes in other areas. It was not merely that the healthier, socially more stable were the patients who improved with respect to their drinking; rather, there was a complex positive relationship among all these factors.

There were two impressive individual statistics. Improvement in drinking was related to improvement in interpersonal relationships for 55 per cent of the patients. Similarly, 57 per cent of the patients who improved in drinking also improved in their work adjustment. The reader is reminded that these "improvements" referred to diminution in the gross or overt troubles in these areas of living. Concretely, it usually signified that the person who no longer was actively alcoholic was not fighting as unreservedly and irritably with his peers, his family, and his spouse as he had before. However, the depth or quality of his interpersonal relationships was not measured by these indices, nor were positive elements of his occupational adjustment, for example, the level of his occupational aspiration or his underlying attitudes towards workmanship.

Finally, these data inferred that changes with respect to drinking were only a partial predictor of the change in the alcoholic's life situation. There was a considerable number of patients who were improved with regard to their drinking but who none the less continued to function at an impaired level (12 to 32 per cent) for the five areas described in Table 32, some even deteriorated (4 to 24 per cent) despite their improvements in drinking. On the other hand, there were patients who continued to have severe drinking problems but who nevertheless improved in their health, social stability, interpersonal relations, work adjustment, and work status.

(g) Over-all Adjustment

Because change in drinking was highly interrelated with improvement (or the maintenance of an unimpaired status) in the other areas of the patient's life, these indices were all brought together into an index of over-all adjustment. The latter assessed the extent of impairment in the patient's drinking, health, social stability, interpersonal relationships, and work adjustment through one score which was simply the sum of the patient's impairment in these five indices at intake and at follow-up. Because the maximal score on each of the five indices was six, the maximal score in over-all impairment was thirty. (If the patient was placed in the x position (insufficient data) on one of the component indices, for example, health, he was arbitrarily assigned a score of three points for health in the calculation of the index of over-all adjustment. If there were two or more such component indices for which there were insufficient data at intake or at follow-up, the patient was excluded (assigned to the x position) from the assessment of over-all adjustment.)

The data in Table 33 showed that 13 per cent of the patients received a score of zero to eleven at intake, indicating that they were only slightly impaired in over-all adjustment; because almost all (92 per cent) of the patients had a score of six in drinking status at intake, those patients who fell into this zero to eleven range for over-all adjustment would have had less than or at most an average of one point impairment (that is, minimal impairment) in the other four indices. At the opposite end of the scale, 21 per cent of the patients had marked impairment in over-all adjustment (score of twenty-one to thirty); thus, in addition to impairment in drinking, they would have had at least an average of four points (that is, marked impairment) in the other indices. However, the majority of the patients (64 per cent) fell between these two extremes of impairment at intake.

127

At follow-up, there was a striking increase in the number of patients (for whom data were available both at intake and at follow-up) who were only minimally impaired—from 105 at intake to 220 at follow-up. Furthermore, there was a diminution in the number of cases with maximal impairment in over-all adjustment; this decrease could not be accounted for simply on the basis of differential loss to follow-up, although the latter was partially a factor. The analysis of change in over-all adjustment between intake and follow-up (Table 34) indicated that there

TABLE 33

CHANGES IN OVER-ALL ADJUSTMENT FROM INTAKE TO FOLLOW-UP

Over-all adjustment (score on index)	No. of patients (% of respective totals in parentheses)		No. of patients lost to follow-up (% of no. in category at intake in parentheses)
	At intake	At follow-up	
0–11	105 (13)	220 (37)	12 (12)
12–14	177 (22)	94 (16)	29 (16)
15–17	172 (22)	84 (14)	42 (24)
18–20	157 (20)	87 (14)	37 (24)
21–30	166 (21)	84 (14)	62 (37)
Insufficient data	20 (2)	33 (5)	13 (65)
TOTALS	797 (100)	602 (100)	

TABLE 34

PATTERNING OF CHANGES IN OVER-ALL ADJUSTMENT FROM INTAKE TO FOLLOW-UP

Over-all adjustment at intake (score on index)	No. of patients at intake	Over-all adjustment at follow-up (score on index) by no. of patients*					
		0–11†	12–14	15–17	18–20	21–30‡	No data§
0–11†	105	*49*	16	8	12	5	15
12–14	177	73	*27*	20	14	9	34
15–17	172	48	22	*22*	18	13	49
18–20	157	34	16	16	*21*	25	45
21–30‡	166	16	11	16	20	*32*	71
Insufficient data	20	—	2	2	2	—	14
TOTAL	797						

*Figures in italics represent patients whose over-all adjustment was unchanged between intake and follow-up.
†Minimal impairment.
‡Maximal impairment.
§Insufficient data and cases lost to follow-up.

128

was a shift towards less impairment for each grouping of patients —where such change was possible (for example, those who scored zero to eleven at intake could not improve by definition). Despite this general improvement, change in the direction of deterioration also occurred in each group (where such change was possible), although improvement did exceed deterioration in each grouping.

3. SUMMARY

The data indicated that many of the patients who came for treatment to these state-supported alcoholism clinics had *changed* in the interval between intake and follow-up, and that this change often was for the better. However, the proportion of improved patients was not large, and the gain—expressed in terms of the difference between the proportion of improved and deteriorated patients—was usually minor. For example, only 18 per cent of the patients had sustained prolonged abstinence or controlled drinking at follow-up; on the other hand, 13 per cent were institutionalized and 2.4 per cent were deceased at the time of follow-up. Slightly more patients had improved than deteriorated in health (30 versus 26 per cent), in social stability (31 versus 17 per cent), and in work status (25 versus 17 per cent). With respect to interpersonal relationships, there was a somewhat larger positive difference between the proportions of improved and deteriorated patients (35 versus 17 per cent). Considering that alcoholism is a chronic disorder which can lead to social and medical morbidity, it might well have been that, without the timely intervention of the clinics, fewer patients would have improved and that the proportion of deteriorated patients would have been substantially larger.

Although the apparent change in the patient population as a whole was not remarkable, the data did indicate that there was a definite proportion of patients who had improved and/or had continued to maintain an unimpaired status. Furthermore, although there were patients who had improved with respect to only one or another aspect of their functioning and adjustment, by and large improvement in the total life situation tended to be interrelated with improvement in drinking.

129

VI. Predictors of Improvement

1. INTRODUCTION

IN THE preceding chapter, it was reported that a minority, although a far from insignificant proportion, of the patients who came to these special alcoholism clinics because of their serious drinking problems had become abstinent or controlled drinkers for six months or more (the improved drinkers). It was then asked how these patients who had improved with respect to drinking, and who concomitantly had very often improved in other areas of their lives, differed from the patients who continued to have serious drinking problems.

This question was approached from three perspectives: (1) to what extent were the differences in outcome associated with what the patients brought to the clinics—their intake characteristics? (2) to what extent were these differences related to what the clinics had done for these patients—to treatment? (3) to what extent were these differences associated with the interaction between these two sets of variables?

Methodological Note. An examination of the data indicated that the choice of a numerical base for the comparison of proportions posed a dilemma. For example, if the base were taken as the number of patients for whom comparable data were available both at intake and at follow-up, the result was that, in certain respects, some groupings of patients improved more often than other groupings in a manner which was not psychologically or clinically sensible. For example, the patients of lowest social stability (at intake) improved as often with respect to the index of interpersonal relationships (20 of 78 patients, or 26 per cent) as did the patients of highest social stability (59 of 216 patients, or 27 per cent). This distortion resulted from the fact that data on interpersonal relationships at follow-up existed for only half the patients who had low social stability at intake and on whom intake data were available, whereas data existed for four-fifths of the patients who had high social stability at intake.

130

On the other hand, if the ratio of improvement were presented as the number of patients *known* to have improved, to the total relevant numerical population at intake, in effect those patients for whom data were not available at follow-up would fall into the unimproved category with respect to the particular index; that is, those patients who could not be traced or who refused follow-up interviews would be classified as "not improved." Although this inference might not have been universally true—some of the patients might indeed have improved with respect to some of the indices—it was none the less a reasonable proposition. First, these patients were functioning more poorly at intake than were any of the other patients (see Tables 20 and 25); secondly, the fact that they could not be traced by the most diligent and practised efforts of the research associates suggested that their life courses continued (or progressed) out of the pale of minimal social adjustment. Furthermore, the statistical interrelationships obtained by basing the percentages on the first (ratio of improved to number of cases known at follow-up) and on the second (ratio of improved to total relevant population at intake) modes of computation were compared, and it was observed that the latter approach led to a consistent and cumulative story, whereas the former led to many inconsistencies and to the minimization of differences. The authors therefore elected the second approach.

2. PATIENT CHARACTERISTICS AS PREDICTORS
OF OUTCOME

(a) Age

According to the usual expectations of psychotherapists, the younger patient is more likely to improve than is the (presumably) more rigid, middle-aged, involutional, or elderly patient. However, the data which, in the present study, related improvement in drinking to age were in contradition to these expectations. The older patients, those older than fifty-five at intake, improved somewhat more frequently than did the younger patients, those under thirty-five at intake. From the younger age groups to the older, there was a consistent progressive increase in the proportion of improved patients—from 12 to 18 per cent. However, neither the difference between the extreme age groups (oldest and youngest) nor the total distribution of percentage of improved differed enough from chance (t-test former comparison, chi-square

131

for the evaluation of differences within the total distribution) to warrant drawing major conclusions about a relationship between age at intake and improvement in drinking. Conservatively, it might be stated that there was no reason to believe that older patients because of personality "rigidity," customarily associated with aging, were less capable of change in drinking than were the younger patients. To the contrary, it might have been that age and "rigidity" *per se*, by encouraging the use of the mechanism of "denial," were factors facilitating certain changes in behavior.[40, 41] It might also be hypothesized that, because there was an association between age and the duration of alcoholism (see Table 35), the impact of accumulated pain and suffering associated with life as an alcoholic was the dynamic element promoting improvement in the drinking habits of the older patients.

TABLE 35

RELATIONSHIP BETWEEN AGE AND DURATION OF DRINKING PROBLEM

Duration of drinking problem	Age by no. of patients (% of total in age group in parentheses)			
	Below 36	36–45	46–55	Above 55
Less than 10 years	68 (70)	68 (45)	39 (39)	17 (31)
Longer than 10 years	29 (30)	85 (55)	69 (61)	38 (69)
TOTAL	97 (100)	152 (100)	100 (100)	55 (100)

(b) Sex and Race

There was no relationship between sex and race and the outcome of treatment. The same proportion of men as of women became abstinent or controlled drinkers, although there were some differences within the female patient population (see "Occupational Status" below).

(c) Educational Status

There also was no relationship between the amount of education that the patient had and the outcome of treatment. The college graduate was as likely or as unlikely to improve in his drinking as was the person who had not completed grammar school.

132

(d) *Occupational Status*

Some peculiar data emerged with respect to occupational status and improvement in drinking. Patients who were described as "service workers" improved more often (22 per cent) than did owners of businesses (13 per cent), those in the professions (13 per cent), white-collar workers (13 per cent), or skilled (11 per cent) or unskilled (12 per cent) factory workers; housewives showed the greatest improvement (24 per cent). The data about "service workers" were frankly a mystery; they might have been one of those chance statistical findings with which large statistical investigations are burdened. Concerning the housewives, when they were compared with the women patients who were otherwise employed, the former were found to have improved roughly twice as often as the latter (21 versus 11 per cent). Also, as was noted in chapter IV, the housewives maintained longer contact with the clinics than did any other occupational group, and there were certain other salient differences between their treatment experience and that of the other groups.

A conservative interpretation of these data indicated that a more favorable occupational status (professional, entrepreneurial) was not associated with a better prognosis in the course of alcoholism, except perhaps as this higher status might be associated with other factors.

(e) *Social Stability at Intake*

In contrast to the above demographic variables, the index of social stability at intake and the components of this index taken separately were highly predictive of outcome. Patients who were married, for example, improved with respect to drinking almost twice as often as did the unmarried patients; similarly, patients who were residing in a family setting improved twice as often as did those who were not, and patients who were employed improved roughly twice as often as did those who were not. Also, almost three times as many patients of high social stability improved as did those of low social stability—the proportion of improved patients for the intermediate categories of this index falling stepwise between.

Social stability at intake was also predictive of improvement in other areas of the patients' lives (see Table 36). It was inferred that those patients who were socially stable at intake, that is, immersed in the roles and responsibilities of adult middle-class life, came to the special alcoholism clinics with a different motivation for change and with greater environmental support for sustaining the emotional stress of initiating and sustaining abstinence. It was observed that the patients of higher social stability participated more in the services offered by the clinics and that they were offered different treatment services than were patients of low social stability.

It seemed unlikely that conscious prejudice against the less "established" patients was the basis for this finding. Nevertheless, the alcoholism clinics in general were not organized or prepared to undertake the creation of a stable milieu for these persons, even though the satisfaction of this need might have been infinitely more important and meaningful for the socially disestablished than was the attempt by the clinics to "establish a relationship" or to stimulate introspection into motives and dynamics. However difficult the socially stable alcoholic patients may be to deal with, the chronically dependent, helpless, passive, and very often "inadequate" disestablished persons are vastly more difficult to influence.[42] In chapter VII the authors return to this problem.

3. TREATMENT VARIABLES AS PREDICTORS OF OUTCOME

(a) Extent of Treatment

Extent of treatment was associated with improvement in drinking (see Table 37). (The reader is reminded that the patients were classified in three groups with respect to extent of contact: minimal (one to four visits), moderate (five to ten visits), and persistent (eleven to more than twenty visits).) Only 11 per cent of the group who had minimal contact with the clinics improved in drinking, compared to 15 per cent of those who had moderate contact, and 21.4 per cent of those with persistent contact. Extent of contact with the clinics was also associated with prolonged abstinence at any time during the year between

TABLE 36
Social Stability at Intake as a Predictor of Improvement in Drinking and in Other Areas of Life

Social stability at intake	No. of patients at intake	% of patients at intake who		% of patients at intake who improved or maintained unimpaired status in			
		Improved in drinking in 6 mos. preceding follow-up	Had 6 mos. abstinence at any time	Health	Social stability	Interpersonal relationships	Work adjustment
High	248	23	29	25	63	24	21
High-medium	226	12	18	24	32	18	25
Medium-low	180	10	18	19	27	15	19
Low	139	8	11	10	6	14	16
$chi^2 =$		20.6	15.5	12.3	140.9	8.1	3.7
$p =$		<.01	<.01	<.01	<.01	<.05	n.s. <.30

TABLE 37
Relationship between Extent of Contact with the Clinics and Treatment Outcome

Extent of contact	No. of patients at intake	% of patients at intake who			% of patients at intake who improved or maintained unimpaired status in			
		Improved in drinking	Had 6 mos. abstinence	Showed at least moderate improvement in over-all adjustment	Health	Social stability	Interpersonal relationships	Work adjustment
Minimal	410	11	15	18	31	28	16	21
Moderate	224	15	20	44	43	43	28	32
Persistent	155	21	33	46	45	48	36	33

intake and follow-up; with improvement and/or the maintenance of an unimpaired status in other areas of life; and with improvement as measured by the index of change in over-all adjustment. For example, patients who changed at least moderately in over-all adjustment (that is, dropped an average of at least one point from each of the five component indices), were found far more often among those who had persistent or moderate contact with the clinics than among those with minimal contact ($chi^2 = 37$; $p = .001$).

Although extent of contact was highly related to outcome, *duration* of contact was not; this finding was not entirely surprising, for a patient could come twice to the clinic with as many as eleven months between his first and last visits. Because extent (number of visits) and duration (length of interval between first and last visits) of contact were somewhat correlated, it was only with a sub-sample of the patients that this question could be evaluated statistically; specifically, only those patients who had eleven to twenty visits to the clinics were examined. There were fifty-four such patients who had maintained contact for six months or longer and forty-five who had maintained contact for fewer than six months. No significant or consistent differences in outcome were observed (see Table 38).

(b) Type of Contact

Having established that extent of contact was significantly associated with outcome, it was then asked whether differences in the nature of "long-term contact" influenced outcome. "Long-term contact" referred to those patients who had more than four visits to the clinics (moderate and prolonged contact), that is, approximately half of the patient population.*

(i) GROUP THERAPY. The data indicated that there were no *significant* differences in outcome between those long-term contact patients who received group therapy and those who received individual therapy (see Table 39). There was a trend (not statistically significant) suggesting that, with respect to inter-

---

*"Long-term contact" is intended as a convenient phrase, handier than "those patients who had more than only brief contact with the clinics." The reader is urged to recall this meaning and not to misconceive it as "prolonged treatment," which it usually is not.

TABLE 38

RELATIONSHIP BETWEEN DURATION OF CONTACT WITH THE CLINICS AND TREATMENT OUTCOME FOR THOSE PATIENTS WHO MADE ELEVEN TO TWENTY VISITS

Duration of contact	No. of patients at intake	No. of patients who improved (% of no. at intake in parentheses)		No. of patients who improved or maintained unimpaired status in (% of no. at intake in parentheses)				
		Improved in drinking	Had 6 mos. abstinence	Health	Social stability	Interpersonal relationships	Work adjustment	Over-all adjustment
6 mos. or more	54	12 (22)	17 (32)	29 (54)	22 (41)	21 (39)	15 (28)	18 (33)
Less than 6 mos.	45	7 (16)	14 (32)	19 (42)	22 (49)	11 (24)	15 (33)	16 (35)

TABLE 39

RELATIONSHIP BETWEEN TYPE OF THERAPY RECEIVED AND TREATMENT OUTCOME

Type of therapy received	No. of patients at intake	No. of patients who improved (% of no. at intake in parentheses)		No. of patients who improved or maintained unimpaired status in (% of no. at intake in parentheses)				
		Improved in drinking	Had 6 mos. abstinence	Health	Social stability	Interpersonal relationships	Work adjustment	Over-all adjustment
Group	97	16 (17)	27 (28)	43 (44)	48 (48)	36 (37)	31 (32)	38 (39)
Individual	281	51 (20)	72 (25)	120 (43)	119 (43)	79 (28)	91 (32)	100 (36)

personal relationships, those patients receiving group therapy had improved somewhat more often than had those receiving individual therapy. It was considered fallacious to attach great weight to this finding, because it was known that two special groups of patients, that is, housewives and those of high social stability, participated in group therapy more often than did patients in other groups within the treatment population. However, the data suggested that the value of group therapy for the alcoholic might be that of facilitating maintenance of contact with the clinic (a fact reported in chapter IV) rather than that the group interaction *per se* offered more to patients with drinking problems than did the interactions with individual therapists.

(ii) THE PROFESSIONAL CONTEXT OF TREATMENT. The differences in outcome among those patients who came more than four times to the clinic were, in general, not related to the particular type of professional person by whom they were treated, or indeed to whether or not they had special professional persons care for them at the clinics (see Table 40). But there were two very important exceptions: (1) those patients who were treated by internists (either by an internist alone or by an internist in conjunction with a social worker) included the largest proportion of patients who were improved in five of the six areas presented in Table 40; (2) with respect to the prime issue of helping patients to stop drinking or to become abstinent, the patients treated by internists had a significantly larger proportion of improved patients than did patients seen by any other professional group.

It was interesting that patients seen by psychiatrists did worse with respect to improvement in drinking than did those treated by either internists or social workers. In chapters VII and VIII, after reviewing the case reports of improved and unmodified or deteriorated patients, the authors discuss the significance of this finding.

(iii) DRUG THERAPY. It was observed earlier that patients who, upon entering treatment, received some drugs, stayed in treatment longer than those who did not receive drugs. Length of treatment, however, in turn was related to outcome: those patients who stayed longer improved more often than those who came only for a more limited number of sessions.

138

TABLE 40

RELATIONSHIP BETWEEN THE PROFESSIONAL CONTEXT OF TREATMENT AND TREATMENT OUTCOME FOR THOSE PATIENTS WHO MADE MORE THAN FOUR VISITS

Professional treatment by	No. of patients at intake	No. of patients who (% of no. at intake in parentheses)		No. of patients who improved or maintained unimpaired status in (% of no. at intake in parentheses)			
		Improved in drinking	Had 6 mos. abstinence	Health	Interpersonal relationships	Work adjustment	Over-all adjustment
Internist with or without the supplementary role of a social worker	100	26 (26)	31 (31)	49 (49)	27 (27)	34 (34)	39 (39)
Social worker with or without the supplementary roles of a psychiatrist or an internist	116	18 (16)	29 (25)	56 (48)	35 (30)	30 (26)	41 (35)
Psychiatrist with or without the supplementary role of a social worker	60	7 (12)	12 (20)	29 (48)	18 (30)	19 (32)	22 (37)
No main treatment person(s)	118	18 (15)	27 (23)	47 (40)	42 (36)	37 (32)	44 (37)

But did the drugs themselves contribute to improvement? Was there any evidence that the prescription of drugs was associated with improvement? To answer this question it was necessary to compare patients who obtained drugs with others who did not obtain drugs but were treated for equally long periods of time; to use the technical term, it was necessary to control for extent of contact to evaluate the usefulness of the drugs.

When five types of drugs were compared according to the number of patients who used them and who were improved with respect to drinking, the only consistently useful drug in the management of alcoholism seemed to be antabuse (Table 41). Barbiturates, vitamins, and tranquilizers appeared to be either harmful or impotent, because for each category of extent of contact the patients who did *not* receive these drugs were more often improved in drinking at follow-up than were those who did. Thus, however useful barbiturates, vitamins, and tranquilizers might have been in the management of such crises as impending *delirium tremens*, nausea, vomiting associated with acute alcohol

TABLE 41

IMPROVEMENT IN DRINKING RELATED TO THE USE OF SPECIFIC DRUGS AND THE EXTENT OF CLINIC CONTACT

Drug received	Extent of contact by no. of patients and by % (of that no.) improved in drinking					
	Minimal		Moderate		Persistent	
	No.	% improved	No.	% improved	No.	% improved
TOTALS	244		167		134	
Vitamins						
Some	92	13	74	18	77	25
None	152	22	93	23	57	26
Barbiturates						
Some	25	12	20	20	27	18
None	219	19	147	20	107	27
Antabuse						
Some	24	21	17	41	9	33
None	220	18	150	18	125	25
Tranquilizers						
Some	86	13	104	15	99	21
None	158	22	63	28	35	37
Special						
Some	25	0	24	12	28	32
None	219	20	143	22	106	24

intoxication, or borderline vitamin deficiency states, they did not help the patients to improve in drinking.

Because the tranquilizers are the most widely prescribed psycho-active drugs in use today, the question of their efficacy was studied further. For patients in long-term treatment, whether they were treated by a psychiatrist, internist, or social worker, those who did *not* receive tranquilizers improved more often than those who did receive them (see Table 42). Similar data were obtained when patients were considered from the perspective of reported prolonged abstinence during the year between intake and follow-up. Whatever the professional context of treatment, those patients who received tranquilizers were less often abstinent for six months or more (in the interval between intake and follow-up) than were those patients who did not receive these drugs.

TABLE 42

IMPROVEMENT IN DRINKING RELATED TO THE PROFESSIONAL CONTEXT OF TREATMENT AND THE USE OF TRANQUILIZERS FOR THOSE PATIENTS IN LONG-TERM TREATMENT

Professional treatment	Tranquilizers received, by no. of patients and by % (of that no.) improved in drinking			
	Some		None	
by	No.	% improved	No.	% improved
Psychiatrist	53	8	16	24
Internist	103	23	36	34
Social worker	84	14	70	26

Although these findings were suggestive of the inefficacy of tranquilizers in the management of alcoholism, the data were not sufficiently controlled (as to the type of tranquilizer or the quantity prescribed, the patient's co-operation, willingness, and understanding in following the prescription given to him, duration of use, and so forth) to evaluate the drugs *per se*. Further inspection did show, however, that there were no discernible differences whether sparine, thorazine, compazine, librium, or other tranquilizers were used. Because three of the clinics were university-associated and were active participants in large-scale research projects in psychopharmacology, it was unlikely that the data could be interpreted as reflecting insufficient technical or medical knowledge about these drugs.

141

Because tranquilizers are used primarily to influence anxiety and/or depression, and because other aspects of psychiatric patients' lives may be influenced through abatement of such suffering, the authors also investigated whether the use of tranquilizers affected the patients' health, social stability, interpersonal relationships, and work adjustment (Table 43). Here

TABLE 43

Use of Tranquilizers Related to the Professional Context of Treatment and Treatment Outcome in Areas of Life other than Drinking for Those Patients Who Made Eleven to Twenty Visits

Professional treatment by	No. of patients	% of patients who improved or maintained unimpaired status in			
		Health	Social stability	Interpersonal relationships	Work adjustment
Psychiatrist					
Tranquilizers used	79	48*†	39‡	25†	24‡
Not used	39	28	48	18	28
Internist					
Tranquilizers used	168	47‡	51†	34†	33†
Not used	51	48	41	31	30
Social worker					
Tranquilizers used	160	45†	53*†	23‡	28‡
Not used	93	41	38	31	30
Group therapy					
Tranquilizers used	80	43†	51†	38†	31
Not used	35	42	37	26	31

*Indicates a statistically significant difference ($p = <.05$).
†Suggests the helpfulness of tranquilizers.
‡Suggests that tranquilizers were contra-therapeutic.

the data gave no indication that the use of tranquilizers was consistently a negative influence upon improvement or the maintenance of an unimpaired status in other areas of patients' lives, as was the case with the two indices pertinent to the drinking problem *per se.* Rather, there was the suggestion that tranquilizers might have slightly facilitated the patients' adjustment apart from their drinking problems.

(c) The Clinic as a Determinant of Outcome

Just as there were considerable differences in the administration, policies, staffs, and approach to treatment among the eight clinics studied, so the data showed considerable differences in the outcome of treatment from clinic to clinic (see Table 44). For example, there were almost three times as many patients who had improved in drinking at Clinic G (25 per cent) as at Clinic C (9 per cent) and almost twice as many patients who had improved or had sustained unimpaired status in health at Clinic G (51 per cent) as at Clinic B (27 per cent). It was then asked to what extent these differences could be accounted for by differences in the patients' characteristics at intake, by differences in their participation in treatment, and by differences in their contacts with the clinics.

Because it had earlier been observed that social stability at intake was more highly predictive of outcome than were the other intake variables, the clinics were rank-ordered according to the proportion of patients unimpaired in social stability at intake, as well as according to the proportion of patients whose status was improved or unimpaired in various other categories (see Table 45). Rank-order correlations (*rho*) were then carried out between each of these other categories and unimpaired social stability at intake. The fact that these correlations ranged from .51 to .93 indicated that the relation between social stability at intake and outcome to a large extent accounted for the differences in outcome among the clinics. For example, that Clinic G had many more patients with favorable outcome in the other areas than did the other clinics could be accounted for, to a large degree, by the fact that proportionately this clinic had the highest proportion of patients unimpaired in social stability at intake; and conversely, Clinic C had few patients with favorable outcome because few of them were unimpaired in social stability at intake.

The second major factor associated with outcome was the extent of treatment. Because the interest here was in trying to account, not for differences among patients, but for differences among clinics, the clinics were also rank-ordered according to the proportion of patients who had long-term contact with them (column 3, Table 45). These rankings were then correlated with those of each of the other categories (of favorable outcome) in Table 45, and also with a composite measure of outcome exclusive of change in drinking. This last index was obtained by taking the

143

TABLE 44
COMPARISON OF TREATMENT OUTCOME IN THE EIGHT CLINICS IN THE STUDY YEAR

Clinic	Total no. of patients	No. of patients who (% of clinic's total in parentheses)		No. of patients who improved or maintained unimpaired status in (% of clinic's total in parentheses)			
		Improved in drinking	Had 6 mos. abstinence	Health	Social stability	Interpersonal relationships	Work adjustment
A	84	13 (15.5)	20 (23.8)	23 (27.4)	30 (35.8)	15 (17.9)	24 (29.0)
B	108	11 (10.0)	17 (15.8)	29 (27.0)*	28 (26.0)	10 (9.3)*	22 (20.4)
C	99	9 (9.0)*	13 (13.0)	34 (34.0)	16 (16.0)*	17 (17.0)	22 (22.0)
D	105	11 (10.5)	19 (18.1)	34 (32.4)	28 (26.6)	21 (20.0)	21 (20.0)*
E	100	15 (15.0)	26 (26.0)	33 (33.0)	41 (41.0)	34 (34.0)	26 (26.0)
F	106	17 (16.0)	25 (23.6)	40 (38.0)	38 (36.0)	24 (23.0)	29 (28.0)
G	104	26 (25.0)†	28 (27.0)†	53 (51.0)†	55 (53.0)†	28 (27.0)	37 (36.0)†
H	91	11 (12.0)	9 (10.3)*	38 (42.0)	48 (52.0)	31 (34.0)†	29 (32.0)

*Indicates the clinics with the *lowest* proportion of patients whose treatment outcome was favorable.
†Indicates the clinics with the *highest* proportion of patients whose treatment outcome was favorable.

TABLE 45

THE EIGHT CLINICS RANKED ACCORDING TO THE PROPORTION OF PATIENTS WITH FAVORABLE TREATMENT OUTCOME AND OTHER CHARACTERISTICS

Clinic	Were unimpaired in social stability at intake	Were in long-term treatment group	Improved in drinking	Had 6 mos. abstinence	Health	Social stability	Interpersonal relationships	Work adjustment	Mean rank
					Rank according to proportion of clinic's patients who — Improved or maintained unimpaired status in				
A	3	5	3	3	7	5	6	3	5
B	7	6	7	6	8	7	8	7	8
C	8	8	8	7	4	8	7	6	6.5
D	6	3	6	5	6	6	5	8	6.5
E	4	2	4	2	5	3	2	5	3.5
F	5	7	2	4	3	4	4	4	3.5
G	1	4	1	1	1	1	3	1	1
H	2	1	5	8	2	2	1	2	2
rho with column 2*			*.79*	.51	.56	*.93*	*.74*	*.88*	*.87*
rho with column 3*			.25	−.08	.18	.60	*.76*	.31	.50

*Significant correlations ($p \leqq .05$) are italicized.

mean ranks of each clinic in all of the social indices of favorable outcome. The data were somewhat surprising. Unlike the relatively strong positive rank-order correlations of favorable outcome with social stability at intake, the correlations between long-term contact and favorable outcome were negligible or weak, except in only one of the seven categories. This finding was unexpected, because social stability at intake for individual patients had earlier been discovered to be highly related to extent of contact with the clinics.

To clarify this important discrepancy, the authors studied the combined influence of social stability and extent of contact, and observed an interesting and comprehensible interplay between these variables (see Table 46). For patients unimpaired in social stability at intake there was a highly significant relationship between extent of contact and improvement in drinking, whereas for the impaired patients there was no relationship between these variables.

TABLE 46

EXTENT OF CONTACT AS A PREDICTOR OF IMPROVEMENT IN DRINKING, CONTROLLING FOR SOCIAL STABILITY AT INTAKE (SOCIAL STABILITY DICHOTOMIZED)

	Extent of contact by no. of patients and by no. improved in drinking					
	Minimal		Moderate		Persistent	
Social stability at intake	No. at intake	No. improved (% of no. at intake in parentheses)	No. at intake	No. improved (% of no. at intake in parentheses)	No. at intake	No. improved (% of no. at intake in parentheses)
Unimpaired	104	16 (15)	88	20 (23)	53	20 (38)
Impaired	306	29 (10)	136	14 (10)	108	13 (11)

Because of the small number of patients in certain categories of the statistical analysis, a more detailed breakdown by both social stability and extent of treatment was not feasible. However an expanded analysis by social stability could be made by condensing extent of treatment into two, rather than three, categories, that is, by combining all the moderate and prolonged cases into the single category "long-term treatment," and contrasting these with patients who had only short-term contact

146

(Table 47). The data merely confirmed the previous statistical analysis that for patients unimpaired in social stability extent of contact was a determinant of outcome, and that for other patients it was not.

TABLE 47
EXTENT OF CONTACT AS A PREDICTOR OF IMPROVEMENT IN DRINKING, CONTROLLING FOR SOCIAL STABILITY AT INTAKE (EXTENT OF CONTACT DICHOTOMIZED)

| | Extent of contact by no. of patients and by no. improved in drinking | | | |
| | Short-term | | Long-term | |
Social stability at intake	No. at intake	No. improved (% of no. at intake in parentheses)	No. at intake	No. improved (% of no. at intake in parentheses)
High	104	16 (15)	141	40 (28)*
High-medium	121	14 (12)	103	12 (12)
Medium-low	93	9 (10)	85	9 (10)
Low	92	6 (7)	49	6 (12)

*The patients unimpaired in social stability who had long-term (moderate or persistent) contact with the clinics improved in drinking more often to a statistically significant degree than did those who had short-term (minimal) contact ($d = 13.4$ per cent; $t = 2.5$; $p = <.01$).

In order to determine whether differences in outcome among the clinics persisted even if these predictive factors were controlled, the authors, for the sake of clarifying the issue, hypothesized, first, that the patients who had maintained adequate social stability despite their drinking problems had "a predisposition towards improvement"; secondly, that the patients' motivations to change were further demonstrated by their willingness to attend the clinics more than four times. It should then have followed that when the clinics were compared only for patients who were "prognostically optimal" in these respects (that is, social stability and long-term treatment), the differences among the clinics should have disappeared (see Table 48). However, marked differences among the clinics remained, indicating that length of treatment and predisposition were not the only factors involved.

Before attempting to search for the additional factors that were involved in the differences among the clinics, the authors considered the possibility that these differences might indirectly or

147

subtly still be due to predisposition or motivation. It was speculated that, because improvement in drinking was associated with
social stability at intake and because extent of contact was also
associated with stability at intake, the clinic which dealt with a
large proportion of such prognostically optimal patients would

TABLE 48

CLINIC DIFFERENCES IN PROPORTION OF PROG-
NOSTICALLY OPTIMAL PATIENTS WHO IMPROVED
IN DRINKING

	Prognostically optimal patients	
Clinic	Total no.	No. improved (% of total no. in parentheses)
A	26	5 (19)
B	24	2 (8)
C	16	0 (0)
D	30	6 (20)
E	39	8 (21)
F	24	9 (38)
G	41	13 (32)
H	49	9 (18)

also do better with patients who were prognostically less than
optimal; it was assumed that the latter patients would benefit
from a climate of encouragement, from a greater expectation of
success, and from increased professional morale. However, when
the data for the total intake population, for the patients who were
prognostically optimal, and for the patients who were not prognostically optimal were examined, this hypothesis was not sustained (Table 49). The fact that a clinic had a large proportion
of prognostically optimal patients did not increase the proportion
of improvement either for the prognostically optimal patients or
for those patients who were prognostically not optimal. For
example, Clinic H had the highest proportion of prognostically
optimal patients, but stood fifth with regard to improvement in
drinking for these patients, and seventh for non-optimal patients.

Returning to the question of identifying the factors which
could account for the differences among the clinics (other than
the differences in the patient populations), the authors considered the differences in the specific treatments offered by the
clinics. Because it was known that those treatment variables

TABLE 49
CLINIC DIFFERENCES IN PROPORTION OF PROGNOSTICALLY OPTIMAL AND PROGNOSTICALLY NON-OPTIMAL PATIENTS WHO IMPROVED IN DRINKING

Clinic	Total clinic population	Prognostically optimal patients				Prognostically non-optimal patients		
		Total		Improved			Improved	
		No. (% of clinic population in parentheses)	Rank order	No. (% of total no. in parentheses)	Rank order	Total no.	No. (% of total no. in parenthesis)	Rank order
A	84	26 (31)	4	5 (19)	3	58	8 (14)	2.5
B	108	24 (22)	7	2 (8)	7	84	9 (14)	2.5
C	99	16 (16)	8	0 (0)	8	83	9 (11)	5
D	105	30 (29)	5	6 (20)	5	75	5 (7)	7
E	100	39 (39)	2.5	8 (21)	4	61	7 (12)	4
F	106	24 (23)	6	9 (38)	1	82	8 (10)	6
G	104	41 (39)	2.5	13 (32)	2	63	13 (21)	1
H	91	49 (54)	1	9 (18)	6	42	2 (5)	8

which were most positively related to improvement were treatment with antabuse and treatment by an internist (with or without a social worker), it was anticipated that differences in treatment outcome among the clinics would be reflected by differences in their use of these treatment modalities. This expectation was in fact confirmed by the data. For both the total population and for the population of optimal patients, Clinics F and G stood at the top of the ranking as far as improvement in drinking was concerned, and Clinics B and C at the bottom (see Table 48). As reported earlier in the book, Clinic G made extensive use of antabuse, and almost all of its patients were treated by internists. At Clinic F, although antabuse was rarely used, for many years the central figure at the clinic had been an internist devoted to the understanding of alcoholism. Clinics B and C, on the other hand, relied heavily on the use of tranquilizers, drugs which seemingly offered little in the management of alcoholism. Although internists were directly involved in the treatment of patients at Clinic B, they occupied a secondary position in the clinic; in fact, the patients who were regarded as most likely to profit from treatment were displaced from the mainstream of this clinic's operation for treatment by medical students and psychiatric residents under psychiatric supervision, whereas the other (the majority of the) patients were regarded as research subjects for testing the efficacy of tranquilizers under management of part-time internists. At Clinic C the goal was to involve patients in psychotherapy; tranquilizers, especially librium, were intended to facilitate such involvement.

(d) The Controlled Drinkers

Thus far in this study the authors have regarded as functionally equivalent those patients who were abstinent for at least the six months prior to follow-up and those who were controlled drinkers for at least the same time. Because the general purpose of treatment is to modify the medical and social morbidity associated with alcoholism, either of these outcomes is valuable if there are no significant differences in morbidity between these groups.

In an earlier study[36] the controlled drinkers were still consistently somewhat more impaired at follow-up than were the patients who had become abstinent (see Table 50). (The differences were statistically significant for only two of seven measures employed.) It was therefore asked whether these trends which were observed in only one state alcoholism program also obtained in the present study of patients from eight geographically and socially disparate clinic populations (see Table 51). In each index of favorable outcome employed in this

TABLE 50

PROLONGED ABSTINENCE AND PROLONGED CONTROLLED DRINKING RELATED TO VARIOUS MEASURES OF HEALTH AND SOCIAL ADJUSTMENT AT FOLLOW-UP (AS NOTED IN AN EARLIER STUDY)*

Measures of adjustment	% of abstinent patients	% of controlled drinkers	d	σ	t	p
1. Unconditionally good health reported by patient	62	51	11	10	1	n.s.
2. No medical treatment in past year	69	56	13	10	1.3	n.s.
3. No downward occupational mobility between intake and follow-up	81	81	0	—	—	—
4. No problems getting along at work	67	56	11	10	1	n.s.
5. Not alienated from family at follow-up	98	85	13	6	2	.05
6. Good or fair relationship with spouse at follow-up	66	50	16	10	1.6	n.s.
7. Not at lower end of a scale of social participation	73	44	29	10	3	.001

*Total number of abstinent patients was 55, and total number of controlled drinkers was 41.

d = percentage differences; σ = standard error of difference; t = ratio of percentage difference to standard error of difference; and p = probability level.

TABLE 51

PROLONGED ABSTINENCE AND PROLONGED CONTROLLED DRINKING AT FOLLOW-UP RELATED TO TREATMENT OUTCOME IN FIVE AREAS OF LIVING

Drinking status at follow-up	Total no. of patients	No. of patients who improved or maintained unimpaired status in (% of total no. in parentheses)				
		Health status	Social stability	Interpersonal relationships	Work adjustment	Work status
Abstinent	78	47 (60)	50 (64)	47 (60)	43 (55)	46 (59)
Controlled drinkers	35	17 (49)	18 (51)	18 (51)	19 (54)	17 (49)

151

study, the data indicated that morbidity was slightly less for the abstinent patients than for the controlled drinkers, but that the differences were smaller than in the earlier study, none of them even approaching statistical significance. It could therefore be concluded that, with respect to modification of morbidity, the attainment of prolonged abstinence had no strong advantage over attainment of controlled drinking,* and that the decision to treat these states as functionally equivalent was valid.

Why did some patients become abstinent, and others controlled drinkers? It was found that there were no significant differences between these groups in age, sex, race, educational attainment, social stability, or duration of their drinking problems. There were, however, some important differences in the treatment experience of the patients who became abstinent and those who became controlled drinkers. Of particular note were the differences from clinic to clinic (see Table 52). For example,

TABLE 52

CLINIC DIFFERENCES IN THE MODE OF IMPROVEMENT IN DRINKING

Clinic	Total clinic population	No. of improved patients who were (% of clinic population in parentheses)		Ratio of no. of abstinent to no. of controlled drinkers	Ratio of proportion of abstinent to proportion of total improved
		Abstinent	Controlled drinkers		
A	84	9 (11)	4 (5)	2.2	.69
B	108	5 (5)	6 (6)	.83	.45
C	99	3 (3)	6 (6)	.50	.33
D	105	6 (6)	5 (5)	1.20	.55
E	100	5 (5)	10 (10)	.50	.33
F	106	15 (14)	2 (2)	7.5	.88
G	104	24 (23)	2 (2)	12.0	.92
H	91	11 (12)	—	∞	1.00

at Clinic E one-third of the improved patients became abstinent and two-thirds became controlled drinkers, whereas at Clinic G almost all of the improved patients became abstinent, and only a very small proportion became controlled drinkers.

There also were significant differences between the extent of

*There might have been prognostic advantages, an hypothesis which this study could not examine.

contact of the patients who became abstinent and that of those who became controlled drinkers, the latter maintaining less contact with the clinics than did the former (see Table 53). There did not appear to be any important differences in the patterning of the treatment, but because so few of the patients who became controlled drinkers had long-term treatment meaningful statistical comparisons between the two types of patients could not be made.

TABLE 53

EXTENT OF CLINIC CONTACT RELATED TO THE MODE OF IMPROVEMENT IN DRINKING

Drinking status	Total no. of patients	Extent of contact by no. of patients (% of total no. in parentheses)		
		Minimal	Moderate	Persistent
Abstinent	78	20 (37)	21 (27)	27 (35)
Controlled drinkers	35	16 (46)	13 (37)	6 (17)

The proportion of patients who were treated with tranquilizers differed significantly. Seventy-four per cent of the patients who became abstinent received tranquilizers, whereas only 46 per cent of those who became controlled drinkers received these drugs. (The 28 per cent difference was statistically significant: $p = < .01$.)

(e) The Matched "Success" and "Failure" Samples

Earlier in this chapter the authors presented some conclusions about the influence of certain treatment factors based on a comparison between the treatment experiences of the total improved group (abstinent and controlled drinkers) with that of those patients who did not improve. These evaluations could, however, have been blurred by the grouping together of the abstinent and the controlled drinkers who, as just noted above, had disparate treatment experiences. For this reason, the seventy-eight patients who were observed to be abstinent at follow-up and who had been abstinent for at least the prior six months—the "success" sample—were compared with a matched sample (matched for age, sex, race, social stability, and clinic) of patients who were not abstinent at follow-up and who had not been abstinent for

153

longer than four months at any time in the interval between intake and follow-up—the "failure" sample (Table 54). It was found that the distinctions between the treatment experiences of the improved and unimproved patients were the same as those between the "success" and "failure" samples. For example, the "success" patients maintained contact with the clinics longer than did the "failure" sample. Also, they were treated by internists

TABLE 54

DIFFERENCES BETWEEN "SUCCESS" AND "FAILURE" SAMPLES WITH RESPECT TO EXTENT OF CLINIC CONTACT

Sample	Total no. of patients	Extent of contact by no. of patients (% of total no. in parentheses)		
		Minimal	Moderate	Persistent
Success	78	26 (33)	24 (31)	27 (35)
Failure	78	37 (47)	27 (35)	14 (18)

TABLE 55

UTILIZATION OF TREATMENT RESOURCES (APART FROM THE OUT-PATIENT CLINICS) IN THE INTERVAL BETWEEN INTAKE AND FOLLOW-UP

Treatment resources used	No. of patients in	
	Success sample*	Failure sample*
In-patient settings		
Mental hospitals	2	5
General hospitals	5	8
"Drying-out" hospitals	2	3
NAAAP-correlated in-patient facilities	3	14
TOTAL	12	30
Alcoholics Anonymous	34	14

*Both samples had a total of 78 patients.

far more often than were the "failure" patients (31 versus 14 per cent) ($p = < .01$); they were treated less often with drugs than was the "failure" sample (22 versus 31 per cent), but they received antabuse more often than did the "failure" sample (15 versus 9 per cent), whereas the latter received tranquilizers and vitamins more often than did the "success" sample (respectively, 60 per cent versus 46 per cent ($p = < .05$) and 49 versus 41 per cent).

154

Two interesting facts which were not perceived previously emerged from the statistical analysis. The "success" sample had considerably more patients involved with Alcoholics Anonymous subsequent to intake (44 per cent) than had the "failure" sample (15 per cent) (see Table 55), indicating that the group was actively looking for support in sustaining abstinence. The "failure" patients, on the other hand, made greater use of in-patient facilities subsequent to intake because of their progressive or continuing medical or psychiatric morbidity.

4. SUMMARY

Differences in outcome were not associated with simple bio-social characteristics of the patients; that is, neither age, sex, race, nor educational status was associated with outcome. Occupational status was peculiarly associated with outcome, in that service workers and housewives (22 and 24 per cent respectively) improved more often than did the other occupational groups which ranged from unskilled factory workers to owners of businesses and to professionals (11 to 13 per cent). Of major significance was the fact that differences in outcome were strongly associated with the patient's functional integrity as an adult in society, as measured by the authors' index of social stability.

Differences in outcome were associated with the extent and type of contact with the clinics. The patients who had improved had more contact with the clinics than did the patients who showed no improvement. Although group therapy could be efficacious in maintaining longer contact with the clinics, given comparable duration of contact there were no differences in outcome between patients seen in individual therapy and those in group therapy. The professional context of treatment was predictive of outcome; that is, patients treated by internists were significantly more likely to improve in drinking than were patients treated by other professionals involved in these clinics. Drug therapy, like group therapy, could be efficacious in maintaining longer contact with the clinics, but given comparable contact with the clinics only antabuse seemed consistently to enhance outcome,

155

whereas vitamins, tranquilizers, or sedative drugs could conservatively be described as probably not helpful, with the suggestion that their use might have been contra-therapeutic, especially in relation to improvement in drinking.

There were significant differences in outcome among the different clinics. These differences partially reflected differences in the social stability of the patients who attended these clinics; there were significant correlations among the clinics when they were ranked for the proportion of patients with high social stability at intake and for the proportion with favorable outcome in many aspects of their lives. Further analyses of these data, controlling for the factor of extent of contact with the clinics, indicated that there were great differences among the clinics even for the "prognostically optimal" patients. Although the latter patients almost always had a higher proportion of improvement than did the other patients, the improvement occurred in relation to what the clinic did for them, rather than merely in relation to the patients' predispositions or motivations to change.

When an examination was made of the authors' practice of grouping together the patients who were abstinent and those who were controlled drinkers at follow-up (both maintaining these conditions for at least the prior six months), the data indicated that these groups were functionally comparable as measured by (the absence of) social and medical morbidity. However, there were differences in the treatment experience of these two groups: the abstinent patients maintained contact with the clinics longer than did the controlled drinkers; they received drugs more often than did the controlled drinkers; and the proportion of abstinent to controlled drinkers varied widely among the clinics.

To ascertain whether relations between treatment and outcome might have been masked by grouping together the abstinent and controlled patients, the authors compared matched "success" and "failure" samples. These comparisons supported the earlier findings and supplied some additional significant facts: that the "success" patients were more often involved with Alcoholics Anonymous subsequent to intake than were the "failure" patients; and that the "failure" sample had to make more use of a variety of in-patient facilities subsequent to intake than did the "success" sample.

156

VII. Qualitative Analysis of Cases

1. INTRODUCTION

IN THE preceding chapters of this book, the patients were described in terms of relatively simple variables or categories. Aspects of the treatment they received, their functioning at intake and at follow-up, and the degree to which they had changed in this interval were interrelated through statistical analysis. The data described groups rather than individuals. In this chapter, emphasis is on individual alcoholics as persons and as patients, the sources of data being the clinical protocols which the collaborating clinics prepared at intake, during treatment, and at follow-up. The purpose of this casuistic chapter is to clarify certain more subtle clinical issues and to attain some perspectives beyond the preceding simpler statistical analyses.

2. GENERAL CONSIDERATIONS

Reporting about patients is a selective process. There were roughly 800 patients, any of whom could have been picked for casuistic analysis and discussion. But rather than making random selections from the total group, the authors chose patients from the follow-up groups on which the earlier chapters focussed. The purpose was to illustrate the kinds of human problems that patients presented at intake; how patients participated in treatment; the impact of treatment on their lives; what their modes of living were at follow-up; and what factors seemed to be plausibly related to the change or to the lack of change in their lives from intake to follow-up.

Cases were selected from three follow-up groups:

(1) the patients who were abstinent at follow-up and who had maintained abstinence for at least the prior six months;

(2) the patients who were controlled drinkers at follow-up and who had maintained such a pattern of controlled drinking for at least the prior six months;

(3) the patients who still had a drinking problem at follow-up and who had not maintained sobriety for any interval greater than three months in the interval between intake and follow-up. These patients are referred to respectively as the abstinent patients, the controlled drinkers, and the unmodified (or deteriorated) problem drinkers.*

3. CONCORDANT AND DEVIANT CASES

As indicated in the previous chapter, it was known that the abstinent patients, by and large, were significantly less impaired in their social stability at intake than were the other patients; that they had a greater amount of contact with the clinics; and that there were certain differences in their treatment experiences, especially in the use of antabuse and in treatment by internists. However, it was also known that these differences sometimes applied to those patients who were not abstinent at follow-up; indeed, this overlap was evident in every statistical category pertinent to intake characteristics, treatment experiences, and changes in adjustment in areas of life other than drinking. In short, the differences reported were statistical rather than causal (in the sense of necessary or sufficient causes). Thus, the fact that a particular patient came, for example, fifteen times to a clinic was in itself no assurance that he would become abstinent; rather, the fact that he was a member of the group of patients who came more often to the clinics indicated that the probability of his becoming abstinent was greater than if he had belonged to the group of patients who came less often. The discriminating variables indicated probabilities of outcome.

This chapter describes patients who were *in accord with* and

*Omitted from casuistic review were those cases who were abstinent at follow-up but had not been abstinent for any prolonged period during the interval between intake and follow-up, and those who still had a drinking problem at follow-up but who had had some prolonged period of abstinence in the intervening year.

those who were *deviant from* major predictive trends. Length of contact with the clinic and social stability at intake being considered major predictive variables of change or of favorable outcome, four prognostic groups were defined and are illustrated in Table 56. Those patients who became abstinent belonged to

TABLE 56

PROGNOSTIC GROUPINGS IN RELATION TO TWO MAJOR
PREDICTIVE VARIABLES OF OUTCOME

| | Social stability at intake | |
Length of contact	Impaired	Unimpaired
Brief	Poor	Not-optimal
Long-term	Questionable	Optimal

all four of these groups, although, because the groupings were defined *post hoc*, abstinent patients were more often in the optimal group than in any of the other three prognostic groups. However, as much or more can be learned about the factors enhancing changes in drinking if the treatment experiences of abstinent patients who would not have been expected to improve (especially those in the poor prognosis group) are examined as if the treatment of those patients who were in the optimal group are studied. Conversely, of those patients who continued with an unmodified drinking problem or who did, in fact, deteriorate between intake and follow-up, most were in the poor prognosis group, but many were in the optimal group. Why did these latter patients, who would have been expected to improve, maintain their drinking problem despite the favorable support of their intact social stability together with their willingness to submit to prolonged treatment? In an attempt to clarify some of the issues, this chapter presents a qualitative review of the case material.

4. CONTROLLED DRINKERS

In earlier chapters there have been references to the question of the alcoholic's becoming a controlled drinker. Davies[37] reported eleven such cases and reviewed the literature from diverse sources

159

to support his finding that "genuine" alcoholics could become controlled drinkers without either prolonged institutional care or deep psychotherapeutic modification of personality. In Gerard's and Saenger's earlier study,[39] 41 out of 300 patients apparently had become controlled drinkers and had been observed to have maintained this condition for at least a year prior to the follow-up interviews which were conducted two to eight years after the patients' initial visits to the special alcoholism clinics of the Connecticut Commission on Alcoholism.

The fact that in the present study only 35 out of 797 patients—less than half the proportion in the authors' earlier study—were observed to be controlled or "social" drinkers at follow-up might be due either to the shorter time interval (one year, rather than two, five, or eight years) between intake and follow-up, or to the fact that a more heterogeneous clinic population (clinics of eight state programs rather than only one) were studied. In support of this second hypothesis, Table 52 reported considerable inter-clinic differences in the proportion of controlled drinkers among the improved patients.

This chapter reviews the controlled drinkers in the same framework described at the beginning of the chapter, supplemented by case material to clarify two special questions: (a) were they really problem drinkers at intake? (b) does careful further review of these cases support their identification as controlled drinkers?

5. GROUPED CASE PRESENTATIONS

(a) The Abstinent Patients

In this review of the abstinent patients, vignettes are abstracted from case studies to emphasize those points which most sharply document the emerging picture.

There were only three patients at Clinic C who became abstinent. All three had minimal contact with the clinic: two of them came only once, and the third appeared only four times over a span of five months. All three were moderately to severely impaired in social stability at intake (score four to six on index), although all had continuing contact with family members (not spouses) who had been actively interested in their welfare. These patients thus were deviant successes as described above; that is, because they did not fulfill the major predictive trends for favorable outcome—absence of impairment in social stability at intake and prolonged contact with the clinic—none of them would have been expected to have improved.

What were the circumstances of their lives at intake? Two were chronically ill, receiving public assistance for disabilities for many years: one of these suffered with "service-connected schizophrenia," the other with severe asthma. The third patient had been living on his savings and investments since the death of his wife two years prior to his initial contact with the clinic, at which (former) time his drinking problem had begun; in Knight's schema he would have been regarded as a reactive alcoholic.

How did these patients participate in treatment at the clinic itself? In a word, they partook minimally, but two of them had extensive hospitalizations subsequent to their clinic visits, the first for four months in a Veterans Administration (VA) mental hospital, and the other in various general hospitals. The third patient angrily denied being an alcoholic or having a drinking problem despite arrests for drunken driving, blackouts, episodes of rage while intoxicated, and innumerable episodes of public intoxication.

What were their modes of living at follow-up? The two patients who had had extensive hospitalization had been in the community and sober for more than six months. One of these was under supervision of a guardian appointed by the VA and was obviously wholly dependent on his mother with whom he lived; he was still unemployed, but as sure as was his mother that the government would always take care of him. The other patient became a permanent resident at a mission, but he spent every day with his sister; interpreting his prior drinking as a means for avoiding work, he claimed that he no longer needed to drink because his asthmatic condition had progressed to the point where he was virtually medically unemployable. The third patient, the "reactive" alcoholic, had been completely abstinent since his one clinic visit; he was working with his brother-in-law in a small grocery store which they purchased; he continued to be seclusive and

161

family-bound, having probably shifted his dependence from his deceased wife to his brother-in-law and his sister.

What seemed to have changed these patients' orientations towards the use of alcohol? One patient had clearly given up any attempt to form a life of his own. His latest schizophrenic episode, described by the VA hospital as of hebephrenic type, seemed to have been followed by complete resignation and an acceptance, by both him and his mother, of a socially incompetent life. The next patient was told, and by follow-up accepted, that further alcoholism would kill him, by way of *status asthmaticus*. Because his medical disability had become complete, rather than only partial, his dependency problem seemed to have been solved entirely to his satisfaction! The third patient succeeded in demonstrating that he "is not and never has been" an alcoholic; his visit to the clinic might have communicated to him for the first time that he had a serious drinking problem. He had become abstinent through the use of denial which was supported by the persons who satisfied his evident needs for dependency.

At Clinic D, there were nine patients who became abstinent. At intake, four of these had been totally dependent on VA, Department of Welfare, or family for periods ranging from one to five years. The other patients were economically self-supporting, although in every case working members of the family also were contributing heavily to the support of the household. Other than this dimension of partial or total economic dependence, and perhaps the fact that they were all involved in grossly troubled familial and interpersonal interactions, it would be difficult to generalize about the life situations of the nine patients at intake.

How did they participate in treatment? Three of these patients had only brief contact with the clinic, while the other six visited the clinic as many as seventeen times in the year following intake. Only one of the patients participated in treatment formally identified as psychotherapy. However, this patient, an overt homosexual, twenty-two years of age, gave up his treatment after only eight visits, probably because he was threatened by the tacit implication that he might consider looking into his sexual problem. The rest of the patients were treated by internists, from whom they received drugs and supportive reassurance which they found comforting and which they regarded as helpful to them in sustaining abstinence.

What were their modes of living at follow-up? Four patients who were entirely dependent financially on their families at intake continued to be so at follow-up, and an additional two patients who had been more or less self-supporting at intake became increasingly though not totally dependent on their spouses or their families. One patient who had been married was separated, and although he made conventional statements about wanting to be back with his wife it seemed that the strain of sexuality and family responsibilities were too much for him, and that in fact he was probably better off alone than married. One of the increasingly financially dependent patients, after a year of abstinence, was growing restless with his marriage, saying that the wife he had married when he was a drunkard was not the kind of woman for a sober man. It was the researchers' impression that he had been insulated from his sexual anxieties by the sexual abstinence and avoidance facilitated by his alcoholism, and that, when sober, he would rather be with "the boys" at AA which he visited at least four times weekly. He was also on antabuse which he described as his "life insurance." One patient, a married woman with an alcoholic husband, was once again sober in counter rhythm with her husband. When he drank extensively, she was abstinent and vice versa; for the past eight months he had been drinking heavily, so she became "the good one" who no longer drank.

Of the nine patients, only one, Mr. G.S., was functioning in a manner suggestive of some growth in self-acceptance as well as in social conformity. He worked part-time to supplement his VA pension (for multiple shrapnel wounds and associated facial disfigurement). In place of his prior whoring activities, he had found a mutually supportive relationship (emotionally, not financially) with one girlfriend. Also, because he continued to attend the clinic, the researchers conjectured that he had formed a relationship with his internist, from whom he had received a variety of medications; he was noted none the less to still be overtly very anxious and very "nervous." The other patients were unchanged in their usual relationships, attitudes and values, general level of emotional maturity, and so forth.

How did these patients shift in their attitudes towards the use of alcoholic beverages? Seven of the nine had become abstinent during the month preceding intake, and at their first visits to the clinic had already been abstinent for at least a week. In effect, they were looking for aid in sustaining rather than in initiating abstinence. It was clear in a number of cases that factors external to the treatment experience had been very powerful influences towards initiating as well as towards sustaining sobriety. Five of the patients who were wholly dependent on pensions, public assistance, and/or their families were strongly influenced by a change in the attitudes of their spouses; the latter had finally reached the point of action indicating that they would leave their alcoholic mates if they continued to drink. As noted above, one patient who had been attending the clinic for several months without evident change in her drinking pattern initiated sobriety only after her husband resumed excessive drinking. Another patient became abstinent after his wife left him; it was quite clear that the dissolution of the marriage freed him from certain tensions and anxieties with which he could not cope, and for which his excessive use of alcohol had been an evident means of avoidance and sedation. Another patient was frightened into sobriety, preceding his initial visit to the clinic, by the consequences of a burglary which he had committed in an amnesic state associated with intoxication.

In two cases the motivations for sustaining abstinence were unclear. One patient, Mr. F., appeared remarkably evasive in discussing what had influenced him both to initiate and to sustain his eight months of sobriety. However, it was apparent that, whatever the reasons for his abstinence, they could not be plausibly associated with the clinical interactions which were minimal and which, in the explicit opinions both of the patient and of the clinic, did not in any way touch upon him or his problems. Mr. M.'s abstinence began with an antabuse-alcohol reaction: after becoming terribly ill, vomiting, and almost passing out, he continued the antabuse and ceased drinking. What was unclear from the interviews was why he continued the antabuse and stopped the alcohol. The most atypical patient in this group of abstinent patients at Clinic D was Mr. G.S.; there was no question that the support and encouragement of his physician, with the tacit expectation that his anxiety could be better controlled with the doctor's drugs than with an alcoholic beverage, had been significant in sustaining his sobriety and in helping him move, as described above, towards a more satisfying life.

At Clinic G, where assiduously-sought treatment fees screened out the economically marginal and the grossly unmotivated patients, there were twenty-five patients in the abstinent group. Because of the relatively larger number of cases, the review of this clinic is based on generalizations about the abstinent patients, rather than on brief summaries of each case as was the procedure for Clinics C and D.

The great majority of the patients coming to this clinic were unimpaired or minimally impaired in social stability at intake, and continued so at follow-up, and most maintained contact with the clinic throughout the year between intake and follow-up, keeping appointments which generally were spaced about a month apart. Therefore, very few of the patients here were deviant successes, in contrast to Clinic C where all three were, and Clinic D where six of the nine were. At Clinic G, antabuse, treatment by internists, and the encouragement of attendance at AA played a major role in the out-patient treatment that followed the week of in-patient care which typically initiated their treatment experiences.

The quality of information, from the perspective of depth of psychosocial understanding, reflected the approach of this clinic. There were almost no data in the case records to indicate how or in what manner the clinic or their treating physicians specifically aided the patients to give up drinking. None the less, there were data which permitted inference of the factors which seemed to be plausibly related to the change in these patients' drinking. The patients could be grouped as follows:

(1) There were five patients for whom a total involvement in the activities and philosophy of AA played a role in their initiating and sustaining abstinence.

165

(2) There were eight patients who had entered into a changed life situation in which their very strong dependency needs could be much more completely satisfied. These patients had either given up their marriages, and/or moved wife and all back into the bosom of their parental families who then directed and dominated the course of their lives.

(3) There were three patients who had fallen into altered life situations which gave them status. These patients all happened to be women: one had married for the fourth time and conceived at age thirty-six following her three prior barren marriages; one had become a librarian, an occupation which she perceived as lady-like and incongruent with drinking; the third woman had become a companion to an older wealthy woman, a position which in addition to the status implications also was highly satisfying for her dependency needs.

(4) There were nine patients whose prolonged abstinence could be explained neither by the changing circumstances of their lives, by what the clinic had done for them, nor by AA participation, but rather by the fact that these patients became able to accept the reality of the threat which the continuing use of alcohol had posed for them. These were persons whose continued hold onto jobs, wives, children, or health was dramatically threatened by the continuation of their drinking.

What was the clinic role in these patients' sustaining abstinence? One could not infer that the clinic had applied any "leverage" to the patients—in the sense of highly sophisticated management of their psychotherapy, or clarification of their life situations—to influence them to give up using alcohol, although one could see quite clearly that the clinic had often acted as a supportive influence on the patients' own efforts and motivation to give up drinking.

What were these patients like when they were sober? It was evident that their personalities and manners of relating were unchanged, and that among them there was a great variety of immature, inhibited, or frankly pathological types of living, ranging from the exhibitionistic to the asocial, from the family-bound to the effusively gregarious who leeched indiscriminately onto friends and strangers alike. No attempt was made by the clinic to deal with these kinds of problems in interpersonal relationships; or perhaps an attempt was made *not* to deal with these issues, an approach which was not very fashionable in "psychodynamically" oriented circles, but which the data suggested might have been quite efficient in altering the patients' drinking patterns.

Clinics C, D, and G had in common their strong medical orientation; that is, they depended highly on the primary or adjunctive use of drugs, both for the medical and psychiatric crises associated with alcoholism, as well as for the continued out-patient care of the (hopefully) "dried-out" alcoholics. In contrast, in two other clinics, F and A, the social worker played the central role in patient management, because the exploration of the patients' interpersonal relationships, past and present, was theoretically regarded as extremely important in patient care.

At Clinic F, there were fifteen patients who were prolongedly abstinent at follow-up. Of these, only five actually maintained prolonged contact with the clinic and accepted management by a social worker, even though this approach was the one preferred by Clinic F. What were their treatment experiences? How did they appear at follow-up?

Mr. A.H.L. made eighteen visits to the clinic during the year between intake and follow-up, and was still in treatment at the latter time. His sobriety was initiated by the threat that his role in his family's craft business was dissolving because of his dependence on alcohol. (It was a good business, supporting his, his father's and his brother's families.) After he became abstinent, he became a frightened wreck of a man, afraid to talk to his customers, unhappy, and bored with his life. He turned, apparently successfully, to his wife for comfort and reassurance, and went to the clinic for support in his struggles to stay away from alcohol. He did not like or want AA.

Mrs. O.F. paid thirty-four visits to the clinic, the first ten for individual sessions with the social workers, the next twenty-four as a member of a psychotherapy group. She also was still in treatment at the time of follow-up. She had been sober since her first visit. The group became her social life, and gave some structure and support to her in her isolation.

Mrs. N.F. made more than thirty visits to the clinic, where she seemed to benefit from discussion of her problems, ventilation of feelings, and continued reassurance that she was not crazy. Again, treatment was supportive of her dependency, and there was no indication that this need would not continue indefinitely.

The other two patients benefited from their many visits to the clinic in paradoxical fashion. After Mrs. B. had explored her marital problems in the course of about a dozen visits to the social worker, she was transferred with her husband to a psychiatrist for joint family interviews. There they literally learned to scream at the doctor, to insult and berate him, instead of turning their hostility destructively at each other. They thus constructed a *folie à deux*, in the context of which she initiated her abstinence; by follow-up she had sustained it for more than eight months.

Mr. R.C. visited the clinic fourteen times for exploration of his marital and vocational life. During this period, it was brought out with increasing clarity that he was a passive, effeminate man, burying himself in his work in an attempt to cope with deeply felt anxiety and strain. When the need for psychiatric treatment was presented to him in such a way that he could not rationalize it away, he became sober (he had continued to drink throughout the period that he was seeing the social worker), broke off his relationship with the clinic, and was still abstinent at follow-up eight months later—explicitly to avoid psychiatric treatment. For reasons that could only be conjectured, he was terrified by psychiatrists, and it was this fear rather than the insights obtained during his casework treatment or the relationship with the case-worker which structured his abstinence.

At Clinic A, there were thirteen patients who sustained prolonged abstinence. Of these there were only four who had accepted prolonged and/or continuing treatment by a social worker, even though this was the approach preferred by the clinic. Mr. J.E., for example, came to the clinic following hospitalization for a bleeding peptic ulcer with hemorrhage to the point of shock; he had been placed on the hospital's "critical" list. This experience, together with the fact that he was on the verge of losing his job because alcoholism was affecting the quality of his work as a machinist, initiated his abstinence. In the twenty-six visits he paid to the clinic, he relied on the support of the social worker to help him to maintain his sobriety.

168

Mr. G., a skid-row eccentric, also initiated his treatment following a medical complication of alcoholism, specifically coma associated with liver disease. He too became remarkably attached to the social worker whose acceptance of him in his peculiar manner of living seemed to help him to maintain sobriety and to become somewhat more self-supporting than he had been previously.

Mr. H.J. had been sober for eighteen months preceding his intake to the clinic. It became apparent that he was a paranoid schizophrenic with many obsessional defenses. The supportive attitude of the social workers as well as their assistance in placing him in work where some of his obsessive traits could be socially constructive were indeed helpful for him, not only in sustaining sobriety but in suppressing his manifestations of paranoid ideas.

Mr. S.K. had been abstinent for ten years prior to intake. He came to the clinic for supportive psychotherapy unrelated to drinking, except that he still regarded himself, at age forty-two, as an alcoholic. Here too psychotherapy focussed on his emotional problems and seemed to help him to manage his emotional difficulties.

From the cases cited for Clinics F and A, it could be inferred that, even though casework management was regarded as a prime element in their therapeutic plans, only a minority of the patients who became abstinent did in fact participate demonstrably in casework. The other patients who became abstinent at these clinics, like those at the medically oriented clinics, either had very few visits, using the clinics as way-stations to treatments which they themselves regarded as more effective (for instance, Mr. D.D. at Clinic A came to ask for antabuse, but when he found that the clinic did not give it he went to his own doctor who prescribed it for him) or became sober after significant life experiences subsequent to or independent of their brief contacts with the clinics (for example, if there were an actual threat of loss of support or of life because of continuing alcoholism, or a shift in their life circumstances that increased the satisfaction of dependent needs).

The salient clinical impressions derived from a review of these abstinent patients may be summarized as follows:

169

(1) Those patients who became abstinent were usually more improved in their social adaptation (compared to their social adaptation at intake) than were the patients who did not become abstinent. However, their mental health was minimally altered as measured by the quality of the relationships and/or the degrees of freedom from emotional debilitation. In brief, there was behavioral change but minimal psychological change.

(2) In general, the type of treatment which appeared to offer some predictable success was that which attempted to support behavioral change, especially with regard to drinking. Those attempts which certain of the clinics made to support psychological change were both ineffective and poorly acceptable to the patients, with the significant exception of those few patients who still identified themselves as alcoholics even though they had been abstinent for many years.

(3) The role that forces external to treatment played in supporting behavioral change in regard to drinking was great. Some of the most useful treatment was in conjunction with such externalities; that is, treatment was used to facilitate the patient's acceptance of the harmful impact of his drinking on his life circumstances—not to increase his understanding of his drinking but to help him appreciate the necessity for behavioral change regardless of his needs or motivations for drinking. For example, Mr. Y. at Clinic A was able to initiate abstinence after the social worker helped him to recognize the seriousness of his violent behavior when he was drinking. The continuing contact with the social worker, which he utilized for blowing off steam (as he put it) in order to control his hostile feelings, aided him in sustaining his sobriety. Although he was abstinent, and was no longer the serious threat he had been to his wife and family (on one occasion he actually rendered his wife unconscious by beating her over the head with a hammer), he continued to maintain the dependent and peculiar relationship with his psychotic wife and with his parental family, who were overtly exploitative of him.

When forces independent of and external to treatment by the clinics influenced changes in the patients' drinking behavior, two types of changes in their lives were noted. The first consisted of a decrease of the patients' responsibilities, the parents or the siblings taking over the direction and control of the patients' lives. The second involved events or interactions which established meaningfully, both unambiguously and psychologically, that the psychic costs of the patients' continuing to drink would exceed the value of their continuing to drink. This realization did not mean that such factors necessarily led to abstinence; as noted below, there were patients who continued to drink excessively despite the most severe disruption of their marriages, work, or health.

(b) The Controlled Drinkers

Were those patients who were observed to be controlled drinkers at follow-up actually suffering from alcoholism; had they been "problem drinkers" at intake? Review of the thirty-five cases indicated that, with only one exception, they could be unequivocally classified as having had severe drinking problems at intake, as manifested by chronic intoxication, ill health associated with alcoholism, arrest records, and problems at work or within the family clearly related to their use of alcohol.

There was one case whose alcoholism at intake, and through the year preceding intake, might be regarded as questionable. This male patient at Clinic C identified himself at intake as an alcoholic, not because he was currently drinking, but because he feared that in his social isolation he might be unable to continue his controlled drinking which consisted of a nightly drink or two of whiskey taken for sedation and for alleviation of boredom. Because he was very reticent in his communication with the clinic, there was no explicit history of current alcoholism from this patient; however, it was speculated that he might have been an alcoholic in prior years, based on the facts that he was known to have been a successful salesman of distilled beverages in another state, that he was divorced, and that at the time of intake he was working for the Salvation Army, receiving a meager salary and room and board, and living in one of their domiciles. It was the authors' hunch that this man had arrived at his present social condition very probably because of prior alcoholism.

In chapter VI it was observed that there were two factors which differentiated the controlled drinkers from those who became abstinent, and which, though not statistically significant, were of

171

interest: first, the controlled drinkers tended to be younger than those who became abstinent; secondly, the duration of their prior drinking problems tended to be shorter than that of those who became abstinent.

Were these patients properly classified, at follow-up, as controlled drinkers? The data indicated that these patients had no episodes of intoxication for at least the prior six months; that they were not suffering with any kind of ill health customarily associated with alcoholism; that they had not been arrested, and that there had not been any disturbances in their employment and other social relationships which might be related to the excessive use of alcohol. Furthermore, the data were supported by observations of the total context of the patients' lives, by collateral sources of data, and/or by clinical appraisals and intuition.

The term "controlled drinking" at follow-up did not refer to a single pattern of drinking. Indeed there was a wide range of drinking behavior, from those who drank daily but in relatively small quantities (that is, up to two or three bottles of beer a day), to those at the other extreme who drank rarely, less than weekly and only at social gatherings. In a sense paralleling those of Davies,[37] these findings showed that there were individuals who could shift, at least for a period of six months to a year, to the occasional or regular use of alcohol without directly resuming the grossly maladaptive use of alcohol which had characterized their drinking behavior prior to their visits to the alcoholism clinics. There was therefore no evidence for the hypothesis that the person who is a problem drinker—the alcoholic—can never reach a *modus vivendi* in which he takes one drink, or several drinks, without going on to binges, to intoxication, and so forth.

How did these shifts in drinking behavior come about? From a negative viewpoint, they did not result from the acquisition of broader self-understanding and thus from a secondary diminution of tension and anxiety which left patients free to use alcohol without the danger of regression into "pharmacothymia." Nor did these changes come about through the establishment of relationships with the therapists, in the sense that the reality testing and supportive constraints available through the relationships might act as breaks on otherwise uncontrolled drinking. Nor were the

172

shifts caused by prolonged contacts with the clinics, for as pointed out in chapter VI (see Table 53), those patients who became controlled drinkers made even fewer visits than did those who became abstinent. Of the latter roughly two-thirds had more than brief contact with the clinics, compared to only about half of the controlled drinkers. More striking, however, was the fact that of those patients who came more than four times to the clinics, the controlled drinkers tended towards moderate rather than prolonged attendance, while the abstinent group preponderantly had prolonged rather than moderate contacts. Finally, the changes in drinking behavior did not result from increased physical good health or well-being.

To determine the positive factors involved in these shifts, the authors used the same procedure as they did in the attempt to understand the factors involved in abstinence; that is, all the protocols of patients in the controlled drinking group were carefully reviewed in a search for probable determinants. The following were identified: (1) decreasing physical health; (2) major shifts in life situations; (3) satisfaction of intense dependency needs; (4) capacity for self-control or constraint based on shifts in cognitive awareness about self and alcohol; and (5) multiple influences. Vignettes from case studies illustrate how these factors seemingly influenced the patients' drinking.

Mr. H.J.A., a patient at Clinic C, was fifty-seven years old at the time of intake. He visited the clinic only two times, and was intoxicated on both occasions. Probably because of his chronic tuberculosis, probably because of ill health associated with his episodes of recent intoxication, this patient was then hospitalized for two months. After leaving the hospital against medical advice, he became sober for two months. During the eight months remaining to follow-up, he drank daily, not more than six *glasses* of beer a day, and no distilled beverages. His social adjustment was unchanged: he was still a divorced man who occasionally visited his married daughter; he continued to be unemployed, living on a pension from the Veterans Administration; he had no social interactions apart from maintaining contact with his daughter. He continued to deny that he ever was an alcoholic, despite abundant data indicating that for ten years or more his health, his reputation, his social adjustment, his arrest record were clearly worsened by excessive imbibing. His changed drinking pattern was based on the fact that his stomach no longer could tolerate whiskey; he responded to whiskey by becoming nauseated and weak, and experiencing abdominal pain. That his present drinking pattern was vastly different from that described at intake was learned through the patient's own report, through observations of him, and through corroborative information supplied by his daughter.

Mr. X.Y., a man in his early sixties and a patient at Clinic E, presented a similar picture. Following only two visits to the clinic he was hospitalized because of emphysema and cardiovascular disease. He continued to be socially isolated and unemployed, and an almost daily drinker of beer (one or two glasses); even with the mild intoxication of beer he became dizzy, but when he tried to drink whiskey one drink made him "light-headed," poorly co-ordinated, and weak.

Mrs. F.H., a patient at Clinic E, exemplified changed drinking behavior that was based on a major shift in life situation. A forty-seven-year-old housewife, she began to increase her use of alcohol about four years prior to her first visit to the clinic, drinking regularly at night to help her fall asleep. About one year preceding intake, she began to drink regularly in the daytime, beginning in the morning, neglecting her housework, and becoming isolated. This change occurred in the context of an emotional disorder related to three factors: her menopause and associated nervousness, depression, and hot flashes; her daughter's rebellious association with delinquent young men and disassociation from the patient; and her husband's continuing financial failure and improvidence. Mrs. F.H. visited the clinic nine times in two consecutive months, using the contact to ventilate hostility against her husband and her daughter. She dropped out of treatment despite the fact that there was no resolution of any of her sexual, interpersonal, or economic problems. She then moved to another city about a hundred miles distant where, without benefit of casework, she went through the experience of her daughter's out-of-wedlock pregnancy, delivery, and giving up of the child for adoption. However, she and her husband arrived at some greater mutual understanding, and roughly two months after her last clinic visit (about eight months prior to follow-up) she returned to her drinking pattern of many years before, that is, an occasional drink or two before dinner and sometimes later at parties. The return to social drinking evidently was associated with the restoration of her sense of importance to her husband, the acceptance of cessation of menstruation, and the resolution of her relationship problems with her daughter—the complete giving up of responsibility for her daughter's life and welfare.

Illustrating a shift in drinking pattern that was based on the satisfaction of dependency needs was Mr. C.E.J., a patient at Clinic F. According to both the patient and the family's report to the clinic, he had never taken any alcohol at all until three years prior to his first visit to the clinic, at which (earlier) time he had attempted suicide as a reaction to being divorced by his first wife. In these years, his drinking was unquestionably excessive: there were many binges; he was aggressive when he drank; he had many arrests for public intoxication; he had been placed in several state hospitals with *delirium tremens*; and he had been treated by many private physicians for alcoholism. When he came to the clinic, for a total of three visits spread out over two months, he was brought there by his father and by a probation officer who had begun to take an interest in the patient following his recent arrest for a burglary committed while drunk. He was clearly unmotivated for treatment. His main complaint and rationalization for his alcoholism in these three visits had to do with the fact that he suffered from the lack of a family atmosphere.

Beginning in the month of Mr. C.E.J.'s visits to the clinic, his father, for whom he had worked in desultory fashion, began to succeed in his trucking business and required the patient's services regularly and for long hours. A few months later the patient had a "total paralysis" of both legs, probably hysterical and successfully treated by "painful injections in the back." Also in this month, he met and married a young widow who was noted to be quite a "bossy" person, yet accepting of the patient's extreme demands for companionship; for example, in her seventh month of pregnancy, she got up, apparently willingly at 5:30 A.M., to go fishing with the patient prior to his day's work. She was his entire social life. With her he drank beer at meals, and occasionally a few beers at night while watching television. Therefore, because of his father's increased need for him and because of his wife's dominance and concomitant emotional support, the patient was able, after the month of intake, to shift from a clearly excessive use of alcohol to the controlled drinking described above. Parenthetically, the probation officer continued to see him on a regular basis. However, it would seem that, just as a shift in his life circumstances satisfying his dependency needs was vastly supportive of his controlled drinking, the loss of his wife, his job, or the explicitly controlling role of his probation officer might precipitate another binge. In any case, for almost a year he had been able to sustain controlled drinking.

Mr. E.G., a patient at Clinic D, was a forty-eight-year-old Negro, married and usually regularly employed. Because of a depression, which was precipitated by the loss of a job he had held for many years, he began to drink excessively less than one year prior to intake. He drank in three-day cycles: the first day, he drank whiskey to the point of intoxication; the next day, badly hungover, he could not work or seek work; the third day, he recuperated; and the fourth day, he again initiated the cycle, beginning to drink alone in order "to forget" his problems. He came to treatment after he had been admitted (via the police) to the psychiatric in-patient pavilion in a state of acute intoxication with hallucinations. Because he had been neglecting his diet throughout the previous nine or ten months, he was physically run down. The arrest and hospitalization made quite an impact on him, and he recognized that drinking was not solving his problems, even though he felt better when he was drunk. Consequently, after his first visit to the clinic, which occurred the day of his discharge from the in-patient pavilion, he drank, according to himself and to his wife, only a few beers each week. His drinking was part of his meager social life with his friends in the neighboring saloon. He no longer drank any distilled beverages.

Why had Mr. E.G. shifted from his deviant use of alcohol to social drinking, to the drinking pattern which he had maintained for at least the fifteen prior years? He was noted to be a simple man who had little education, was rather schizoid in his personal

176

relationships, and tried to maintain himself and his family with minimal trouble or fuss. It seemed that his recognition of the fact that drinking whiskey would get him into further trouble sufficed to stimulate the acceptance of a different attitude towards the use of alcoholic beverages. It was not until three or four months subsequent to his controlled drinking that this patient was able to find work again; for the next six months to follow-up, he was regularly employed. Therefore, the change in his drinking behavior occurred *prior* to the shift in his life's circumstances.

Most of the patients who shifted from uncontrolled to controlled drinking did so in the context of multiple determining factors; that is, they had the benefit of shifts in their life situations, increased satisfaction of their dependency needs, and/or increased physical ill health associated with alcoholism—all or any combination of which supported their quite conscious resolutions to continue drinking but in a different manner.

The characteristic psychological defense which the controlled drinkers used to maintain themselves was denial; they relied heavily on their capacity to utilize "will power." Characteristically, they were without insight into the motivations of the current or prior drinking, except in the crude sense that they might have recognized some reactive elements to their problems (that is, there might have been precipitating events or circumstances to which they could refer and rationalize their drinking problems), or that they might have tried to find some excuse for their previous drinking patterns. They were not at all introspective, not concerned with the subtler motivations which led them to turn to alcohol for the resolution of emotional problems (if they accepted that they ever had any).

What was the quality of their adjustments as controlled drinkers? Like the patients who had become abstinent, many controlled drinkers showed improvement in certain of the outer circumstances of their lives. From society's perspective, they were causing less trouble for themselves and for the people around them. However, the quality of their personal relationships and their psychosocial integration was still characterized as immature, deviant, or troubled, and there were no significant changes in their values. Thus, as with the abstinent patients, there was certain

177

evidence of behavioral changes, but no indication of psychological or emotional changes.

How did controlled drinkers participate in treatment? As noted above, their participation in treatment was even more meager than that of those patients who became abstinent. With regard to the quality of their relationships with the clinics, for the most part these patients tended to denigrate their contacts with the clinics, seeing them, in accord with their utilization of denial, as meaningless or possibly harmful experiences for them. There were two cases who were able to use continuing contacts with the clinics for emotional support, and three patients who, in addition to the controlled drinking which they utilized to alleviate or to minimize tensions or anxieties, took a variety of tranquilizers prescribed for them by the clinics, or by their own physicians.

(c) The Unmodified or Deteriorated Drinkers

When it was reported earlier (chapter vi) that only a relatively small proportion of the patients (about 18 per cent) improved with respect to their drinking, these patients were contrasted in a number of ways with those patients who continued to drink excessively and who were institutionalized in consequence of their drinking problems. It is not the intention here merely to re-emphasize the factors discerned in the statistical analysis, but rather to review the case material of that sample of unmodified or deteriorated problem drinkers who were comparable to the improved patients with respect to age, sex, race, social status at intake, and so forth, and to focus on two related questions: why did these patients not continue their contacts with the clinics? and why were they not motivated to stop drinking?

The first fact which emerged was that many of the unimproved patients would not permit the follow-up interviewer to find out what they thought or felt about their continuing drinking. Although they would readily indicate that they were doing badly with respect to their drinking, their health, their social relationships, they were angry and resentful at being perceived as deviant or maladjusted, and were defensive about their drinking problems; they were not "happy" drinkers. They did not need to deny or specially minimize their drinking problems, but they charac-

178

teristically tried to deal with them psychologically through deny-
ing or minimizing their significance. However, enough of these
patients gave data or presented explicit thoughts and feelings
about their continued drinking, so that reasonable inferences
could be drawn.

Mr. M.A., for example, when visited by a physician from
Clinic H following an episode of hematemesis, resentfully
promised to make an appointment at the clinic. He did not do so.
His wife, however, did call several times, tearfully indicating her
distress, her dependence on her husband who was ten to fifteen
years older than she, and her inability to influence him in any way.
The patient thus continued to deny the existence of his drinking
problem as well as his need for treatment. When his life situation
was examined in greater detail, it became possible to formulate
some reasonable hypotheses about why he continued to drink.

Mr. M.A. married his third wife only two years before his first
visit to the clinic. They had a child who was a year old at intake
and whose subsequent growth and development seemed to
parallel an increase in his father's drinking. It was speculated that
Mr. M.A. had regressed—turned more to oral satisfaction—in
response to his wife's increasing interest in their child, and in
response to her inability to clarify her own position with respect
to his drinking or to seek alternatives for herself from the rhythm
of his binges, hangovers, social isolation, and periods of recovery.
He experienced her as rejecting him through her weakness. It was
as if he could not sustain himself without her sturdily setting
limits for him. However, his wife suffered from diabetes, was
emotionally labile, timid, and dependent on her husband, and was
no source of strength, direction, or support for him whatsoever.
Concerning Mr. M.A.'s mother (and stepfather) at whose home
he lived with his wife and son, the data suggested that she was
neutral, indifferent, or satisfied with him and his alcoholism,
because he continued to go to work even though he neglected or
mistreated his wife.

There was therefore a striking absence of forces inhibiting his
drinking, or encouraging him to modify his behavior or attitudes
towards his drinking. There was interest on the part of his wife,
unaccompanied by strength, but there was no such interest on

179

the part of his mother who clearly was the central figure in this household. It was speculated that this continued drinking might have been his solution to the problem posed by his wife's desire to establish a home independently of her in-laws (that she wished to do so was manifest) and by his own willingness to benefit from a generous rental agreement which his mother probably offered to keep him in the household.

There were other patients like Mr. M.A., who lived in a social milieu characterized by the passivity and/or the subtle support for continued drinking provided by adult figures around them. However, unlike Mr. M.A.'s situation which was evaluated largely by *inferences* drawn from certain factual data, the situations of most of these other patients were quite explicit in the follow-up material; that is, the patients, spouses, and other family members described their acceptance of the patients' drinking problems with emphasis on the fact that occupational adjustment had not been jeopardized by drinking. In a number of cases, there were even notable improvements in occupational adjustment despite continuation or even increase in drinking. However, the important fact was that the spouses and other family members did not object to the patients' isolated evening drinking or weekend binges, and were not concerned that the drinking might indeed become worse, that health might become jeopardized, that social relations were impoverished.

In some instances, this passive acceptance of the patient's drinking was immersed in the culture of poverty—in lower-lower class family living. Mr. D.K.K., for example, was an unemployed automobile mechanic at intake and had been separated for six months from his wife and nine children (four of whom were with his wife, and five placed temporarily in foster homes). He drank throughout the day, drinking whatever he could get, and in the weeks prior to intake restricting himself to wine because of its low cost. He came to the clinic because of paresthesia and chills which he imputed to his excessive drinking and deficient diet. He was hospitalized through the agency of the clinic because of these complaints, treated successfully for them, and discharged to the community after a three-week hospitalization. Thereafter, he returned to drinking. Several months later, a charitably disposed former employer allowed him to live in a shack behind his garage in return for the patient's services as night watchman. Still drinking, Mr. D.K.K. was given the opportunity to do chores around the garage and ultimately filled in for an employee who left. At the time of follow-up he was earning $65 a week (early 1961) and was back with his wife and nine children whom he could support adequately in terms of what they regarded as an acceptable style of living. His wife was delighted with this improvement in their situation. However, he drank throughout the day both at the job and afterwards; he worked six days a week for long hours, and the seventh day he spent drinking with casual acquaintances.

A second framework for continued drinking differed in the direction of forces. Whereas the emphasis above was on *passive acceptance* of continuation, in other instances it was observed that some patients continued to drink as a result of the *active encouragement* of their milieu. Usually this support was provided by an alcoholic spouse but in some instances by friends or relatives, who encouraged the patient to deny the significance of his or her stress, to evaluate symptoms as prowess, or to strive for a type of "controlled" drinking in which constant sedation by alcohol was maintained without slipping over the line to become physically unco-ordinated, aggressive, or comatose. However, despite the patient's intention, he was not able to adhere to this role, and did exhibit behavioral difficulties clearly associated with drinking. Mrs. J.F., for example, a thirty-seven-year-old white married woman (in her third marriage) drank throughout the year between intake and follow-up; drank while taking thorazine from the clinic's physician to help her sober up; drank before, between, and after her three stays at the correlated in-patients facilities of this state's program; drank with her husband and her father-in-law, until she separated from her husband roughly one month prior to the follow-up. At this time she did not stop drinking, instead she moved in with an elderly gentleman who served her drinks throughout the day in accord with his personal theories about the treatment of alcoholism. Her brief period of employment during the year was as a barmaid.

The third context in which continued excessive drinking

181

occurred was escapist; that is, because of drinking the patient had lost his job, his family, his savings, and his home, and, without any interest in exploring his own participation in his by now precarious life, he turned with greater intensity to the relief from distress (depression, resentment superimposed on a wounded narcissism) which he obtained from drinking, and to the company of those similarly occupied.

The fourth, and least common context among the group of patients studied by these clinics, could be characterized as an attempt to achieve diminution of tension associated with neurotic problems. Mr. G.B., for example, was a twenty-nine-year-old Negro high-school graduate, a highly skilled sheet metal mechanic, a married man, and the father of one child. At intake he had had a drinking problem for only one-and-a-half years, although he had been drinking since age eighteen. When, in the course of an examination for life insurance, it was discovered that he had cirrhosis of the liver, he had himself admitted to the in-patients facility for a week's drying out. Here he sought antabuse as a source of self-control. He did not want to be an alcoholic, and made many visits to the clinic in the year between intake and follow-up. Through this year, his drinking oscillated between antabuse-supported abstinence and prolonged periods of excessive drinking with binges, blackouts, and so forth.

The external facts of race, education, occupation, and marital situation were of particular interest in Mr. G.B.'s case because they pointed to the problem areas with which he struggled. He belonged to the Negro middle class of his community, having been born in a New England town where he was one of the two Negroes in his high-school class. He struggled to be good, controlled, and ambitious at the behest of his religious, hard-working, exacting mother to whose training he related his own tense attempts to do things perfectly. He was fearfully preoccupied with violence; for example, when his sister was "almost raped," instead of beating up the man Mr. G.B. went on a binge because he feared he would lose control and kill the offender.

He began drinking while in the air force, although in the six years that he was thus employed he had no disciplinary problems and worked his way up to staff sergeant. In the racially segregated town in which he lived, housing for Negroes was scarce. When he and his wife were forced to leave their comfortable apartment because of the needs of the landlord, he became desperate, and again the struggle to control his anger precipitated a binge. Parenthetically, the case illustrated the role of antabuse in supporting the conscious decision to give up drinking. When the course of Mr. G.B.'s life brought him into situations which stimulated anger and resentment, he forgot to take his antabuse. By the time his tension had grown to the point where he could not cope any longer, his antabuse level was sufficiently low to permit him to drink without an alcohol-antabuse reaction. Another aspect of his drinking was important. Drinking for him symbolized freedom. When he drank he associated with jazz circles where drinking was the rule. When he was sober he was the "good Negro," church-going, diligent in his work, and rather sad. He needed psychotherapy, and probably would have benefited further from deeper exploration of his defences, underlying conflicts, and conflicting identifications. His work, however, required frequently changing schedules. Although his employer regarded him as a good worker and was willing to let him take time off from work at his own (the patient's) expense so that he could go for treatment at regularly committed hours, this practice created hardship for his wife and child because his income was only marginally adequate for their needs.

It is important to emphasize the rareness of this case. Mr. G.B. was verbal, intelligent, and motivated to attain abstinence, and his drinking was clearly associated with intrapsychic conflict. As is discussed in the final chapter of this book, the management of such cases should not be taken as typical of the patients usually encountered in the out-patient clinics of the state programs, even though they unfortunately tend to become the model into which the clinics would like to fit all of their cases.

The salient clinical impressions derived from the above review of patients who continued with their drinking problems may be summarized as follows:

(1) There was usually a striking absence of forces directing the patient towards attaining or initiating sobriety. In some of the cases, there was a passive acceptance of the continued drinking problem; in others there was an actual environmental support of the patient's denial of alcoholism and continuation of a life in which the taking of alcoholic beverages was the central fact.

(2) The use of alcohol for sedation, as well as the social life of the saloon continued to be extremely attractive to these patients. They did not want to give up drinking. Their drinking might indeed have been a problem for the community, for their families, or for their fellow employees, but for these patients the balance between the adaptive and the disruptive elements in their continuing drinking was still heavily weighted in favor of the adaptive. In the great majority of such cases, the depression-alleviating and the humiliation-soothing functions of alcohol were the predominant features. In a very few cases, the use of alcohol was an important feature in the resolution of neurotic conflicts.

VIII. Summary and Discussion

THE SPECIFIC aims of the study reported in this book were: first, to develop a body of research instruments which could be used in follow-up studies of patients who had drinking problems and who were treated in the major out-patient and associated in-patient facilities of state-supported alcoholism programs; secondly, to utilize these instruments in a follow-up study of a diversified population of alcoholics who were treated in a variety of settings and with different emphases and methods of treatment. In this final chapter, the major findings of the study are summarized briefly; later, the authors present the inferences and implications which were evolved in the course of the research and the data analysis, and which seemed pertinent to the clinical management of certain aspects of alcoholism. Even though the reader may not accept the conclusions drawn by the authors, it is hoped that the body of data, the tabulations, and the statistical comparisons presented in earlier chapters will serve as a dependable source of scientific discussion and clarification for all concerned with the problem of alcoholism, and that the data will be employed in future research and practice.

1. THE MAJOR FINDINGS

(a) The Sample

Although the methodological details of this study will not be reviewed here, none the less it is necessary to remind the reader that the sampling of the alcoholic population which was explicit in the study design imposed certain limitations on the general applicability of the findings. The data referred to a special group of patients, those who were well enough to come to state-supported alcoholism services; for example, the sample contained

185

extremely few patients with the more extreme medical, neurologic, and psychiatric complications associated with alcoholism,
such patients being found more frequently in institutions for the
chronically ill, or in other medical speciality clinics. Furthermore,
only a small group of clinics within the state-supported alcoholism
programs of the United States collaborated in this research; the
reader is referred to chapter II of this book for a discussion of
these clinics' special characteristics. But more germane to the
question of the breadth of validity is the fact that an undefined
proportion of patients with drinking problems may go to private
clinics, to individual medical practitioners, to social agencies,
or to psychiatric clinics, in all of which the drinking problems are
handled within a framework of treatment that encompasses
patients with a variety of emotional disorders and problems of
living. In these different settings, different emphases and methods
of treatment, or even the same methods, may have remarkably
different consequences. Hence, each of the summarizing statements reported below should be understood as explicitly pertinent
to the special conditions of this study. The reader will have to
decide from his own experience whether or not they can apply
to other arenas of experience and interaction with patients with
drinking problems. To what extent the sampling limitations affect
the findings can be specifically elucidated only by study focussed
on this issue.

(b) The Patients at Intake

There were considerable individual differences among the
patients at intake, in respect both to the duration of their drinking problems and to the extent to which they were dependent—
at that time—on alcohol. Most of the patients felt that they had
had difficulties which were associated with the excessive use of
alcohol for more than five years, and only a very few, less than
3 per cent, believed that they had used alcohol to excess for less
than a year. Their physical health, typically, was not impaired
except for transitory (usually associated with episodes of intoxication or with binges) disturbances of sleep and appetite. Their
drinking was most often solitary (true of 37 per cent of the

patients) or with casual companions (34 per cent), rather than in social, religious, or dietary contexts which might encourage "normal drinking." Although the patients seldom frankly denied that they had problems with drinking, they did not accept the idea that they must stay away from alcoholic beverages. A few boldly denied their inability to control their intake of alcohol, or stated that they did not whether or not they could do so, because they had achieved relief of mental or bodily distress through drinking.

There were marked differences in the outer aspects of the patients' social adjustment (marital, educational and employment status, residential stability); thus, the clinics served every extreme of society, from the successful member of the business or professional community to the derelict on skid-row. In contrast to these marked differences in social stability, the patients regularly were observed to have serious difficulties in their personal relationships and in their occupational functioning. The incidence of divorce, for example, was about twice as high as that of the general population, and those who were living with their spouses were often having serious marital problems at the time of their initial visits to the clinics. Their social activities and participation were meager: only one-third had a social life with friends or family, or with Alcoholics Anonymous, and only one-seventh participated in social activities with both family and friends. With respect to their work, less than half of the patient population was employed at intake, and even these patients often had serious difficulties at work associated with their drinking.

(c) Participation in Treatment

Consistent with the general experience of all the professions concerned with the alcoholism problem, the patients surveyed in this study usually did not sustain a prolonged relationship with the clinics that were treating them. Only about one-fifth of the patients attended the clinic for ten or more visits, or continued to keep appointments as long as six months after their initial visits. By examining the interrelationships between variables describing the patient's status at intake, the treatment provided for him, and the extent of his contact with the clinic, the authors discerned certain factors enhancing the patient's continuing contact with the clinic.

In the initial evaluation of the patient, that is, in the first few visits to the clinic, a diagnostic evaluation by a physician (internist or psychiatrist) did not guarantee the patient's continuing association with the clinic, but the absence of such evaluation strongly enhanced the likelihood that he would break contact. Also, it was extremely important that the patient be given some medication directly related to his suffering with alcoholism, but it was striking that the patient's attendance at the clinic was not influenced by any one drug more than any other, or by several types of drugs in combination rather than only one; examination of the data consistently showed significant differences in the extent of contact with the clinics only between patients receiving some drugs and those receiving no drugs. The involvement of collaterals (spouses or other relatives) in the evaluation of the patient enhanced his continuing attendance at the clinic, as did assignment of the patient to a group for continuing discussion of his or his fellows' drinking and other problems.

Of the many ways of describing the patient's social status and functioning, the authors' index of social stability (based on marital, employment, and residential status) was most highly associated with the extent of the patient's contact with the clinic. Specifically, the less impaired the patient was in social stability, the greater the extent or duration of his contact with the clinic. Finally, there was an interesting indication that the patient's social stability influenced the treatment offered to him. It was noted that the probability of a patient's being seen by a physician, assigned to group therapy, and, even to a lesser degree, offered drugs was diminished in accord with the degree of his impairment in social stability.

(d) The Patients at Follow-Up

Many of the patients were noted to have changed significantly from their status at intake. A very few had died in the interval between intake and follow-up. In the month preceding the follow-up, some of the patients were in institutions; only about a third were known to have continued to be problem drinkers in the community; and about another third were abstinent or controlled drinkers. The status of about a fourth of the patients was unknown, because they could not be traced, or, in a small minority of cases, because they refused to co-operate with the follow-up procedure. The inability to obtain a follow-up study of a patient was associated with two factors: first, the degree of impairment in his social functioning at intake—the greater the patient's impairment in social stability, interpersonal relationships, or work adjustment at intake, the greater the probability that he would not be studied at follow-up; second, the extent of contact with the clinic—the fewer his visits to the clinic, the less likely that he would be included among the patients studied at follow-up.

Reviewing the patient's drinking status, the authors noted that a small, though far from insignificant proportion (about 18 per cent) of the patients had become abstinent, or were controlled drinkers, for at least the six months prior to and including the period of the follow-up study.

With regard to the patient's functioning in the areas of health, social stability, interpersonal relationships, and work, there was a considerable proportion of patients who had changed since intake, many for the better, many for the worse. What was most striking was that improvement in these areas of living was highly associated with improvement in drinking status. For example, for the patients who became abstinent or controlled drinkers, 55 per cent improved in their interpersonal relationships as measured by the authors' index, while only 6 per cent became worse. Of the patients who had shown no improvement in their drinking in the interval between intake and follow-up, 15 per cent improved with respect to their interpersonal relations, but 16 per cent deteriorated. The "gain" of improvement over deterioration was 49 per cent for the patients whose drinking improved, but minus one per cent for those whose drinking problems were unmodified or worse.

(e) Predictors of Improvement

Four factors were major predictors of improvement in drinking and, secondarily, of the patient's improvement in the other aspects

189

of his living. These were the extent of the patient's contact with the clinic, treatment by an internist, the use of the drug antabuse, and the patient's social stability at intake. However, some factors which were associated with the extent of the patient's contact with the clinic did not in themselves affect outcome. For example, group therapy enhanced the likelihood that the patient would continue attending the clinic, but when patients were matched for extent of contact there were no differences in outcome between patients seen individually and those seen in a group. Although the patient's attendance at the clinic was enhanced by his having received some drug or medication from the clinic, only the use of antabuse was correlated with improvement in drinking. For all the other drugs, there were no differences in outcome between those who did and those who did not receive them. Paradoxically, those patients who did not improve in drinking had received tranquilizers more often than those who did.

Two of the factors, extent of contact with the clinic and the patient's social stability at intake, were noted to be significantly correlated. When these factors were controlled, it was feasible to evaluate their separate influence on outcome. Here an interesting finding emerged. For those patients who were not impaired in social stability at intake, there was a progressive increase in the proportion of improved patients as contact with the clinics increased. For those patients who were impaired in social stability at intake, there were no differences in outcome with increasing contact with the clinics. The authors regard this finding as rich with implication, and return later in the chapter to a discussion of it.

(f) Case Analyses

Subsequent to the study of the interrelationships among the statistical categories descriptive of the patients at intake, in treatment, and at follow-up, the case records of three groups of patients were read to formulate further explanatory hypotheses and to gain some broader perspectives on the complexities of alcoholism and its treatment. These three groups were the patients who had sustained abstinence for at least the six months prior to follow-up, the patients who had been controlled drinkers in this period, and the patients who showed no prolonged modification—or deterioration—in their drinking problems in the year between intake and follow-up.

First of all, it was noted that very few of the patients who improved with respect to their drinking problems could be regarded as changed in their mental health. They did not manifest an enhanced capacity for self-realization or an increased utilization of genital modes (in the psychoanalytic sense) of satisfaction or object-relationships; nor had they acquired increased tolerance for their own limitations and for the vicissitudes of living. To the contrary, the majority of the patients who improved with respect to their drinking problems, continued to suffer with such indications of maladaptation or mental illness as seclusiveness, extreme dependency, eccentricities of character, unmodified involvements in pathologic marital relationships, anxiety, and depression. Thus, the very real changes in the patients' social adjustment and functioning which were associated with abstinence or controlled drinking were not corollary with or consequent upon inner or psychological change.

Secondly, the patients' and the clinics' reconstructions of the forces which helped initiate or sustain abstinence or controlled drinking characteristically emphasized the important role of changed life circumstances or of external interventions in the changed drinking behavior. Modifications in self-awareness or enhanced self-esteem acquired through relationships with the clinics or with a particular therapist were rarely, rather than regularly, cited as factors in the patient's changed drinking behavior. Some of the more frequently cited altered life circumstances and interventions were described as follows: (a) increased ill-health, usually but not necessarily connected with alcoholism; (b) increased satisfaction of dependency needs through a changed environment; and (c) increasing intolerance by family and community to the patient's excessive drinking, so that the patient faced the prospect of loss of sources of satisfaction and security were he to continue drinking. This latter factor operated most strongly in the converse, that is, when the patient's personal environment was tolerant of his drinking, or supportive of it, he continued to drink despite social or medical complications which brought him into treatment.

Thirdly, looking at the patients' interactions with the clinics, the authors noted that the types of treatment which were best utilized by the patients were those which attempted to support the patient's efforts and his environment's interest in the diminution of his drinking; the less the clinic became involved in the intricacies of the determinants of the patients' symptoms, relationships, or defenses, the more likely was the clinic to succeed in supporting change in drinking behavior. Although there were exceptions to this generalization, they were few. This point is discussed again later in this chapter.

Fourthly, data pertinent to the concept of "controlled drinking" were reviewed on a case basis. It was noted that patients with an unquestionable history of alcoholism did become controlled drinkers. Such controlled drinking varied from occasional drinking of beer or distilled beverages at social gatherings to the daily use of small quantities of alcohol without evidence of "loss of control."

2. DISCUSSION: INFERENCES AND IMPLICATIONS

Why did only about half the patients maintain more than a perfunctory contact with the clinics? Why were the patients so loath to regard themselves as in need of help? Why was it so difficult to modify the drinking behavior of most of the patients? Perhaps these questions could be phrased with equal, or even greater precision, in the converse. Why did so many of the patients maintain more than a perfunctory contact with the clinics? Why were there any patients who regarded themselves as in need of help? Although there is no unitary or inclusive theory of the etiology and psychodynamics of alcoholism, at least the psychiatric literature has consistently emphasized the concept that patients who use alcoholic beverages to excess do so in order to satisfy many conscious and unconscious psychologic needs through the pharmacologic, symbolic, and communicative (interpersonal) effects of the use of these substances. Reviewing the formulations of a number of psychiatric clinicians, Zwerling[7] discerned a common framework in all their theories: that the use of alcohol, for the problem drinker, ". . . relieves the sense of aloneness, places an instantaneously available source of pleasure at his disposal, permits the mastery and simultaneously the expression of unmanageable hostile feelings, and has a virtually built-in and guaranteed array of sufferings and punishments which serve both to appease the conscience mechanism and to feed back stress stimuli for continuing the cyclic addictive process" (p. 546). In brief, there is nothing desirable, from the alcoholic's inner viewpoint, to merit abandoning his crutch, his cross, and his delight.

It is essential to recognize that the concept "alcoholism is a disease" may correspond to the authors' and their colleagues' evaluative perception of alcoholism, but not necessarily to the patient's. One may note that alcoholic beverages play an extremely important role in the patients's life, that they are, in fact, causing distress to his "smooth social and economic functioning," and potentially to his health and longevity. However, the patient does not regard himself as diseased or distressed until the balance between the adaptive versus the disruptive elements in his drinking is perceived by him to have shifted towards the disruptive.

It is for this reason, the authors believe, that patients whose drinking exists against a background of social stability, are more likely than the socially unstable patients to accept themselves as candidates for treatment of their alcoholism. Their social and economic functioning is still "smooth" enough to perceive the jars and shocks which a binge or an episode of intoxication, or prolonged social withdrawal into excessive drinking, brings into the course of their lives; that is, the potential of loss, or the threat of loss, of the constraints and supports of marriage, a job, and a home is still relevant psychologically.

The importance of this threat of loss was clearly emphasized by Pfeffer et al.,[43] who noted that the threat of job loss—and with it the loss of retirement and medical benefits—contributed significantly to the treatment of alcoholics employed in industry. Of 180 patients referred (because their drinking was interfering with their work performance) for treatment to the Consultation Center for Alcoholism, only 13 per cent refused treatment. Similarly, 82 per cent were entered into a program of treatment following preliminary psychiatric and medical interviews and examinations, and 76 per cent of all patients referred were able to remain on their jobs because of abstinence from alcohol or markedly increased control. In short, where external factors unequivocally demanded rectification of the patient's drinking behavior, the patient's motivation for change was evident. When such unequivocal demands were withdrawn, the patient's "motivation" for treatment could become negligible. Thus, of twenty patients who were discharged by their companies after Pfeffer's group had made the initial evaluations for treatment, none was willing to return for treatment despite the already established relationship with the clinicians, and despite serious attempts to encourage them to return. The explicit value of the clinic program for them was to protect their investment in the position with the firm; with this loss, the "need" for treatment dissipated.

To recapitulate, for the patient who has found alcoholic beverages to be an extremely valuable and important element in his adaptive (conscious and unconscious) processes, the typical inner motivation for treatment is negligible. In the present authors' opinion, this negligible motivation should be regarded as an essential element in the clinical problem—not as an independent variable reflecting bad judgment, bad character, or "untreatability." Operationally, the clinic should address itself directly to tipping the balance of forces in the patient's drinking problem so that his perception of alcoholic beverages becomes more invested with threat of loss than with satisfaction. The above observations are consistent with those of other authors, who stress the importance of threat as a factor initiating marked changes in an alcoholic's drinking problem.

It must be emphasized that there is a great difference between threatening the patient and helping him to invest his perception of alcoholic beverages more with threat than with pleasure. In fact, a number of treatment approaches are implicitly based on this reasoning. Conditioned-aversion treatment attempts to imbue the drinking experience with threat, specifically of intense gastric distress, by developing a "conditioned reflex" between inbibing a drink and the emetic effect of apomorphine or emetine. Antabuse treatment explicitly threatens the drinker with punishment should he drink alcoholic beverages, specifically with a widespread sympathetic nervous system disturbance beginning with flushing, tachycardia, and perspiration, and extending to vasomotor collapse, convulsions, or even death. Both of these psychopharmacologic methods* require some motivation towards abstinence on the part of the patient.

The most demonstrably successful techniques employed by the clinics could best be characterized in the authors' opinion as controlling or as supporting. The patient's acceptance of the drug antabuse was a dramatic instance of his willingness to be "controlled." The usefulness of any or all of the drugs prescribed by the clinics was, in general, to facilitate maintenance of contact with the clinics; giving the patient a drug served as a concrete indication of the clinic's supportive and "giving" attitudes. From reviewing the case records, from informal interactions with the clinic staffs in discussing those patients whose drinking behavior had been curtailed or minimized, the authors believe that the kind of verbal or personal interactions which were most useful for the patients also could be characterized as "controlling and supporting."

Those communications which stressed the reality of the patient's difficult life situation and the role of his drinking behavior in perpetuating these difficulties were highly acceptable to him, because they indicated the clinic's interest in having him change; on the other hand, those interactions which attempted to explore the subtler determinants of the patient's involvement in his difficult life situation were highly unacceptable, because they indicated, quite properly, that the clinic was interested in understanding (as a method for achieving certain shifts in the balance of forces in the patient's mind) rather than being directly inter-

*Consistent with the data in this book, the greatest proportion of patients described as improved or helped through these means are those whose social stability is not impaired—those who seek to give up drinking to obviate loss of status, affection, or support. Neither conditioned-aversion treatment nor antabuse treatment create this motivation; they supplement it through the use of an adjunctive threat.

195

ested in the patient's welfare. For example, when the internist communicated that drinking was harmful for the patient's well-being, the patient was gratified to have a benevolent authority intervene on his behalf; but when the psychiatrist inquired, hypothetically, into a patient's associations in order that the tension experienced prior to a binge might be elucidated, he was threatening the patient's attempt to maintain a defensive isolation of his drinking behavior from the totality of his life. Similarly, it was noted that the most "successful" clinic was the one where the psychoanalytic model played the least role in the training, outlook, practice, or interests of the staff. This observation suggests that the more one is committed to the value of depth of understanding of human motivation and behavior, the more difficult it may be to meet effectively the treatment expectations of the alcoholic patient at a clinic, because the orientation of the patient characteristically is to minimize the emotional depths and complexity of his drinking problem.

To enhance the patient's perception of threat or disruption of his drinking pattern, the clinician can establish a relationship with him through the acceptance of the patient's needs for support and control, and can therefore gradually assume the role of an auxiliary ego—an ego which focusses its interest on the clearer recognition of the manifold ways in which alcoholic beverages have made the patient's life more difficult. By paying attention to those aspects of the drinking problem, the therapist may paradoxically teach the patient not to regard his drinking as a symptom in the medical or psychoanalytical sense of the term, but rather as a mode of behavior to be abjured.

To engage a patient in the investigation of his own behavior as a symptom, or group of symptoms, rooted in a complex cognitive-emotional framework requires a great deal from the patient. It requires that he have a sturdy investment in introspection, a capacity for the delay of gratification, and a strong interest in the strengthening of his inner sources of support and control. It also requires an environment that is capable of tolerating and protecting him until changes in his cognitive-emotional framework lead to modification in his life-style. Very few of the patients known to these clinics°even approached the satisfaction of such requirements.

Some years ago, Tiebout[44] came to the conclusion that the psychiatrist should look to what the patient consciously believes about himself and his drinking, rather than to what the then current psychiatric and psychoanalytical theory and practice have taught him. From his experience with these patients, he emphasized such concepts as "hitting bottom,"† compliance, and surrender, terms which play an important role in the code of beliefs practised by Alcoholics Anonymous. What Tiebout pointed out was that the patient must learn from experience and from the therapist that he cannot continue to try to live with alcohol— he must learn to live without it. Prior to accepting this approach, no amount of exploration of "causes" is meaningful or effective in influencing the patient's drinking behavior. Where the present authors would disagree with Tiebout is in the assumption that alcohol is in fact the patient's problem and that it can be remedied by total abstinence. It is the authors' experience that the use of alcohol by a patient with a serious drinking problem is only one facet in his highly complex psychosocial adaptive processes. It may be useful to present the patient with the shibboleth that he will be well—or better off in some important ways—by living without alcohol, but it is not scientifically complete or entirely accurate.

Reflecting on the clinical protocols assembled in this study, especially in the context of today's more advanced knowledge of social psychiatry and ego psychology, the authors would agree with much of what Tiebout emphasized out of his experience, but they would be inclined to add an additional set of statements about the phenomenon of alcoholism and its treatment:

(1) Factors outside of the clinic-patient interaction have a

°Even in the psychoanalytically-oriented staff working with Pfeffer,[43] the majority of the patients were purposefully assigned for directive, supportive rather than analytic psychotherapy, and only 10 per cent for individual analytic psychotherapy.
†Parenthetically, the authors noted the experience of "hitting bottom" was alluded to extremely rarely by the patients or by the clinics in reconstructing the events and experiences which led to a changing of the patients' attitudes towards their drinking problems.

crucial role to play in enhancing the disruptive or threatening value of alcohol for patients with drinking problems, and hence in initiating and/or sustaining abstinence. The exploration of techniques which the clinic can use to strengthen the impact of such factors is an insufficiently developed area of research and practice. Many alcoholic patients try to deceive their therapist into believing—as they themselves would like to believe—that their drinking "really" does not jeopardize their health, social relationships, and employment.

(2) For the most part, it is the community, rather than the drinker, which is distressed by the excessive use of alcoholic beverages.

(3) It may be true that the alcoholic *ought* to regard himself as burdened by the medical-psychiatric *saequelae* or correlates of his drinking; however, the patient for the most part does not strongly share the community's negative attitudes towards his drinking—its co-ordination–impairing, vocation-interfering, aggression-enhancing concomitants—until he can perceive his drinking as threatening to his security or to his self-image. In a certain proportion of cases, the alcoholic may finally grow to share strongly these negative attitudes, but, until then, a splendid capacity for rationalization, denial, or minimization will sustain his drinking. Because the community incurs the burden—that is, of drunken driving, disturbance of the peace, hospital costs, welfare costs for neglected children, and so forth—it may be sound clinical policy to let treatment begin when the patient is ready, but it is probably poor social policy to avoid intervention in the hope that medical measures will obviate social control. The authors believe that the community might play an important role in the modification of patients' drinking problems by supplying elements of constraint and support through modes of social control—sanctions—which are tolerant of the person with the drinking problem, but which do not countenance those aspects of the drinking behavior which threaten the health or welfare of others. (The authors are not suggesting that the harassment techniques which have been focussed, with so little success, on opiate addicts, be applied to alcoholics.)

(4) As has been shown elsewhere,[39] the attainment of absti-

nence is not equivalent to the attainment of happiness. To the contrary, many patients who become abstinent live in considerable desperation (see chapter vii). Nor is the attainment of abstinence equivalent to the attainment of self-realization. When a man of limited interpersonal, intellectual, or artistic attainments gives up problem drinking, he still will not, as in the anecdote about the patient with the badly fractured wrist who is to be operated upon by a renowned orthopedist, be able to play the violin that he had not played before. The only values of abstinence are that the patient may live longer, stay out of institutions, and hopefully cause less overt suffering for persons in his immediate environment. The authors wish to emphasize that they consider these values as the only *direct* probable consequences of abstinence as such. Perhaps alcoholic patients might be better helped, if these limited goals were explicitly accepted.

(5) Because the medical profession cannot, except in an exceptionally few cases, modify the dependency problems, narcissism, sexual fears, and ambiguous identifications which commonly precede the drinking problem and continue, often with renewed vigor, following abstinence, a treatment orientation geared to what the patient can use and accept will have to be developed. Some of the acceptable modes of interaction for the patient, as inferred from the protocols assembled in this research are suggested in the following paragraphs.

Of importance in this regard is support, both personal and pharmaceutic, against the rigors of abstinence. Apart from the specific content of the interactions and communications with the treating person, the patients are more likely to respond favorably to an atmosphere in which the therapist is seen as a person imbued with authority, a parental surrogate, who offers not only interest but *direction*. In general, the clinic faces the problem of sustaining the patient while helping him to develop alcohol-free techniques for coping with or modifying painful experiences (humiliation, anxiety, loneliness, depression) for which he had, in a sense successfully, used alcohol. The "helping" may be focussed on strengthening defenses such as denial or suppression, supporting obsessional trends, offering tutelage and direction in techniques for the dissipation of tension, providing diversionary activities of a recreational or avocational nature, and, in a minority of cases, providing analytic psychotherapy for the clarification of intrapsychic conflict.

For patients whose lives are relatively filled by the commitments, gratifications, worries, entertainments, preoccupations and responsibilities of marriage, work, and family, the out-patient clinic can provide direction, support, and understanding which can help them survive the rigors of abstinence. As noted above for these patients, whom we have termed "unimpaired in social stability," the probability of improvement was directly associated with the extent of their contacts with the clinics. The out-patient clinic had an obvious utility and relevance for their treatment, though undoubtedly much still needs to be learned about their management. Perhaps a systematic application of the approach defined in the preceding paragraph might substantially raise the proportion of improved patients among this group.

On the other hand, for those patients who lacked either marriage, work, or residence in a familial setting (approximately 70 per cent of the clinic population), the extent of attendance at the clinic was not at all associated with improvement. This finding suggests that, although the clinic might be of benefit for occasional patients in this group, there is something intrinsically lacking in the experience which the out-patient structure can provide for the patients whose social stability is impaired.

These data were not easily interpreted. However, it seemed certain that the findings could not be accounted for by social class differences, because the statistics describing the relationship between outcome and clinic attendance for the skid-row patients (those who were neither married, nor employed, nor living in a familial setting) were no different from those describing the patients who were impaired with respect to only one of these three parameters. Furthermore, educational and occupational levels, both indices of social status or class, were related neither to outcome nor to attendance at the clinics.

To account for the different relationships between attendance at the clinics and outcome for the patients impaired in social stability at intake, the authors offer the following hypothesis: (1) for those patients who lack the constraints of marriage, work,

200

and family, it is surmised that there is a vastly greater probability that their milieu will lack forces directing them towards initiating and/or sustaining abstinence (a lack noted among the unimproved or deteriorated patients in this study); (2) it is expected that these patients are more likely to place themselves in settings in which there is actual environmental support of their continued drinking.

It is known that drinking alcoholic beverages is a major element in the life structure of the homeless skid-row men. Although systematic data on the question are not available, it is surmised that for those patients who, though they are not on "skid-row," are either unemployed, unmarried, or without familial ties of residence, drinking is also likely to play a time-filling, diversionary, or masculinity-asserting function, which may be relatively harmless, perhaps, for the non-alcoholic man, but disruptive for the alcoholic. The absence of any one of these three common structuring factors (marriage, work, family) in daily adult life in modern society may simply outweigh the directive and supportive potential which the clinics might play in the one or two hours available to the patient in the course of a week. If the clinic—or some comparable institutional entity—could provide the relevant structuring influences, it might be possible to influence more predictably the drinking problems within this group of patients.

Some acknowledgment for this point of view has been expressed by those clinics which try to provide a lounge, occupational therapy, or recreational facilities for their patients on an out-patient basis. However, in the authors' experience, these programs are predominantly diversionary, for they do not acquire for the patient a sense of importance or cruciality in his life, specifically some sense of relevance to his struggle to achieve or sustain abstinence. Furthermore, these out-patient programs lack authority to maintain the patient's presence or to bring him there.

Many in-patient facilities for treatment of alcoholism explicitly recognize the need for providing a structure of recreational activity, occupational training, and exploration of group interaction processes to supplement their educational and psychotherapeutic processes. In a discussion related to a formal research study of the outcome of treatment in out-patient facilities, it may seem irrelevant to insert remarks or opinions about in-patient programs for alcoholism. However, it is the authors' hypothesis that, for the patient who lacks the structuring influence of marriage, regular employment, and familial residence, a preliminary in-patient experience of a special type might provide the basis for continued out-patient treatment which would be demonstrably relevant to change in his functioning.

Two predominant types of in-patient facilities were utilized by the out-patient clinics in the state alcoholism programs which were studied. One type is used for psychiatric emergencies, for "drying out," or for diagnostic (predominantly medical) studies. The duration of hospitalization is measured in days, and any patient with a drinking problem might be admitted once or many times for these short-term services or goals. However meaningful or useful this type of hospitalization might be in the treatment of a patient, it clearly does not sufficiently contribute to the development of structure in the patient's life.

The other type of in-patient facility is rather selective in its intake policies. For the most part, patients who are impaired in social stability have a poor likelihood of admission to these facilities in which duration of hospitalization is measured in weeks—usually four to six. In addition to caring for the patients' medical-psychiatric crises or problems, a program of relatively intensive group and individual education and therapy is provided along with recreational and vocational activities. Unfortunately, these more prolonged in-patient programs are usually geographically, often administratively, and not infrequently philosophically separated from the preceding or following out-patient care. Certainly, the rate of return to out-patient care following these in-patient experiences is recognized to be low. Most crucial, in the authors' opinion, is the fact that, when the patient is discharged from the in-patient service, the developing associations with other patients and with staff are usually—and often permanently—interrupted. Also, the structuring of daily experience, which the authors believe these patients impaired in social stability require, is abandoned just as it is beginning, and the patient is perforce thrust back where he came from, hopefully—

but not likely—having attained some impetus to continue with treatment.

It thus follows that, for patients impaired in social stability, merely providing an in-patient experience which parallels the style or goals of these two types of existent in-patient services for alcoholics would not be especially useful. On the basis of the authors' own reading in the field of social psychiatry,* and the fresh viewpoints which they have had the good fortune to acquire in discussions abroad in Holland† and Yugoslavia,‡ it is suggested that patients impaired in social stability might benefit from a treatment program with the following characteristics:

(a) There should be preferential admission for patients who are impaired in social stability, so that they, and their needs, would set the tone of the institution, rather than play a role in which they are tolerated, somewhat like the poor relative at the wedding.

(b) Patients should be admitted to the hospital which is located in the same community as that in which they subsequently will seek employment and residence.

(c) Duration of hospitalization undoubtedly should be in excess of six weeks; three to six months would be a more appropriate minimal period to achieve the goals discussed below.

(d) There should be care for the patients' medical-psychiatric crises or problems; subsequently, a program of relatively intensive group and individual education and therapy should be provided along with recreational and vocational activities. Extensive use should be made of such modalities as patient government, patient clubs, and patient-organized work and recreation programs to aid in the establishment of group identity and of group support. The hypothesis is proposed that these patients need forces in their

*Cumming and Cumming, *Ego and Milieu*, New York: Atherton Press, 1963, has been an especially stimulating influence to our thinking in this regard.
†W. K. Van Dijk, Een catamnestisch onderzoek na 12 maanden bij 51 klinisch behandelte alcoholisten. (Nederlands Tijdschrift voor Geneeskunde, 105, 40, 1961, pp. 1974–81.)
‡In the summer of 1964 Gerard had the opportunity to visit Dr. Vladimir Hudolin, chief of the neuropsychiatric division within the general hospital, Zagreb, Yugoslavia (Bolnice "Dr. M. Stojanovic"), and to observe his large-scale social-psychiatric program for the treatment of alcoholism.

milieu which will direct them towards sustaining abstinence. Lacking family and close ties of friendship or of regular association, they need to become part of a sub-culture which offers them the benefits of the common structuring factors in daily living which they have not been able to acquire, or have lost, and the opportunity to provide such structure for their fellows.

(e) A variety of intermediary programs (night hospital, day hospital, half-way houses) should be developed between full in-patient and out-patient care.

(f) There should be over-all integration of both in-patient and out-patient care by the same clinicians and administrators, so that the patients would not be exposed to differing sets of assumptions and care in accord with their location in in-patient facilities, night hospitals, half-way houses, and so forth.

(g) An important feature of the program should be the exploration and, where appropriate, implementation of the reinvolvement of the patient with his family; casework and family treatment would be necessary components of this program.

(h) Such a program as described above would require the development of a staff capable of accepting men and women of prolonged deviant life-styles and/or lower social class origins. The buildings, furnishings, clothing, language, and food should reflect such acceptance. The imposition of conventional middle-class aseptic clinical expectations, roles, and relationships would undermine the possibility of helping these patients. Flexibility in roles and relationships between patient and staff is essential (for example, reports[45] of the recent experience of rehabilitation institutions such as Fountain House in New York City).

(i) Without laboring the point further, what is needed is the application of the social psychiatric experiences of the past two decades (from Maxwell Jones' "therapeutic community"[46] through the English "day hospital" to Brager's[47] utilization of indigenous non-professionals) to the problem of the socially disestablished alcoholic. Application should not be haphazardly piecemeal, but integrated, well-planned with full realization of the experimental nature of such a program. Concomitant with the development of such a program, which we have outlined only in the most general form, scientific evaluation of the process and its outcome should be carried out. This assessment should be done in an administrative context which permits flexible, but not impulsive, modifications in the program. It is the authors' opinion that, if the emphasis is on "successful" service rather than on research, neither the community nor the staff could or would tolerate the problems of caring for this important component of the alcoholic population for which ordinary clinical settings have proved so unrewarding.

APPENDIX

RESEARCH INSTRUMENTS AND MANUALS
FOR PERSONNEL OF ALCOHOLISM SERVICES
PARTICIPATING IN THE NYU-NAAAP FOLLOW-UP STUDY

Phase I: Collection of Intake and Treatment Data
(Manual and Instruments)

Phase II: Collection of Follow-Up Data
(Manual and Instruments)

Phase I: Collection of Intake and Treatment Data (Manual and Instruments)

INTRODUCTION

THE GENERAL objectives of this study are two-fold: first to conduct a follow-up study of the outcome of treatment of patients with drinking problems, treated in tax-supported alcoholism programs; and secondly, to develop a common framework for the description of patients and their treatment which can be used for future research in this field.

The study is being conducted under the auspices of the North American Association of Alcoholism Programs and the New York University Center for Applied Social Research. A grant-in-aid to this research was made by the National Institute of Mental Health, and in February 1957 work began on this project. The personnel conducting the study are: principal investigators, Gerhart Saenger, Ph.D. and Donald L. Gerard, M.D.; research social workers, Miss Renee Wile and Miss Lucille Grow.

The specific aim of this study is to ascertain the nature and degree of change in patients with a drinking problem treated in NAAAP clinics, in relation to three groups of factors: (1) the social and medical-psychiatric characteristics of the patient and his drinking problem; (2) the treatment setting; (3) the length and type of treatment received.

This research is dependent on the use of uniform recording procedures by the collaborating clinics in which certain data are obtained for each patient in a sample of their cases. These recording procedures have been developed and tested in four clinics. They have been developed with an eye to both the requisites of research and the possibilities of carrying out research studies in on-going clinic operations. It is obvious that the quality of the research and the significance of its findings are inherently dependent on the degree of interest and co-operation the clinics are able to bring to their part of the work.

The first two years of the study have been devoted to the pilot phase, which involved the following:

(1) Development of forms and procedures to describe the patient, his treatment, and his post-treatment status at follow-up. Basically, the

problem has been to discover what data about research patients can be recorded systematically, regularly, and consistently by the clinics without upsetting their usual work.

(2) Study of the problems of tracing, locating, and interviewing patients six months or a year after intake.

(3) Planning the main study on the basis of experience in the pilot phase.

The four clinics which participated in the pilot phase are: the New Haven out-patient clinic maintained by the Connecticut Commission on Alcoholism; the State University Alcoholism Clinic at Kings County Hospital, Brooklyn, financed by the New York State Interdepartmental Health Resources Board; the Alcoholic Rehabilitation Clinic maintained by the Department of Health of the District of Columbia; and the combined in-patient and out-patient service at the Medical College of Virginia Hospital, Richmond, conducted by the Division of Alcohol Studies and Rehabilitation of the Virginia Department of Health.

The general design of the study assumes that each clinic will, on the average, take on nine new cases each month for the research project. An intake study and a continuing record of the individual treatment of each such patient will be undertaken during the first year of the project (1959). The second year of the project (1960) will be devoted to follow-up studies approximately one year after the patients' first visits to the clinic; for example, the patients who enter the research sample in January 1959 will be followed up in January 1960. There is reason to believe that one year of follow-up will be highly informative from a scientific and clinical perspective. A one-year follow-up is all that can be accomplished within the limits of this project, apart from the possibility of a small-scale study, two or three years after intake, of some of the patients studied in the pilot phase. In addition, however, the intake study and the treatment record and the data obtained at the one-year follow-up offer an excellent baseline for later follow-up by the individual clinics of these same patients at intervals of more than one year.

The third year of the project (1961) will be focussed on a statistical analysis of the data from the collaborating clinics, the preparation of a report, and consultation with the clinics in order to design future research and to aid in clinic development and planning based on the results of this study.

In order for an NAAAP clinic to participate in this study, it is necessary administratively to plan on devoting to the project a full eight hours of professional staff time per week for a two-year period. This includes occasional intra-staff conferences and inter-staff (research staff–clinic staff) conferences.

The research team is prepared to spend as much time as is necessary

210

with the collaborating clinics to explain the content and the use of the research instruments; to develop sampling procedures with each clinic, in the light of the clinic's particular circumstances and characteristics; to work with the entire staff of the collaborating clinics in general, and in particular with a liaison person from each clinic; to prepare reports on the results of the research; and in general to be as useful as possible to aid the collaboration.

PART I. DESIGN OF THE STUDY

(a) *The Sample*

1. CONSIDERATIONS IN THE CHOICE OF THE SAMPLE. In order to compare, evaluate, and measure the many factors involved in the outcome of treatment of patients with drinking problems, a large sample is needed. Exactly how large it need be depends on the statistical analysis to be undertaken. Certain comparisons can be done with a small sample. For instance, to relate the outcome of treatment to the number of clinic visits, three groups of patients, each about 30 in number, could be compared. The first group (hypothetically) would consist of those who have come only one time to the clinic, the second group 2 to 5 times, and the third group 6 or more times. Then the frequency could be noted with which, for instance, patients in these three groups were abstinent, continued to drink but with evident modification of their drinking problem, or were unchanged in this area of their lives. A total sample of 90 cases would suffice for this statistical analysis; on the basis of the frequency distribution a conclusion could be reached as to whether or not the number of visits has any predictive value of change in the patient's drinking problem.

But this simple analysis would perforce have to ignore other important variables. For example, earlier studies indicate that socio-economic status may be a predictor of change in the drinking problem. Now, to see whether the number of clinic visits is a predictor of change independently of socio-economic status, it would be necessary to make the following statistical breakdowns:

One clinic visit	Low socio-economic status	30
	Middle socio-economic status	30
	Upper socio-economic status	30
2–5 clinic visits	Low socio-economic status	30
	Middle socio-economic status	30
	Upper socio-economic status	30
6 or more clinic visits	Low socio-economic status	30
	Middle socio-economic status	30
	Upper socio-economic status	30
TOTAL		270

211

Next, it might be desirable to investigate the influence of a particular treatment emphasis on changes in drinking problems in relation to both socio-economic status and the number of clinic visits. Assuming three categories of treatment emphasis were constructed, three times the prior number of cases would be needed, or 810.

In certain instances these hypothetical comparisons can be made with less than 30 cases in each major subclassification. However, the closer we approach 30 cases, the more reliable the inferences can become.

Since the objective is to relate variations in the outcome of treatment to the manifold differences in the social and medical characteristics of the patients and also to the manifold differences in the treatment they received, it is clear that a large sample is necessary to study any particular relation while controlling—or holding constant—other important variables. On the basis of these considerations, a sample of 1,200 cases is far from excessive, and a sample much smaller than this might seriously hamper the study.

2. SELECTION OF THE SAMPLE. In order to secure a sample of about 1,200 patients, collaboration with at least twelve clinics is planned. This reduces the number of cases to be studied for research purposes by each clinic to manageable proportions, makes it possible to obtain a more detailed picture of the total work of the different types of NAAAP clinics, and insures maximum variations in types of patients. Each participating clinic, therefore, will study approximately 100 first-admission patients; that is, nine new cases will be added each month in each clinic for a twelve-month period. In order to make each clinic sample representative of its total intake, procedures will be worked out individually with each clinic to assure that any patient admitted to the clinic has an equal chance to appear in the sample, and at the same time to adjust individual sampling procedures to the demands of smooth clinic operations.

(b) Collection of Data

The study is designed to ascertain the extent and type of change, after a period of one year measured from intake, of patients who differ in regard to social background and pathology and who are exposed to different types of treatment. It is planned, therefore, to collect information about: (1) the social background and status of the patient at intake; (2) the type and length of treatment; (3) changes in the patient's status—that is, the extent of relative movement between intake and follow-up. Special forms are used to record information on each of these subjects. A general description of the forms follows. Detailed instructions about their use will be provided in part II, section C of this manual.

1. INTAKE INFORMATION. The data to be collected at intake fall into

two categories: (a) data identifying the patient's socio-economic status, residence, and familial connections; and (b) data describing the patient's drinking problems and life patterns at the point where treatment was begun.

The identifying data are collected during the first visit of the patient to the clinic and entered on an intake information form. Since a substantial number of patients fail to return after their first visit to a clinic, some information about the patient's drinking and occupational status is also obtained and recorded, along with some brief general observations of the patient's appearance and behavior at the first visit to the clinic.

A more detailed instrument, the case review, is used to describe the patient's life patterns and drinking problems at the point where treatment was begun. It is a narrative which is designed to provide a baseline description of the patient, against which his pattern of living and general adjustment at the time of the follow-up study can be compared. There is also a check list of about a dozen topics, which abstracts some specific data from the narrative case review. The case review will be supplemented at the time of follow-up by an additional section dealing with the clinic's estimate of the patient's treatment experience, his reasons for continuing or withdrawing from treatment, and all additional material gathered in the course of treatment but *not* covered in the case review at the time of intake.

2. TREATMENT INFORMATION. Information concerning the actualities of the patient's treatment experience is entered on the treatment record. The form is designed to describe in simple and general terms what was done for the patient and what happened in each contact the patient had with the clinic. Observations of the patient and some of his reactions to the treating person are also recorded. The form consists of a check list to be filled in after each formal contact of the patient with a treating person, regardless of his professional identification.

In addition, a separate form has been devised for those patients who receive group therapy, to provide some information about their participation in and reaction to that form of treatment.

3. FOLLOW-UP DATA. During the second year of operations, patients admitted during the first year will be traced and be identified in the following manner: (a) those resident in the same area (state) as at intake; (b) those who have died; (c) those who are out of state or out of the area; (c) those who are not traceable. Those patients who are resident within the same area (state) as they were at intake will be interviewed once. For those patients who have died, death certificates, other public records, and whatever information is available about the circumstances of the death and its relation to alcoholism will be collated.

The extent of change in the status of patients between intake and

213

follow-up will be measured by comparing the status of the patient at the beginning of the treatment (baseline data) with his status at follow-up. For this purpose, the case review will be used as a follow-up interview guide, to assure comparability of the information obtained at intake and follow-up. In addition, the same check list used at intake will be filled in and that part of the intake information form which summarized observations of the patient will be used at the time of the follow-up interview.

(c) Clinic Staff Time Required during the First Year

Estimates collected in the pilot phase of this study in four clinics indicated that the average number of clinic visits was six per case. The time required to process research cases averaged approximately two hours per case—that is, 5 to 10 minutes for the intake information form, 90 minutes for the case review and check list, and 24 minutes for the six treatment records per case, requiring about 4 minutes each.

During the first year of operation the total amount of time a clinic will need for recording the data about research patients should amount to about 200 hours, or approximately 4 hours of staff time per week. Allowing an additional three hours per week for conferences, planning the sample, and the time of the co-ordinator or liaison staff member, the eight hours of staff time per week mentioned above should be ample.

PART II. RESEARCH PROCEDURES IN THE CLINIC

(a) Personnel and Supervision

The research staff will make preliminary arrangements with the heads of the participating clinics to be followed by regular visits of research staff members. During these visits, joint meetings will be held with the clinic administrators and staff members for discussion of procedures and review of initial recording experiences.

In each participating clinic the director is to appoint a special liaison person, whose duties include the facilitation of communication between the clinic and the research office in New York, as well as the co-ordination of the research within the clinic. During the first year of the study, the liaison person will see that:

(1) The sampling procedure is carefully followed in selecting the cases for the research sample, and the research office is notified of the names and case numbers of the patients in the sample.

(2) All participating staff members are informed which cases are included in the research sample.

(3) A treatment record (or group therapy form) is filled in every time a person in the research sample is seen by a staff member.

214

(4) The case review and check list are completed as early as possible, that is, as soon as all information asked for has been completed.

(5) At the point of follow-up the person in charge of tracing will make a final review of the case.

(6) All data are collated and forwarded to the research office in accordance with the research schedule.

During the second year of the study, the liaison person will be in charge of the tracing, the arrangement of appointments with traced sample cases, the assignment of staff members for interviews, and seeing that the cases are written up and sent to the research office.

(b) Sampling Procedures

A routine method of selecting patients for participation in the research will be set up in each clinic in such a way as to obtain as representative a sample as possible of their intake, thus avoiding any bias which might be introduced by selecting "good" patients or "bad" patients. Once this routine is determined, it is essential that it be followed without exception.

The clinic cards and folders for these research cases will be marked so that each person handling the records will realize that these patients are research cases and that special forms must be completed on them.

Each month the research office in New York will send a "new case list" form, in duplicate, to the liaison person in each clinic. The names and clinic case numbers of the patients chosen for the study during that month, and the number of interviews each had, should be entered on that form, and one copy should be returned to the research office at the end of the month and one copy kept in the clinic.

In addition, each month the New York office will send an "old case list" form, in duplicate, to each clinic, on which the names of all the research patients in prior months will be listed. The number of interviews conducted with each of those patients during that month should be entered, and one copy of the form should be returned to New York at the end of the month, and the other kept at the clinic.

(c) Research Forms

For each case chosen in the study sample, data are to be gathered and recorded on specially prepared forms. In general, these forms are self-explanatory. If any problems arise in using them, these can be discussed with the research staff by mail, telephone (SPring 7–2000, extension 8237), or in conference.

1. INTAKE INFORMATION FORM. This form is designed to record identifying data about the patient. It should be filled out by the person who usually collects identifying data for the clinic at the patient's first visit to the clinic. If the patient is too ill and/or intoxicated, the

215

information for this form may be obtained from the person accompanying the patient to the clinic. This form is sent to the research office in New York along with the case review and check list when they are ready. Many clinics find it desirable to keep a copy of the intake information form in their permanent files.

2. TREATMENT RECORD FORM. This form is to be filled out by the interviewing person, regardless of professional orientation, EACH TIME the patient is seen for an *individual* interview in the *12-month period following his intake*. It should be filled out immediately after the interview, while the information is still fresh in the interviewer's mind. In the event that a patient is seen by two professional persons during the same visit, a form is to be completed by each interviewer. At the patient's first visit to the clinic, a treatment record is filled out in addition to the intake information form. At that time, questions 9, 10, and 11 should be left blank. *At all other times, no questions should be left blank.*

If a relative of the patient is seen, only the top segment (items 1–6) on the first page of the Treatment Record are to be completed. However, in addition to writing the name of the patient, on that same line write the name of the relative and his relationship to the patient. This same procedure is followed if an interested person, such as a minister, physician, employer, or agency representative is seen. If a joint interview with patient and a relative is held, the entire form is filled out as it relates to the patient, inserting "joint interview, patient and relative" under "Purpose."

If a patient is hospitalized as part of the treatment program of the clinic, special arrangements for the use of the treatment record will be worked out by the research staff for the in-patient services connected with the clinic.

These treatment records should be kept in the clinic until the case review (see below) is written. When the case review is sent in, all treatment records completed by then should also be sent to New York, and thereafter the treatment records should be sent in each month with the old case lists.

3. GROUP THERAPY FORM. This form is to be used for each research patient who is being seen in group treatment. It is to be filled out each time the patient attends the group, and should be kept in the clinic until the case review is written. When the case review is sent in, all group therapy forms completed to that date should also be sent to New York. Group therapy forms completed subsequent to the time of the case review should be sent to New York each month with the old case lists.

If the patient is being seen individually as well as in the group, the treatment record form should also be filled out for these individual interviews.

216

4. CASE REVIEW. There are two parts to the case review: (1) a narrative not unlike diagnostic summaries used in clinic settings; and (2) a short check list. The case review is designed to record the patient's situation when he comes to the clinic. This should be recorded as fully as possible as soon as the relevant data have been collected, but not later than six weeks following intake. The emphasis of these data should be on the patient's *situation during the year before he was seen at intake*, not on changes in the first few weeks of treatment.

The case review, designed to record in one document *all information about* the status of the patient at and *in the year preceding intake*, is to be written up by one person especially designated for this task by the clinic. Since it is the task of this person to obtain and integrate all information about the patient collected by various staff members—for example, internist, psychiatrist, psychologist, social worker, or public health nurse—it has appeared advantageous to designate a person who has interviewed the patient and thus would already have this information about a given case.

The case review should be completed as soon as all information required in it has been collected. This may be after one, two, three, or more visits. In any case, the person in charge of completing the case review should do so within six weeks following the patient's first clinic visit. In some of the settings in which the pilot study was done, it was found feasible to do this after a single clinic visit and an interview focused on the case review data.

The information for the case review should be collected during the natural course of the interview, whenever the opportunity for exploring a particular area of life presents itself. The participating staff members should keep in mind that many patients appear in the clinic only once or a few times. Unless complete information about these cases is available, it will not be possible to ascertain the effects of short-term treatment. Since the pilot study indicated that short-term treatment may often be related to a change in attitude and behavior, it is desirable to obtain complete information as early as possible.

5. CHECK LIST. The check list is not designed for use in the interview, but is to be filled out at the time when the case review is written, in accordance with what the patient has told clinic personnel about himself. Although the data in the case review describe the year prior to the intake, the check list focuses, with one explicit exception, on a shorter time period—*the month before intake.* Please check whichever category best describes your understanding of the patient's situation in the month preceding intake.

The check list is a way of abstracting some data from the case review write-up and should not be used as a substitute for it, because a wider range of data is needed than is included in the check list.

On the first page of the check list, a "binge" is defined as a sustained period of drinking, of more than 24 hours' duration. An "episode of intoxication" is defined as a period of drinking for less than 24 hours. In case of doubt, check "episode."

If the patient has been employed for part of the month prior to intake and unemployed for part of the month, check both on question VI.

It is recognized that sometimes it is extremely difficult to collect data on patients with drinking problems. However, please attempt insofar as possible to cover all areas in the case review, as this material is crucial to the study. When data on a given topic are not available, *please explicitly say so in the narrative.* It is important to know whether lack of data is due to oversight or to some other problem. Therefore, please state the reason for your inability to collect data in a given area mentioned in the check list. Each topical area of the case review narrative should be written up separately, and introduced by the proper heading. Two copies of the narrative and one copy of the check list should be sent to the research office as soon as it is written, together with the intake information form and all the treatment records, both individual and group, up to that time.

(*d*) *Summary of Record-Keeping and Transmittal*

Title of form	Filled out	Transmitted to New York
Intake information form	Day of first visit to the clinic	With the case review
Treatment record	Immediately after each interview	With the case review, and thereafter each month with case list Forms
Group therapy form	Immediately after each group session	With the case review, and thereafter each month with case list Forms
Case review	As soon as feasible— at latest, 6 weeks after intake	As soon as written, in duplicate, with forms listed above, plus check list
Check list	Immediately after case review narrative is written	With the case review
New case list	End of month	End of month
Old case list	End of month	End of month, with all treatment records accumulated to date

All correspondence should be sent to the Center for Applied Social Research, New York University, 41 Fifth Avenue, New York 3, New York. Mail should be addressed to whichever member of the research staff seems most relevant for the purposes of the correspondence. If there is any question as to who is most relevant, address Miss Renee Wile or Miss Lucille Grow, to whom all forms should be sent. Telephone calls should be made person to person to SPring 7–2000, extension 8237.

PART III. SAMPLES OF RESEARCH FORMS

1. INTAKE INFORMATION FORM

Completed by: _____

Title: _____

Name of Clinic: _____

Date of Intake: _____

Clinic Case No: _____

We should like to have the following social data systematically obtained (and recorded) at the first interview:

1. PATIENT'S NAME _____
                    (Last)   (First)   (Middle or Maiden)

2. ADDRESS: _____
           (Number)   (Street)   (City)   (State)

3. NOW RESIDING WITH: _____ RELATIONSHIP: _____

4. IS THERE A WORKING ADULT, other than the patient, in the patient's household now? Yes ( ), No ( ). If yes, relationship to patient: _____

5. NAME AND ADDRESS OF NEAREST RELATIVE: _____

   Relationship to patient: _____

6. SEX: Male ( ), Female ( )

7. RACE: White ( ), Negro ( ), Other: _____ ( ), NR ( )

8. RELIGION: Catholic ( ), Protestant ( ), Jewish ( ), None ( ), NR ( ), Denomination (e.g. Baptist, Presbyterian): _____

9. DATE OF BIRTH: _____ NR ( ) _____

10. PLACE OF BIRTH: (Country—or if United States, name of state) OF:

    Patient: _____ Father: _____ Mother: _____

11. MARITAL STATUS: Single ( ), Divorced ( ), Separated ( )
                     Married ( ), Widowed ( ), NR ( )

12. FULL NAME OF SPOUSE: _____
                     (Last)   (First)   (Middle or Maiden)

13. NUMBER OF CHILDREN: _____ AGES: _____

14. CURRENT EMPLOYMENT STATUS OF PATIENT:

    ( ) (a) Employed

    ( ) (b) Unemployed

    ( ) (c) Housewife. (A person is designated as a "housewife" when she is married and living with her husband and not on the labor market. If the wife is employed or just temporarily unemployed, she is not a "Housewife," and her occupation should then be noted.)

219

(a) *If patient is employed:*
(1) Name and address of employer: _____

_____

(2) Occupation; what type of work does he do on this job? _____

_____

(3) How long employed there? _____

(4) Is the job: Full-time? ( ) Part-time? ( ) Sporadic? ( )
NR? ( )

(5) Salary: (Stated salary, or the interviewer's best estimate of salary.
Fill in whatever applies. If occasional worker, estimate annual
income.)

$_____ $_____ $_____
    Per Week   Per Month   Per Year

(b) *If patient is unemployed:*
(1) How long since last permanent employment? _____
(Exclude temporary jobs.)

(c) *If patient is housewife:*
(1) How long since she was last on the labor market? _____

15. PATIENT'S USUAL OCCUPATION (Job at which he has spent the major part of
his working life, or for which he is trained):

_____

(If patient is a housewife, enter husband's usual occupation on this line.)

16. EDUCATION: ( ) None   ( ) Some College
                                              ( ) Completed college
            ( ) Some grammar school
            ( ) Completed grammar school   ( ) Other:_____
            ( ) Some high school
            ( ) Completed high school

17. SOURCE OF REFERRAL TO CLINIC: _____

OBSERVATIONS

In all cases, the interviewer should briefly describe
the patient in terms of each of the following:

18. PERSONAL HYGIENE AND GENERAL APPEARANCE: _____

_____

19. APPARENT STATE OF HEALTH: _____

_____

20. CURRENT DRINKING STATUS (sober, hungover, etc.): Include your own observations and also whatever the patient tells you about his drinking on that day,
whether he drank or not, how much, and what effect it had on him:

_____

21. SYMPTOMS OBSERVED RELATED TO ALCOHOLISM (tremors, etc.): _____
_____ None observed ( )

22. ATTITUDE TOWARD CLINIC TREATMENT (defensive, co-operative, confused, passive, etc.) _____
_____ Not observed ( )

23. STATEMENTS OF PATIENT ARE CONSIDERED:
( ) Largely reliable
( ) Doubtful
( ) Unreliable
( ) No judgment possible

24. INFORMATION ON THIS FORM WAS OBTAINED FROM:

( ) Patient

( ) Relative: _____

( ) Other: _____
(Preferably this material should be obtained from the patient. However, it is also possible to obtain it from the person who accompanies the patient at intake. The source of the material should be noted.)

---

2. TREATMENT RECORD FORM

---

1. NAME OF PATIENT: _____
(last)   (first)   (middle or maiden)

2. INTERVIEWER: _____ CLINIC TITLE: _____

NAME OF   CLINIC   DATE OF
3. CLINIC: _____ CASE NO.: _____ INTERVIEW: _____

4. INTERVIEW BEGAN AT: ____ AM ( ) PM ( )   ENDED AT: ____ AM ( ) PM ( )

5. PLACE OF CONTACT: Out-patient facility ( ),   In-patient facility ( )
Patient's home ( ),   Other: _____( )

6. PURPOSE OF INTERVIEW: _____

I. CONTENT

1. Obtained new social and/or medical data?   Yes ( ),   No ( )

2. Specific prescriptions or recommendations:
(a) Were any drugs prescribed in this interview?   Yes ( ),   No ( )
If yes, either check all the following which apply, or write in the ones prescribed.
(1) ( ) Any vitamin
(2) ( ) Any amphetamine

```
(3) (  ) Antabuse
(4) (  ) Any barbiturate
(5) (  ) Mephenesin or tolserol
(6) (  ) Compazine
    (  ) Frenquel
    (  ) Atarax
    (  ) Sparine
(7) (  ) Thorazine (chlorpromazine)
    (  ) Any rauwolfia (serpasil, etc.)
    (  ) Meprobomate (miltown or equanil, etc.)
    (  ) Deprol
(8) (  ) Endocrine drugs, related to thyroid
    (  ) Endocrine drugs, related to adrenal
    (  ) Endocrine drugs, related to pituitary
(9) (  ) Placebo
(10) (  ) Special clinic compound (Specify name or number)
```

(11) Others. Specify: _____

(12) Is this prescription part of a controlled study of a particular
     drug?   Yes ( ),   No ( )
(b) Were dietary prescriptions or recommendations made? Yes ( ), No ( )
(c) Did you discuss or arrange that the patient begin
    psychotherapy and/or supportive therapy?   Yes ( ), No ( )
(d) Did you discuss, arrange or recommend hospitalization? Yes ( ), No ( )
(e) Other recommendations? (e.g., group therapy, etc.)   Yes ( ), No ( )

    If yes, specify: _____

3. Was the patient's use of any medication prior to this clinic
   discussed?   Yes ( ), No ( )

4. Were data obtained on patient's physical condition?   Yes ( ), No ( )
   If yes:
   (a) Evaluation did not suggest need for special medical examination? ( )
   (b) Evaluation suggested current need for special medical examination? ( )
   Résumé of any salient information from routine or special examination that
   was made: _____

5. Discussed and/or advised patient regarding practical
   problems?   Yes ( ), No ( )
                        Discussed   Advised action
   If yes, which?   ( ) (a) Finding employment   ( )
                      ( ) (b) Problems in current jobs   ( )
                      ( ) (c) Family life   ( )
                      ( ) (d) Social life   ( )
                      ( ) (e) Financial problems, maintenance, etc. ( )
                      ( ) (f) Post-hospital planning   ( )
                      ( ) (g) Health   ( )
                      ( ) (h) Housing   ( )
                      ( ) (i) Other: _____   ( )

6. Discussed and/or advised patient regarding current
relationships?   Yes ( ), No ( )
   Discussed   Advised action
   If yes, which?   ( ) (*a*) Spouse   ( )
                       ( ) (*b*) Parents   ( )
                       ( ) (*c*) Siblings   ( )
                       ( ) (*d*) Children   ( )
                       ( ) (*e*) Drinking partners   ( )
                       ( ) (*f*) Fellow workers   ( )
                       ( ) (*g*) Occupational supervisor-boss, foreman
                                 etc.   ( )
                       ( ) (*h*) Other: _____( )

7. Patient discussed earlier relationships and experiences?   Yes ( ), No ( )
   If yes: ( ) (*a*) In adult life
                       ( ) (*b*) During school years
                       ( ) (*c*) During pre-school years

8. Patient discussed his drinking problem   Yes ( ), No ( )
   If yes, discussed (*a*) its origin and development   Yes ( ), No ( )
                       (*b*) its present status   Yes ( ), No ( )

9. (*Leave blank for first visit to clinic and in-patient interviews.*)
   Information obtained indicated that (in the interviewer's judgment)
   patient has had alcoholic beverages in the interval between this and
   the last visit to the clinic   Yes ( ), No ( )

10. (*Leave blank for first visit to clinic and in-patient interviews.*)
    If he has been drinking in this interval, has he—
    (*a*) lost time from work through drinking?   Yes ( ), No ( )
                                                        Not discussed ( )
                              Not applicable, unemployed ( )
    (*b*) been arrested in the interval for drinking   Yes ( ), No ( )
                                                        Not discussed ( )
    (*c*) been hospitalized in the interval for drinking   Yes ( ), No ( )
                                                        Not discussed ( )

11. (*Leave blank for first visit to clinic and in-patient interviews.*)
    Discussed the patient's symptomatology in the interval between this and his
    last visit to the clinic. Yes ( ), No ( ), Not applicable ( )
    If yes, what areas of symptomatology were discussed?
        ( ) (*a*) Somatic expressions of anxiety
        ( ) (*b*) Symptoms of physical ill health
        ( ) (*c*) Sleeping difficulties
        ( ) (*d*) Appetite
        ( ) (*e*) Symptomatology related to alcoholism, e.g. hangover,
                  insomnia, tremors, blackouts, convulsions, DTs etc.
        ( ) (*f*) Other: _____

II. OBSERVATION OF PATIENT DURING INTERVIEW

In each scale below, check the item(s) which in your opinion best fits the patient.
An entry is required in *each* scale. All data apply to current interview only.

1. Predominant pattern of verbal communication (check at least one):
   ( ) (*a*) Constricted
   ( ) (*b*) Restrained

( ) (c) Some give-and-take
( ) (d) Freely communicative
( ) (e) Garrulous
( ) (f) Circumstantial and "windy"
( ) (g) Fluctuating, varying, inconstant
( ) (h) Other (specify): _____

2. Predominant mood during interview (check at least one)
( ) (a) Depressed
( ) (b) Sad, fearful of future
( ) (c) Neutral
( ) (d) Happy
( ) (e) Gay
( ) (f) Euphoric
( ) (g) Labile, inconstant, fluctuating
( ) (h) Other (specify): _____

3. Desire for treatment:
(a) Does the interviewer think the patient wants treatment?
Yes ( ), No ( ), Unclear ( )
(b) Does the interviewer think the patient comes to the clinic
( ) voluntarily
( ) through coercion
( ) elements of both present
( ) no data

4. Suspiciousness:
(a) Does the behavior of the patient indicate that he
( ) trusts the interviewer
( ) is slightly suspicious of the interviewer
( ) is very suspicious of the interviewer
( ) Other (specify): _____

5. Does the patient behave toward the interviewer in
( ) (a) An overtly friendly manner
( ) (b) A friendly but reserved manner
( ) (c) A deferential and/or excessively polite manner
( ) (d) A sarcastic or rude manner
( ) (e) An openly antagonistic manner
( ) (f) Other (specify): _____

6. During this interview was patient
( ) sober
( ) has had some alcohol
( ) hungover
( ) intoxicated
( ) unclear

III. COMMENTS

_____
_____
_____
_____

3. OUT-PATIENT GROUP THERAPY FORM

NAME OF   CLINIC
1. PATIENT: _____, 2. CASE NO: _____,

3. AGE: _____, 4. SEX: _____, 5. NAME OF CLINIC: _____,

6. NAME(S) AND PROFESSIONAL DISCIPLINE (CLINIC TITLE) OF THERAPIST(S)
LEADING GROUP:

_____,_____
_____,_____

7. DATE OF THIS GROUP SESSION: _____, 8. NUMBER IN ATTENDANCE: _____,

9. BEGAN AT: _____ AM ( ), PM ( )   ENDED AT: _____ AM ( ), PM ( )

PARTICIPATION

1. Did the patient answer any questions about his own life experiences, relationships, or feelings put to him by
   (a) any other patient   Yes ( ), No ( )
   (b) a therapist   Yes ( ), No ( )

2. Did he ask any questions about the life experiences, relationships or feelings
   (a) of any other patient   Yes ( ), No ( )
   (b) of the therapist(s)   Yes ( ), No ( )

3. Without being formally asked to do so, did he speak about his own drinking
   problem?   Yes ( ), No ( )
   If yes: (a) Did he discuss it for the
                  time of his life before he
                  came to the clinic?   Yes ( ), No ( )
              (b) Since coming to the
                  clinic?   Yes ( ), No ( )

4. Without being formally asked to do so, did he speak about his problems or
   difficulties at the present time?   Yes ( ), No ( )
   If yes: did he discuss problems or difficulties in the areas of
              (a) work   Yes ( ), No ( )
              (b) parents   Yes ( ), No ( )
              (c) spouse   Yes ( ), No ( )
              (d) children   Yes ( ), No ( )
              (e) other relatives Yes ( ), No ( )
              (f) other persons in his life Yes ( ), No ( )

5. Without being formally asked to do so, did he express some ideas, opinions or
   feelings about other patients':
              (a) drinking problems   Yes ( ), No ( )
              (b) other problems in life Yes ( ), No ( )

EMOTIONAL REACTIONS

1. Did the patient have any outburst of hostility or aggression in the course of
   this session?   Yes ( ), No ( )
   If yes: Indicate by a check whether this was:
                              Verbal   Actions and gestures   Physical contact
   (a) toward another patient: _____   _____   _____

   (b) toward a therapist: _____   _____   _____

225

2. In your opinion, did he act as though he was responsive to the group interaction?
Yes ( ), No ( )
If no: Do you think he was predominantly:
(check as many as needed)

(a) bored	Yes ( ),	No ( )
(b) uninterested	Yes ( ),	No ( )
(c) withdrawn	Yes ( ),	No ( )
(d) other expression of unresponsivity	Yes ( ),	No ( )
(e) actually responsive but pretending not to be	Yes ( ),	No ( )

3. *If yes:* In your opinion, did he act interested in the group interaction:
    (a) all or most of the time   ( )
    (b) part of the time   ( )
    (c) never   ( )

ALCOHOL USE

1. In this session was there evidence that the patient:
    (a) had had alcoholic beverages since the last visit to clinic ( )
    (b) had been abstinent since the last visit to clinic ( )
    (c) use of alcohol unclear ( )
    (d) not applicable ( )

4. CASE REVIEW

INSTRUCTIONS

The case review is intended for use in the intake phase of this study. A case review should be written for each research patient after intake—whenever it is feasible, but within six weeks after the date the patient is first seen.

The questions asked in each area of the patient's life are not intended to *limit* your study, but rather to serve as a guide for recording what you have learned. Any other data obtained in the course of your contact with the patient would be most welcome and useful and should be recorded.

The questions in this case review are intended for use in a great variety of clinics. They may be less sophisticated or less complex than the information you customarily collect about your patients. This form represents a minimal picture of the patient's life and circumstances, which all clinics will obtain in common. Any information you report beyond this would also be useful in the study.

Although the questions listed in this form are more or less specific in phrasing, they are intended only as guides to the type of information sought, not as direct questions to be answered in a word or two. Completing this case review entails a sympathetic inquiry into each of the listed areas of the patient's life. It does not entail cross-examining the patient or doing a systematic questionnaire-type inquiry into every detail.

The information should be sought and discussed whenever it appears most practical and advantageous to do so, rather than at any fixed time. Whether all or most of the information can be collected at the first interview will depend on your judgment of the situation. Of course, the earlier the data can be collected the better, since this will minimize the chance of missing valuable information if the patient does not return.

If for some reason you are not able to obtain data in a particular area, *indicate in your case review* that you were not able to get that information rather than leaving it unmentioned.

The questions relating to changes in the patient's life are to be considered as referring to the year preceding intake.

The case review should be typed in triplicate, so that two copies can be sent to the research study office and one copy kept in your own files. Use a separate sheet for each topical heading—for example, all the material on health goes on a page headed "I. HEALTH." Please record also the time required to write this case review.

SCHEDULE OF AREAS TO BE COVERED

Identifying Data
At the beginning, please list *all* of the following:
1. Full name of the patient: last name, first name, and middle or maiden name.
2. Clinic case number.
3. Date of intake.
4. Date this form was written.
5. Name and clinic title of the person writing the case review.
6. Time used in writing the case review.
7. Name of your clinic.

Subject Areas

I. HEALTH
How has the patient been feeling during the year prior to intake? Please indicate something about his sleeping and eating patterns, as they are important general indications of his state of health.

Has he had any particular health problems? Has he sought medical attention during the past year, and if so, for what? Was he treated by a physician or a clinic, or has he been hospitalized during the past year.

II. DRINKING
During the year prior to intake has the patient had any problem with drinking? How long has he had such a problem?

Has his drinking affected his sense of well-being or his health? Has it had any unpleasant effects or caused difficulties in his work, family relations, or social relations?

Where and with whom does he usually drink? During the past year, has he had any trouble with the police or been arrested for his drinking? What does he regard as the basis for his drinking?

III. FAMILY RELATIONSHIPS
With whom does the patient live? How does he get along with the people with whom he lives and how do they get along with him? Has there been any change in the relationships in the past year? Does the patient have any other living relatives? How does he feel about them and what is their feeling about him?

IV. SOCIAL RELATIONSHIPS
What are the patient's activities and relationships apart from work? What does he do in his spare time and with whom?

Does he have any social relations with persons outside his family? What is the nature and closeness of these relationships?

227

V. OCCUPATIONAL ADJUSTMENT

What is the patient's work like now, and has it changed during the year prior to intake? Is he satisfied with his job and well adjusted or does he have problems at work?

What are his personal relationships at work? How much does he earn, and what does he think about his earnings?

VI. TREATMENT EXPERIENCE

During the year prior to intake has the patient had any treatment for his drinking problem? If so, where was it, what kind of treatment did he get, and what is his attitude toward it? Was the treatment helpful or not? (The term "treatment" is used here in a very loose sense, meaning any attempt on the part of a person or an institution to influence him with regard to his drinking problem. This would include experience with A.A., with ministers, with clinics, physicians, social agencies, etc.)

VII. OBSERVATION OF THE PATIENT

Describe the patient's rapport and his reactions to interviewers during the intake period in terms of the presence or absence or degree of cooperativeness, friendliness, interest in communicating about himself. Are there areas the patient attempts to cover up or deny?

VIII. EXTENT OF ACTIVITY

How many interviews has the patient had with clinic staff members? How many have members of his family had? How many appointments has the patient failed to keep? What other activity has occurred in this case? (Telephone calls, letters, conferences, etc.—with patient or others, such as agencies, minister, employer, etc.)

IX. CLINIC STAFF'S IMPRESSION OF PATIENT'S TREATABILITY

What is your impression of the patient's motivation for treatment, for giving up drinking, for coming to the clinic during the treatment period, and what would you speculate as to the likelihood that he will continue to maintain contact with the clinic? Does the information he has given you appear to you to be an accurate picture of his situation?

X. COMMENTS ABOUT THE PATIENT NOT OTHERWISE INCLUDED

---

5. CHECK LIST

NAME OF PATIENT: _____

(last)   (first)   (middle or maiden)

NAME OF CLINIC: _____ CLINIC CASE NO: _____

NAME OF PERSON FILLING OUT FORM: _____ DATE FILLED OUT: _____

I. DRINKING PATTERN DURING PAST MONTH (*check only one from 1. to 5.*)

1. Patient has been abstinent   ( )

2. Patient does not claim abstinence, but has no drinking problem, and has no trouble related to drinking within or outside the family   ( )

228

3. Patient has a drinking problem, but does not have any trouble related
   to drinking within or outside the family   ( )
   If this is so, he has been drinking (*check as many as apply*, (*a*) *to* (*f*)):
   ( ) (*a*) daily
   ( ) (*b*) has had at least one binge (more than 24 hours duration)
   ( ) (*c*) has had at least one episode of intoxication (less than 24
        hours duration)
   ( ) (*d*) "sneaked" drinks
   ( ) (*e*) drinks for sedation of nervousness or bodily discomfort
   ( ) (*f*) no record

4. Patient has a drinking problem, and has trouble related to his drinking problem
   within or outside the family   ( )
   If this is so, he has been drinking (*check as many as apply*, (*a*) *to* (*f*)):
   ( ) (*a*) daily
   ( ) (*b*) has had at least one binge (more than 24 hours duration)
   ( ) (*c*) has had at least one episode of intoxication (less than 24 hours
        duration)
   ( ) (*d*) "sneaked" drinks
   ( ) (*e*) drinks for sedation of nervousness or bodily discomfort
   ( ) (*f*) no record
   If this is so, he has problems (*check either or both*):
   ( ) (*a*) within the family
   ( ) (*b*) outside the family

5. Drinking problem not evaluable; patient intoxicated   ( )

II. REASONS FOR DRINKING IN PAST MONTH (*check as many as apply*)
   ( ) 1. Relief of psychological symptoms
   ( ) 2. Relief of physical symptoms or discomfort
   ( ) 3. "Can't stop"
   ( ) 4. No need to stop (because his drinking is under control or he does
        not regard self as an alcoholic, etc.)
   ( ) 5. Poor environmental situation
   ( ) 6. Says he "doesn't know why he drinks."
   ( ) 7. Other: _____
   ( ) 8. No information
   ( ) 9. Not drinking

III. IF PATIENT IS DRINKING, would you characterize him as a person who has done
    most of his drinking in the past month (*check only one*)
   ( ) 1. By himself
   ( ) 2. With casual acquaintances
   ( ) 3. With close or intimate friends
   ( ) 4. With his family
   ( ) 5. Not determinable—not clear
   ( ) 6. Not applicable—not drinking

IV. PATIENT'S DESCRIPTION OF HEALTH STATUS WITHIN PAST MONTH (*check only
    one*)
   ( ) 1. Unconditionally describes his health as good.
   ( ) 2. Conditionally describes his health as good, e.g. "I feel really fine,
        but . . ."

229

(   ) 3. Describes his health as fair, i.e. he manages to get along despite what are, or what he regards as illnesses.

(   ) 4. Describes his health as poor; his life is hampered by what are, or what he regards as illnesses.

V. STATUS OF MEDICAL TREATMENT WITHIN THE PAST YEAR (If no. 1 is checked, no. 2 and no. 3 must be blank. Both no. 2 and no. 3 may apply. If so, check both.)

(   ) 1. Has had any in- or out-patient medical treatment for any illness in the past year (omitting what the patient regards as or calls colds, cuts, bruises, etc.)

(   ) 2. Has had out-patient treatment for illness in the past year (omitting what the patient regards as or calls colds, cuts, bruises, etc.). If so, indicate here briefly what the patient recalls the illness or symptoms to have been (in whatever terms he uses, e.g. lung trouble, pneumonia, etc.) _____

(   ) 3. Has had in-patient treatment for illness in the past year. If so, indicate briefly what the patient recalls in his terms as illness or symptoms and get the name of the hospital for our own check:

_____

_____

VI. EMPLOYMENT STATUS IN PAST MONTH (*check all that apply in the past month*)

(   ) 1. Permanent job—own business

(   )   Permanent job—employed

(   ) 2. Part-time job

(   ) 3. Special employment situation—freelance

(   )   Special employment situation—seasonal employment or lay-off

(   ) 4. Housewife. (Check this only if she has had no work other than this in the past month. Women who have worked other than as a housewife in the past month should be checked in the other categories of jobs, as with men patients.)

(   ) 5. Temporary job

(   ) 6. Working, but details are unknown

(   ) 7. Unemployed, on the labor market

(   ) 8. Not working—ill

(   ) 9. Not working—retired

(   ) 10. Refused information

VII. DESCRIBE PATIENT'S JOB in terms of title and the kind of work he does (e.g. "grocery store stock clerk," not merely "clerk." If patient is not presently employed, describe here his last job:

_____

_____

VIII. PROBLEMS IN JOB IN PAST MONTH (*check as many as apply*)

(   ) 1. No problems, gets along fine

(   ) 2. Occasional friction with fellow workers

(   ) 3. Occasional friction with boss

230

( ) 4. Occasionally has trouble with work, job
( ) 5. Occasional absences
( ) 6. Frequent trouble with fellow workers
( ) 7. Frequent trouble with boss
( ) 8. Serious difficulty in doing work, accidents, etc.
( ) 9. Frequent absences
( ) 10. Refused information
( ) 11. Not applicable—not working or a housewife

IX. PATIENT'S RELATIONSHIP WITH HIS FAMILY IN PAST MONTH (*see instructions below*)

	Mother	Father	Spouse	Children
Good	( )	( )	( )	( )
Medium	( )	( )	( )	( )
Poor	( )	( )	( )	( )
Out of Touch	( )	( )	( )	( )
Not Applicable	( )	( )	( )	( )
No Information	( )	( )	( )	( )

Instructions for Family Relationships (please check separately for each family member)

Good—his relationship with family member is good or satisfactory. He has no complaints, does not see himself as having any problems with them.

Poor—his relationship with family member is poor or unsatisfactory. He complains about them and considers that he has a problem with them.

Medium—is to be used when the relationship is neither good nor bad. There can be minor difficulties, or the relationship can be good at times and bad at others.

Out of touch—is defined as "out of communication with the family members" either verbally or in writing.

Not applicable—Family member is deceased or never existed.

X. PATIENT'S STATEMENT REGARDING FRIENDS APART FROM WORK (*check only one*)
( ) 1. Has no friends
( ) 2. Has only casual friends
( ) 3. Has close friends (one or more)
( ) 4. No information

XI. PATIENT DESCRIBES HIS SOCIAL ACTIVITIES IN PAST MONTH AS FOLLOWS (*check as many as apply*)
( ) 1. Patient in jail, hospital, or other institution
( ) 2. Described as solitary, T.V., movies, reading, etc. alone
( ) 3. Associates with casual drinking companions
( ) 4. Social activities include some or several of the following:
    ( ) (*a*) social activities with family members—entertaining friends, visiting friends, dances, movies, church, etc.
    ( ) (*b*) social activities with other than family members—visiting, dates, organizational activity
    ( ) (*c*) A.A. activities—meetings and 12-step work
    ( ) (*d*) other (specify): _____
( ) 5. No information

6. NEW CASE LIST

CLINIC: _____ MONTH: _____ YEAR: _____

In accordance with our regular sampling procedure, the following new admissions have been added to the research sample:

	DATE OF INTAKE	CLINIC CASE NO.	NAME OF PATIENT	NO. OF VISITS THIS MONTH
(1)				
(2)				
(3)				
(4)				
(5)				
(6)				
(7)				
(8)				
(9)				
(10)				
(11)				
(12)				

At the end of each month, send this list, in duplicate, to:

Appropriate person
Research Center
41 Fifth Avenue, Suite 1-E
New York 3, New York

232

7. OLD CASE LIST

CLINIC:_____ MONTH:_____ YEAR:_____

Please enter below the number of visits this month for each of these patients in the research sample, and at the end of the month return this list, in duplicate, to the appropriate person at the Research Center, 41 Fifth Avenue, Suite 1-E, New York 3, New York, along with the Treatment Records and/or Group Therapy Forms for these patients.

CLINIC CASE NO.	NAME OF PATIENT	NO. OF VISITS THIS MONTH

Phase II: Collection of Follow-up Data (Manual and Instruments)

INTRODUCTION

THIS MANUAL is for use in the second phase of the study, the follow-up of study patients. The purpose of the follow-up phase is to collect systematically the same type of data which we have obtained at intake (e.g., information on employment, drinking, family situation, and other areas of adjustment) in order to evaluate changes which have occurred during the year which has passed since the patients first came to the clinics.

At this time we should like to re-emphasize that it is very important to re-interview at follow-up all study cases seen at intake. The cases which are difficult to find may be those transient persons close to a "skid-row adjustment." Their omission from the study, however, might provide us with too favorable a picture of the total outcome of treatment provided by the participating clinic. We are also exceedingly interested in obtaining full data about all areas of life from the patient and, whenever possible, also from other persons close to him. In this way we can best describe for all patients interviewed, the changes which have occurred in their lives during the past year.

The manual contains the forms and instructions which are needed for the purposes of the follow-up phase of work:

1. PRE-FOLLOW-UP SUMMARY: Instructions are given for recording of new information which has come to your attention about the patient from the time the case review was written to the time when tracing and follow-up is initiated.

2. TRACING INSTRUCTIONS. The tracing instructions describe hints for locating the patient based on our experience during the pilot study.

3. TRACING FORM. This form is to be used to advise us of the status of tracing and interviewing on each patient. Space is provided for recording the steps taken in tracing any information learned about the current status of the patient during tracing.

4. INTERVIEWING INSTRUCTIONS. The interviewing instructions describe payments for interviews and persons to be interviewed.

5. FOLLOW-UP REVIEW INSTRUCTIONS. These instructions concern the topics to be covered in the follow-up review. Recording methods are described.

234

6. FOLLOW-UP CHECK LIST. The purpose of the follow-up check list is the same as the purpose of the check list filled out at intake. Again it should not be considered a substitute for but a supplement to the follow-up review.

7. FOLLOW-UP OBSERVATION SHEET. The purpose of the follow-up observation sheet is to record observations of the patient during the follow-up interview.

RESEARCH FORMS AND INSTRUCTIONS

1. PRE-FOLLOW-UP SUMMARY

Prior to initiating tracing operations, a pre-follow-up summary should be written which should be concerned with the interval between intake and the time you begin the tracing operations, roughly a 12-month interval. This summary should contain the following information:

I. DATA MODIFYING THE CASE REVIEW

Look over the research case review and the clinic record. Briefly report anything learned from the patient, or other sources about his functioning in the year prior to intake which either fills out or supplements what was told us in the case review. For instance, if there was no report about his social relations *prior to intake* at the time the case review was written, and if data was obtained about this aspect of the patient's life subsequently, please report this material in this pre-follow-up summary. We also are most interested in any material that may alter information given in the earlier case review. For instance, if you learn that the patient has been married twice instead of once as he had told you at intake, please indicate this in the pre-follow-up summary.

II. TREATMENT EXPERIENCE

If the patient is no longer attending the clinic what are your impressions and ideas about why he discontinued? If he is continuing to attend the clinic what do you think his motives, goals or attitudes might be for doing so? Since coming to you, describe what important changes in his attitudes or in his life situation have occurred in regard to the following:

1. Health
2. Drinking behavior
3. Living arrangements
4. His parental or marital situation
5. Social life
6. Employment
7. Means of support
8. Any other areas not included

III. DATA FROM OTHER SOURCES

(a) Have you heard of any important changes in the patient's attitudes or in his life situation since he came to you, from sources *other* than the patient? Indicate the information and approximately when this information was obtained and indicate the sources, e.g., family member, grapevine of other patients, other agencies, or interested persons in the community, etc.

(b) What inquiries have you had about the patient from clinics, agencies, hospitals or interested persons in the community? Summarize the nature of the inquiry and indicate the approximate date.

(c) Has he been hospitalized or incarcerated since he came to the clinic subsequent to your writing of the case review? Where? What for? How long?

2. TRACING INSTRUCTIONS FOR FOLLOW-UP

The patients to be traced and interviewed each month are the patients who were seen at intake 12 months previously. For instance, the tracing of patients who were seen at intake in January, 1959, would begin in January, 1960. However, if by chance it is not possible to find a January, 1959, intake patient in January, 1960, efforts to find and interview him should continue through the tracing year. For those clinics which did not begin in January, 1959, the first group of cases to be traced and interviewed would be those patients seen at intake during the first month that the clinic participated in the study.

TRACING METHOD AND HINTS
The tracing of patients no longer in touch with the clinic should, of course, proceed on an individual basis and at the discretion of the clinic worker who best knew the patient. On the basis of our previous experience in the pilot study and other follow-up studies we thought it might be useful to offer a few suggestions.

In general, it seems to provoke less anxiety in patients, particularly those who may not be doing well, to begin the tracing by telephone, whenever this is possible. In this way any questions as to why the clinic continues to be interested in the patient may be answered immediately. We have found that a certain number of patients are pleased at the evidence of interest in them. If it is necessary to write to a patient and there is uncertainty as to his current address or if the follow-up letter is returned as "unknown at this address," a "certified letter with forwarding address requested" obtained at the post office can be helpful in securing a new address. If the patient can not be found, it is helpful to be in touch with any family member who knew of the patient's coming to the clinic.

If it is impossible to locate a patient or any member of his family directly, the following sources of information for tracing are suggested: (1) source of referral, (2) courts, social agencies or hospitals where patient is known, (3) A.A. or skid-row grapevine.

In the event that all of these courses give no clue as to the whereabouts of the patient it is important to clear all otherwise untraced patients with: (1) the Bureau of Vital Statistics to find out whether or not the patient has died in the interim, (2) with the Social Service Exchange, should this be possible and, (3) where these exist, with a General Index of Persons known to the penal system or the state hospitals.

CORROBORATIVE DATA IN TRACING
In the course of tracing the whereabouts of a patient, it is frequently possible to get information regarding the present status of the patient. We are providing a tracing form for the clinic workers to record any such information. Although we realize this is an extra burden, particularly when the patient is subsequently interviewed, we are particularly interested in any information about the patient coming from sources OTHER than the patient since this may clarify or corroborate what he tells you. We would appreciate that the clinic workers be particularly alert to any such information.

TRACING CATEGORIES DEFINED
In using the *tracing form*, the status of the cases should be checked in one of the tracing categories:

(a) *Tracing Status*
1. Ready for interview
2. Deceased. What did you learn of the circumstances leading to his death?

What is the cause of death listed on the death certificate? Did his drinking problem have any apparent relationship to his death?

3. Out of state

4. In state but not geographically accessible

For designations 3 and 4, what were you able to learn about his moving away from the vicinity of the clinic which might cast some light on his current status? Geographically inaccessible refers to those patients who are now living too far away from the clinic to make a visit feasible and where there are no other interviewing personnel available in that area.

5. Untraceable

Indicate sources utilized to trace the patient. What have you been able to learn about his possible or probable work, drinking, life status informally in the course of attempting to trace him? e.g. "The last time I saw Joe," his ex-wife said, "was in September '59—he was on a binge then."

(b) *Interview Status*

1. Interviewed

2. Refused

What do you know about the basis of this refusal? Do you have some ideas, from the nature of his refusal, which might cast some light on his current status?

USE OF TRACING FORM

At the end of each month, please send a tracing form describing tracing status for cases traced during that month. If patient is traced as "ready for interview" and then interviewed in the same month, the tracing form should be marked with "ready for interview" and "interviewed" both checked. If the tracing form is marked under (a) ("ready for interview") but interview will not take place until the following month, no additional tracing form will be sent but we will expect a follow-up interview, check list, and observation sheet. In the event a "ready for interview" patient refuses to be interviewed, a second tracing form should be sent indicating the circumstances of the refusal in the appropriate place. Only persons traced can be considered refusals, of course.

In the event a patient categorized as untraced, refused, out-of-state, or geographically inaccessible becomes available for interview at a later date, please send another tracing form describing the circumstances, and then send us the interview material.

---

3. TRACING FORM

PATIENT: _____ CLINIC: _____

TRACER: _____ DATE OF INTAKE: _____ DATE OF TRACING: _____

STEPS IN TRACING:

DATA ON STATUS OF PATIENT LEARNED DURING TRACING (If deceased, give details of death.) (Use back of page when necessary.)

Data   Source of data

RESULTS:

(a) *Tracing Status*
   1. Ready for Interview   ( )
   2. Deceased   ( )
   3. Out of State   ( )
   4. In state but not geographically accessible   ( )
   5. Untraced   ( )

(b) *Interview Status*
   1. Interviewed   ( )
   2. Refused   ( )

---

4. INTERVIEWING INSTRUCTIONS

The follow-up phase of the study should ideally consist of an interview with the patient, either in the clinic office or at his home and corroboration of his current status by his family member or other interested person.

PAYMENT

The study will pay $3.00 for each completed clinic interview, $3.00 for each home visit and an additional $7.00 for each patient interviewed at home. For example, if two home visits are made and patient is interviewed at the time of the second visit, the payment will be $6.00 for the two home visits and $7.00 for the interview, a total of $13.00.

Travel outside the city will be paid for at the rate of 10c a mile.

PATIENTS CURRENTLY IN TREATMENT

In the event that a patient is in treatment at the time of follow-up, the follow-up review and check list may be written by the therapist from the data already known to him, or depending on the situation an evaluative interview may be used for obtaining any missing data.

The observation sheet should be filled out from data obtained in one interview during that month.

TELEPHONE INTERVIEWS

If the patient refuses to be interviewed in person, a telephone interview is acceptable *only* if (a) sufficient data is available to cover the follow-up review and (b) this information indicates that the status of the patient is the same or worse than at the time of intake. We cannot accept telephone statements indicating improvement without the minimum corroboration of the interviewer's estimate of the patient's reliability in a face to face contact.

238

It is, of course, convenient to have the patient come to the clinic for an interview. However, if the patient fails to appear for an appointed interview, we have in the past found it timesaving in the long run to arrange the second appointment at the home of the patient and so eliminate the possibility of further failed office appointments. Although patients may not be willing to make the effort to come to the clinic, they are usually more welcoming of a home visit or, at worst, hesitate to throw the worker out of their home. We are asking that at least 3 home visits be attempted before a case is considered as "interview refused."

INTERVIEW WITH FAMILY MEMBERS

If the patient's whereabouts is unknown and a family member exists, the family member should be interviewed.

PATIENTS IN INSTITUTIONS

If the patient is traced to an institution, hospital, jail, etc., it is expected that he be interviewed there. We have found that institutional administrative personnel are cooperative in arranging such an interview. If the institution is too far distant from the clinic, data provided by the institution personnel and/or family may be used. If the condition of the patient is such, i.e., psychotic, that his statements are not oriented, data should be obtained from institutional personnel.

PATIENTS OUT OF CITY BUT IN STATE

If the patient is out of the clinic city but is traced to another residence within the clinic state, wherever possible the patient should be seen. Where there are other state clinics such as in Connecticut or Virginia, it might be feasible or convenient if arrangements could be made for the clinic nearest the patient to interview him.

Where it seems feasible to the clinic, other agencies may be asked to interview out-of-town but not out-of-state patients.

PATIENTS OUT OF STATE

Out-of-state patients will be traced and any data obtained in the course of tracing will be recorded but they will not be interviewed.

RECORDING

The content of the interview covers the same areas as those included in the case review. In addition, the follow-up observation sheet and the follow-up check list should be completed. The observation sheet should be used to record data about the status of the patient on the day of the interview. The follow-up interview should cover the year between intake and follow-up. The check list should cover the month before the follow-up interview, with two exceptions:

(1) "I. DRINKING PATTERN."

There is an addition here. If 1. ("Patient has been abstinent") is checked, indicate how long abstinent. If 2. ("Patient does not claim abstinence but is understood to have no drinking problem") is checked, indicate the number of months he has had no drinking problem. (Please keep in mind that this section should be checked in accordance with *your understanding*.)

(2) "V. STATUS OF MEDICAL TREATMENT WITHIN THE PAST YEAR" refers to *year* between intake and follow-up.

You will note that the check list has spaces for indicating the person seen and the place of the interview. Because of the many possible sources of data, it is important for us to have this information on every case.

If the patient and family member are both seen, the check list should record your understanding of the situation. If only a family member is seen, the check list should be filled out in accordance with the information given by the family member. If the only source of information is a community person or agency, a check list should be filled out in accordance with their report.

If patient and other source both give data, please say patient and other person.

5. FOLLOW-UP REVIEW

INSTRUCTIONS

The follow-up review should be written as soon as possible after the interview with the patient.

As on the earlier case review, the questions asked in each area of the patient's life are not intended to limit your study but rather to serve as a guide for recording what you have learned from the patient or others about the patient. Any additional data obtained in the course of your contact with the patient would be most welcome and useful and should be recorded.

If for some reason you are not able to obtain data in a particular area, indicate in your follow-up review that you were not able to get that information rather than leaving it unmentioned.

The questions relating to changes in the patient's life refer to the year between intake and follow-up.

The follow-up review should be typed in triplicate, so that two copies can be sent to the research study office and one copy kept in your own files for your own research and internal uses. Use a separate sheet for each topical heading; e.g., all the material on health goes on a page headed "I. HEALTH."

Any information you have from someone other than the patient should be included on the appropriate page of the follow-up review. This material should be in a separate paragraph with source of data clearly marked, particularly if the patient is also seen.

Whenever possible, we would like direct quotes from the patient.

As in other summaries, please state reasons whenever data is unavailable on a particular topic.

SCHEDULE OF AREAS TO BE COVERED

Identifying Data

At the beginning, please list *all* of the following:

1. Full name of the patient: last name, first name, and middle or maiden name. If patient and other person or agency reports, give name of both patient and other person or agency.
2. Clinic case number
3. Date of follow-up
4. Date this form was written
5. Name and clinic title of the person writing the follow-up review
6. Time used in writing the follow-up review
7. Name of your clinic

Subject Areas

I. HEALTH

How has the patient been feeling during the past year? Please indicate something about his sleeping and eating patterns, as they are important general indications of his state of health.

240

Has he had any particular health problems? Has he sought medical attention during the past year, and if so, for what? And where? Was he treated by a physician or a clinic, or has he been hospitalized during the past year?

II. DRINKING

Review the patient's drinking or abstinence pattern for the past year. Has his drinking affected his sense of well-being or his health? Has it had any unpleasant effects or caused difficulties in his work, family relations, or social relations?

Where and with whom does he usually drink? During the past year, has he had any trouble with the police or been arrested for his drinking? What does he regard as the basis for his drinking? If he has been abstinent, for how long? Why?

III. FAMILY RELATIONSHIPS

With whom does the patient now live? Is there a working adult other than the patient in the home? How does he get along with the people with whom he lives and how do they get along with him? Has there been any change in the relationships in the past year? Does the patient have any other living relatives? Is he in touch with them or not? If yes, how does he feel about them and what is their feeling about him?

IV. SOCIAL RELATIONSHIPS

What are the patient's activities and relationships apart from work? What does he do in his spare time and with whom; his family, alone, with friends?

Does he have any social relations with persons outside his family? What is the nature and closeness of these relationships?

V. OCCUPATIONAL ADJUSTMENT

What is the current employment status of the patient and has it changed during the past year? If so, how many jobs has he had in the past year? If employed, what does he do? Is he satisfied with his job and well adjusted or does he have problems at work?

What are his personal relationships at work? How much does he earn and what does he think about his earnings? If unemployed, why is he unemployed and for how long has he been unemployed?

VI. TREATMENT EXPERIENCE

What does he say about his clinic experience with you? Was it helpful? Does he wish to resume?

During the past year, has the patient had any treatment for his drinking problem *other* than at your clinic? If so, where was it? What kind of treatment did he get and what is his attitude toward it? Was the treatment helpful or not? (The term "treatment" is used here in a very loose sense, meaning any attempt on the part of a person or an institution to influence him with regard to his drinking problem. This would include experience with A.A., with ministers, with other clinics, physicians, social agencies, etc.)

VII. OBSERVATION OF THE PATIENT

Describe the patient's reactions to interviewer during the follow-up interview in terms of the presence or absence or degree of cooperativeness, friendliness, interest in communicating about himself.

VIII. RELIABILITY

Are there areas the patient attempted to cover up or deny? Did his statements and manner impress you as reliable, doubtful or unreliable? Does the information he has given you appear to be an accurate picture of his situation?

IX. PROGNOSIS RE DRINKING

If patient has been abstinent for six months or more what is your impression of the patient's motivation for giving up drinking, and what would you speculate as to the likelihood that he will continue to be abstinent? If he is drinking, do you think he will become abstinent or do you think he will continue drinking?

X. COMMENTS ABOUT THE PATIENT NOT OTHERWISE INCLUDED

6. FOLLOW-UP CHECK LIST

NAME OF PATIENT: _____

         (last)   (first)   (middle)

PLACE OF INTERVIEW: Institution (   ); Clinic (   ); Home (   ); Other_____

NAME OF CLINIC: _____ CLINIC CASE NO.: _____

NAME OF PERSON FILLING OUT FORM: _____ DATE FILLED OUT: _____

I. DRINKING PATTERN DURING PAST MONTH (*check only one from 1. to 5.*)
  1. Patient has been abstinent.   ( )
    If so, for how many months? _____

  2. Patient does not claim abstinence, but is understood to have ( )
    no drinking problem, and has no trouble related to drinking
    within or outside the family.
    If so, for how many months? _____

  3. Patient has a drinking problem, but does not have any trouble ( )
    related to drinking within or outside the family.
    If this is so, he has been drinking (*check as many as apply, (a) to (f)*):
      ( ) (a) daily
      ( ) (b) has had at least one binge (more than 24 hours' duration)
      ( ) (c) has had at least one episode of intoxication (less than
              24 hours' duration)
      ( ) (d) "sneaked" drinks
      ( ) (e) drinks for sedation of nervousness or bodily discomfort
      ( ) (f) no record

  4. Patient has a drinking problem, and has trouble related to his ( )
    drinking problem within or outside the family.
    If this is so, he has been drinking (*check as many as apply, (a) to (f)*):
      ( ) (a) daily
      ( ) (b) has had at least one binge (more than 24 hours' duration)
      ( ) (c) has had at least one episode of intoxication (less than
              24 hours' duration)
      ( ) (d) "sneaked" drinks
      ( ) (e) drinks for sedation of nervousness or bodily discomfort
      ( ) (f) no record
    If this is so, he has problems (*check either or both*):
      ( ) (g) within the family
      ( ) (h) outside the family

  5. Drinking problem not evaluable; patient intoxicated   ( )

242

II. REASONS FOR DRINKING IN PAST MONTH (*check as many as apply*)
( ) 1. Relief of psychological symptoms
( ) 2. Relief of physical symptoms or discomfort
( ) 3. "Can't stop"
( ) 4. No need to stop (because his drinking is under control or he does not regard self as an alcoholic, etc.)
( ) 5. Poor environmental situation
( ) 6. Says he "doesn't know why he drinks."
( ) 7. Other: _____
( ) 8. No information
( ) 9. Not drinking

III. IF PATIENT IS DRINKING, would you characterize him as a person who has done most of his drinking in the past month (*check only one*)
( ) 1. By himself
( ) 2. With casual acquaintances
( ) 3. With close or intimate friends
( ) 4. With his family
( ) 5. Not determinable—not clear
( ) 6. Not applicable—not drinking

IV. PATIENT'S DESCRIPTION OF HEALTH STATUS WITHIN PAST MONTH (*check only one*)
( ) 1. Unconditionally describes his health as good
( ) 2. Conditionally describes his health as good, e.g. "I feel really fine, but . . ."
( ) 3. Describes his health as fair, i.e. he manages to get along despite what are, or what he regards as illnesses.
( ) 4. Describes his health as poor; his life is hampered by what are, or what he regards as illnesses.

V. STATUS OF MEDICAL TREATMENT WITHIN THE PAST YEAR (If no. 1 is checked, no. 2 and no. 3 must be blank. Both no. 2 and no. 3 may apply. If so check both.)
( ) 1. Has not had any in- or out-patient medical treatment for any illness in the past year (omitting what the patient regards as or calls colds, cuts, bruises, etc.).
( ) 2. Has had out-patient treatment for illness in the past year (omitting what the patient regards as or calls colds, cuts, bruises, etc.). If so, indicate here briefly what the patient recalls the illness or symptoms to have been (in whatever terms he uses, e.g. lung trouble, pneumonia, etc.). _____
( ) 3. Has had in-patient treatment for illness in the past year. If so, indicate briefly what the patient recalls in his terms as illness or symptoms and get the name of the hospital for our own check:

_____

_____

VI. EMPLOYMENT STATUS IN PAST MONTH (*check all that apply in the past month*)
( ) 1. Permanent job—own business
( ) Permanent job—employed
( ) 2. Part-time job
( ) 3. Special employment situation—freelance
( ) Special employment situation—seasonal employment or lay-off

243

(   ) 4. Housewife. (Check this only if she has had no work other than this in the past month. Women who have worked other than as a housewife in the past month should be checked in the other categories of jobs, as with men patients.)
(   ) 5. Temporary job
(   ) 6. Working, but details are unknown
(   ) 7. Unemployed, on the labor market
(   ) 8. Not working—ill
(   ) 9. Not working—retired
(   )10. Refused information

VII. DESCRIBE PATIENT'S JOB in terms of title and the kind of work he does (e.g. "grocery store stock clerk," not merely "clerk." *If patient is not presently employed, describe here his last job*:

_____

_____

VIII. PROBLEMS IN JOB IN PAST MONTH (*check as many as apply*)
(   ) 1. No problems, gets along fine
(   ) 2. Occasional friction with fellow workers
(   ) 3. Occasional friction with boss
(   ) 4. Occasionally has trouble with work, job
(   ) 5. Occasional absences
(   ) 6. Frequent trouble with fellow workers
(   ) 7. Frequent trouble with boss
(   ) 8. Serious difficulty in doing work, accidents, etc.
(   ) 9. Frequent absences
(   ) 10. Refused information
(   ) 11. Not applicable—not working or a housewife

IX. PATIENT'S RELATIONSHIP WITH HIS FAMILY IN PAST MONTH (*see instructions below*)

	Mother	Father	Spouse	Children
Good	( )	( )	( )	( )
Medium	( )	( )	( )	( )
Poor	( )	( )	( )	( )
Out of touch	( )	( )	( )	( )
Not applicable	( )	( )	( )	( )
No information	( )	( )	( )	( )

Instructions for Family Relationships
(*please check separately for each family member*)
Good—his relationship with family member is good or satisfactory. He has no complaints, does not see himself as having any problems with them.
Poor—his relationship with family member is poor or unsatisfactory. He complains about them and considers that he has a problem with them.
Medium—is to be used when the relationship is neither good nor bad. There can be minor difficulties, or the relationship can be good at times and bad at others.
Out of touch—is defined as "out of communication with the family member" either verbally or in writing.
Not applicable—family member is deceased or never existed.

244

x. PATIENT'S STATEMENT REGARDING FRIENDS APART FROM WORK (*check only one*)
( ) 1. Has no friends
( ) 2. Has only casual friends
( ) 3. Has close friends (one or more)
( ) 4. No information

xi. PATIENT DESCRIBES HIS SOCIAL ACTIVITIES IN PAST MONTH AS FOLLOWS (*check as many as apply*)
( ) 1. Patient in jail, hospital or other institution
( ) 2. Described as solitary, T.V., movies, reading, etc. alone
( ) 3. Associates with casual drinking companions
( ) 4. Social activities include some or several of the following:
    ( ) (*a*) Social activities with family members—entertaining friends, visiting friends, dances, movies, church, etc.
    ( ) (*b*) Social activities with other than family members—visiting, dates, organizational activity
    ( ) (*c*) A.A. activities—meetings and 12-step work
    ( ) (*d*) Other (Specify): _____
( ) 5. No information

7. FOLLOW-UP OBSERVATION SHEET

PATIENT'S NAME: _____ CLINIC: _____

CASE NO.: _____ INTERVIEWER: _____

In all cases, the interviewer should briefly describe the patient in terms of each of the following on day of follow-up interview.

1. PERSONAL HYGIENE AND GENERAL APPEARANCE: _____

_____

2. APPARENT STATE OF HEALTH: _____

_____

3. CURRENT DRINKING STATUS (sober, hungover, etc.): Include your own observations and also whatever the patient tells you about his drinking on that day, whether he drank or not, how much, and what effect it had on him:

_____

_____

4. SYMPTOMS OBSERVED RELATED TO ALCOHOLISM (tremors, etc.): _____

_____ None observed ( )

5. ATTITUDE TOWARD FOLLOW-UP INTERVIEW (defensive, co-operative, confused, passive, etc.): _____

_____ None observed ( )

6. STATEMENTS OF PATIENT OR INFORMANT ABOUT HIS FUNCTIONING IN THE PAST YEAR ARE CONSIDERED:

( ) Largely reliable
( ) Doubtful
( ) Unreliable
( ) No judgment possible

7. INFORMATION ON THIS FORM WAS OBTAINED FROM:

( ) Patient
( ) Relative: _____
( ) Other: _____

(Preferably this material should be obtained from the patient. If patient is not interviewed, only questions 6. and 7. need to be filled out. Question 6. should be filled out for person interviewed.)

References

1. WORLD HEALTH ORGANIZATION: Second Report of the Alcoholism Subcommittee, Expert Committee on Mental Health. W.H.O. Tech. Rept. Series no. 48, 1952.
2. KELLER, M.: Definition of Alcoholism. Quart. J. Stud. Alc. 21: 125–34, 1960.
3. Alcohol, Science and Society: Twenty-Nine Lectures with Discussions as Given at the Yale Summer School of Alcohol Studies. New Haven: Quarterly Journal of Studies on Alcohol, 1945.
4. McCARTHY, R. G., and DOUGLASS, E. M.: Alcohol and Social Responsibility: A New Educational Approach. New York: Thomas Y. Crowell and Yale Plan Clinic, 1949.
5. Alcoholics Anonymous: The Story of How Many Thousands of Men and Women Have Recovered from Alcoholism. New York: Alcoholics Anonymous Publishing, 1955.
6. Alcoholics Anonymous Comes of Age: A Brief History of A.A. New York: Alcoholics Anonymous Publishing, 1957.
7. ZWERLING, I.: Psychiatric Findings in An Interdisciplinary Study of Forty-Six Alcoholic Patients. Quart. J. Stud. Alc. 20: 543–54, 1959.
8. BURNETT, F. M., and GREENHILL, M. H.: Some Problems in the Evaluation of an Inservice Training Program in Mental Health. Am. J. Pub. Health 44: 1546–56, 1954.
9. FELIX, R. H., and CLAUSEN, J. A.: The Role of Surveys in Advancing Knowledge in the Field of Mental Health. Pub. Opinion Quart. 17: 61–70, 1953.
10. KOTINSKY, R., and WITMER, H. L. (eds.): Community Programs for Mental Health. Cambridge: Harvard Univ. Press, 1955.
11. ROSENFELD, E.: Social Research and Social Action in Prevention of Juvenile Delinquency. Soc. Problems 4: 138–48, 1956.
12. HOLT, R. R.: Problems in the Use of Sample Surveys. In KOTINSKY, R., and WITMER, H. L. (eds.): Community Programs for Mental Health. Cambridge: Harvard Univ. Press, 1955, pp. 325–58.
13. STRAUS, R., and BACON, S. D.: Alcoholism and Social Stability: A Study of Occupational Integration in 2,023 Male Clinic Patients. Quart. J. Stud. Alc. 12: 231–60, 1951.
14. GERARD, D. L.: Intoxication and Addiction: Psychiatric Observa-

tions on Alcoholism and Opiate Drug Addiction. Quart. J. Stud. Alc. 16: 681–99, 1955.

15. ISBELL, H., FRASER, H. F., WIKLER, A., BELLEVILLE, R. E., and EISENMAN, A. J.: An Experimental Study of the Etiology of "Rum Fits" and Delirium Tremens. Quart. J. Stud. Alc. 16: 1–33, 1955.

16. SCHILDER, P.: Zur Lehre von den Anamnesen der Epileptiks Epileptischer, von der Schlafmittelhypnose und vom Gedaechtnis. Arch. Psychiat. Nervenk. 72: 323–25, 1924.

17. IVY, A. C., GROSSMAN, M. I., and BACHRACH, W. H.: Peptic Ulcer. Philadelphia: Blakiston, 1950.

18. HOLLINGSHEAD, A. B., and REDLICH, F. C.: Social Class and Mental Illness: A Community Study. New York: Wiley, 1958.

19. U.S. DEPARTMENT OF HEALTH, EDUCATION, AND WELFARE. Vital Statistics of the United States 1960, vol. II, Mortality (part B). Washington, D.C.: Government Printing Office, 1963.

20. MERTON, R. K.: Social Theory and Social Structure. Glencoe: Free Press, 1957.

21. POPHAM, R. E.: The Jellinek Alcoholism Estimation Formula and Its Application to Canadian Data. Quart. J. Stud. Alc. 17: 559–93, 1956.

22. KLINEBERG, O.: Race Differences. New York: Harper, 1935.

23. BALES, R. F.: Cultural Differences in Rates of Alcoholism. Quart. J. Stud. Alc. 6: 480–99, 1946.

24. SNYDER, C. R.: Alcohol and the Jews: A Cultural Study of Drinking and Sobriety. Glencoe: Free Press, 1958.

25. KELLER, M., and EFRON, V.: The Prevalence of Alcoholism. Quart. J. Stud. Alc. 16: 619–44, 1955.

26. GERARD, D. L., and SAENGER, G.: Follow-up Study of Patients Seen by the Connecticut Commission on Alcoholism, 1948–1957. Unpublished MS.

27. BAILEY, N. B.: The Family Agency's Role in Treating the Wife of an Alcoholic. Social Casework 44 (5): 273–79, 1963.

28. McCORD, W., and McCORD, J.: Origins of Alcoholism. Stanford: Stanford Univ. Press, 1960.

29. BRILL, N. Q., and STORROW, H. A.: Social Class and Psychiatric Treatment. Arch. Gen. Psychiat. 3: 340–44, 1960.

30. MOORE, R. A., BENEDEK, E. P., and WALLACE, J. G.: Social Class, Schizophrenia and the Psychiatrist. Am. J. Psychiat. 120: 149–54, 1963.

31. DAVIES, D. L., SHEPHERD, M., and MYERS, E.: The Two-Years' Prognosis of 50 Alcohol Addicts after Treatment in Hospital. Quart. J. Stud. Alc. 17: 485–502, 1956.

248

32. Gibbins, R. J., and Armstrong, J. D.: Effects of Clinical Treatment on Behavior of Alcoholic Patients: An Exploratory Methodological Investigation. Quart. J. Stud. Alc. 18: 429–50, 1957.
33. Gerard, D. L., and Saenger, G.: Interval between Intake and Follow-up as a Factor in the Evaluation of Patients with a Drinking Problem. Quart. J. Stud. Alc. 20: 620–30, 1959.
34. Keller, M., and Seely, J. R.: The Alcohol Language. Toronto: Univ. of Toronto Press, 1958, Brookside Monograph no. 2.
35. Jackson, J. K.: Types of Drinking Patterns of Male Alcoholics. Quart. J. Stud. Alc. 19: 269–302, 1958.
36. Knight, R. P.: The Dynamics and Treatment of Chronic Alcohol Addiction. Bull. Menninger Clinic 1: 233–50, 1937.
37. Davies, D. L.: Normal Drinking in Recovered Alcohol Addicts. Quart. J. Stud. Alc. 23: 94–104, 1962.
38. Kendell, R. E.: Normal Drinking by Former Alcohol Addicts. Quart. J. Stud. Alc. 26: 247–57, 1965.
39. Gerard, D. L., Saenger, G., and Wile, R.: The Abstinent Alcoholic. Arch. Gen. Psychiat. 6: 83–95, 1962.
40. Kahn, R. L., and Fink, M.: Personality Factors in Behavioral Response to Electroshock Therapy. J. Neuropsychiat. 1: 45–49, 1959.
41. Kahn, R. L., and Fink, M.: Prognostic Value of Rorschach Criteria in Clinical Response to Convulsive Therapy. J. Neuropsychiat. 1: 242–45, 1960.
42. Pittman, D. J., and Gordon, C. W.: Revolving Door: A Study of the Chronic Police Case Inebriate. Glencoe: Free Press, 1958.
43. Pfeffer, A. Z., et al.: A Treatment Program for the Alcoholic in Industry. J. Am. Med. Assoc. 161: 827–36, 1956.
44. Tiebout, H. M.: The Syndrome of Alcohol Addiction. Quart. J. Stud. Alc. 5: 535–46, 1945.
45. Dincin, J.: Utilization of Professional Staff in Psychiatric Rehabilitation. Social Work 10 (1): 51–57, 1965.
46. Jones, M.: The Therapeutic Community. New York: Basic Books, 1953.
47. Brager, G.: The Indigenous Worker: A New Approach to the Social Work Technician. Social Work 10 (2): 33–40, 1965.